Drupal for Designers

Dani Nordin

O'REILLY®

Beijing · Cambridge · Farnham · Köln · Sebastopol · Tokyo

Drupal for Designers

by Dani Nordin

Published by O'Reilly Media, Inc., 1005 Gravenstein Highway North, Sebastopol, CA 95472.

O'Reilly books may be purchased for educational, business, or sales promotional use. Online editions are also available for most titles (*http://my.safaribooksonline.com*). For more information, contact our corporate/institutional sales department: 800-998-9938 or *corporate@oreilly.com*.

Editors: Julie Steele and Meghan Blanchette		**Indexer:** Angela Howard	
Production Editor: Rachel Steely		**Cover Designer:** Karen Montgomery	
Copyeditor: Audrey Doyle		**Interior Designer:** David Futato	
Proofreader: Kiel Van Horn		**Illustrators:** Robert Romano and Rebecca Demarest	

July 2012:   First Edition.

Revision History for the First Edition:
    2012-07-11   First release
See *http://oreilly.com/catalog/errata.csp?isbn=9781449325046* for release details.

ISBN: 978-1-449-32504-6

[LSI]

1342017109

Table of Contents

Part III.   Setting Up a Local Development Environment

Part IV.   Prototyping in Drupal

Foreword

Giving a web designer Drupal is like handing a child an empty paper towel roll and telling them to go play. Some kids look at the tube, turn it over in their hands, and look at you with confusion—or annoyance—as if to ask: "What am I supposed to do with *this*?" But the creative kids see much more than an old piece of gluey cardboard. With a little imagination, they know that by simply peeking through it, the tube is transformed into a telescope. Suddenly, the playground is now a bustling harbor, and perched atop the slide, they are captaining the most feared pirate ship at William Howard Taft Elementary. Stick a handle through the middle, and it's a rolling pin. Add a cone to one end and some fins to the other, and it's a rocket.

Then there's the kid who uses it to roll up a hundred-foot-long sheet of perforated paper towels and sells it back to you at a premium because it's "artisan-crafted." That kid is a born marketer. We're not going to talk about him. Walk away.

Like the empty paper towel roll, Drupal can both confuse and delight. With more than 15,000 modules, it can be extended to do virtually anything—assuming you have the patience to figure out how. This is what makes the role of a Drupal designer so rare and unique—so much so, in fact, that we don't call them "designers." We call them "themers." Some CMS communities—WordPress, Joomla, or Expression Engine, for example—often separate designers from developers according to who does what with Photoshop files: designers make them, and developers chop them up into HTML, CSS, and code to create a functioning website.

Drupal's theming system, however, is so *robust*—that's developer speak for "overly customizable, complicated, and obtuse"—that it requires a vast array of skills to master, partly because Drupal uses a lot of arrays. (Zing!) Drupal *themers* work with HTML, CSS, and PHP. They create and chop up Photoshop files. They are designers and site builders, both describing and implementing functionality using Drupal's vast collection of modules, custom PHP, "hooks," "overrides," and all kinds of technical stuff you'll come to know and love (or loathe).

That's why this book is so important. Designing for Drupal requires knowledge of both design and code, colors and conditionals, people and processors. So if you're new to Drupal, welcome! Please ignore the gallows humor in the previous paragraph. Drupal is great! If you're already a Drupal pro and picked up this book to see how other folks do it, we should get together and do what Drupal experts do best: complain about Drupal.

All kidding aside, Drupal is an amazing platform built and supported by more than 17,000 talented designers and developers. It can power websites ranging from personal homepages and homeowners' associations to television networks and international publications like *The Economist*. This book will do more than any other to ease Drupal's learning curve. It will also introduce you to the Drupal community and its brilliant, opinionated, passionate, and funny themers.

So, read and explore. Be the creative kid on the playground. With a little practice, you can turn that cardboard tube into a microphone. Or megaphone. Or lightsaber. Or an improbably large toothpick.

And when you're done with your cardboard tube metaphor, please get involved in the Drupal community. Please don't squander that big, juicy brain of yours in isolation. Share your creativity and fresh ideas. We need you.

—Todd Ross Nienkerk
Partner and co-founder, Four Kitchens
Austin, Texas
April 29, 2012

Introduction

If you're reading this book, you're probably a web designer who has heard of Drupal, wants to get started with it, and may have even tried it out a couple of times. And you might be frustrated because even if you're used to code, Drupal has thrown you a major learning curve that you hadn't expected. And just when you think you've gotten a basic site together, now you have to figure out how to make it *look* right—and the whole process starts over again.

Yep, I've been there too. That's why I wrote this book.

This book, which brings together the first three *Drupal for Designers* guides with some new material, a more logical flow, and better grammar, is for the solo site builder or small team that's itching to do interesting things with Drupal but needs a bit of help understanding how to set up a successful Drupal project. It's for the designer who knows HTML and CSS, and is willing to learn a bit of PHP, but doesn't want to have to learn how to speak developer in order to parse Drupal documentation. Most importantly, this book is for those who want to use Drupal to make their vision a reality, but need help working their minds around the way Drupal handles design challenges.

What I present here are not recipes for specific use cases; although recipes can be useful, experience has shown there's rarely just one way to accomplish an objective in Drupal. Rather, what I'm offering is context: a way to understand what Drupal is and how it works so that you can get over the hump and start figuring things out on your own. Over the course of this book, I'll help you understand:

- How to uncover the information you need to successfully plan a Drupal project (in Part I)
- How to bring solid UX principles to your team, and what types of deliverables work best with Drupal implementations (in Part I)
- What types of design documents can help you make your vision a reality, and how to use them (in Part II)
- How to set up a local development environment, and work with command-line tools such as Drush and Git to make site building easier (in Part III)

- A few tips and tricks for prototyping solutions in Drupal (in Part IV) and ways to make starting jobs easier (in Part V)
- How to break down your design layouts, select a base theme, and manage the code that Drupal is giving you (in Part IV)
- Options for estimating projects and dealing with tough client situations, and some sample client-facing documents to get you started (in Parts VI and VII)

A Caveat

Although this book offers plenty in the way of real-world examples, advice on how to get things done, and other important issues for Drupal designers, its goal isn't to teach specific project management, design, or site building techniques. Every Drupal designer and site builder has his or her own approach to creating projects, and it's hard to pin down one "right" way to create in Drupal. The key to appropriate planning and design, in my experience, is:

Knowing what you have to create
> This is where the site planning and discovery process, discussed in Part II, is especially useful.

Knowing what you'll need to do in order to get the job done
> This will vary depending on the project, but Parts III and IV will offer some interesting factors to consider.

Knowing how to walk clients through the process
> In Part VI, I share some of my experience from years of working with clients, including proposing and estimating projects, handling difficult conversations, and creating effective documentation.

Developing systems that make it easier to start, implement, and hand off Drupal projects
> You'll find a host of ideas throughout this book that will help you do just that.

In the last section, I share some examples of the client documentation I've developed over six years of running a design studio and estimating Drupal projects. Feel free to use the documentation in that section as a basis for your own project documents.

Focus on Drupal 7

As you will likely notice once you start getting into the practical examples, the site building examples in this book are focused primarily on working in Drupal 7. The reason for this is simple: although I've done a lot of work in Drupal 6, the usability enhancements in Drupal 7, the latest version of the Drupal CMS, have made it my choice for starting new projects. Despite this focus, much of the material in this book is version-agnostic—particularly the parts that focus on user experience, project planning, and design. Even the chapters on setting up a local development environment can be easily adapted for Drupal 6 projects.

About the Case Studies

While we will learn how to install Drupal on a local development environment and get started with installing modules (see Part IV), throughout several of the practical examples in this book we'll primarily be focusing on two real-world projects. Although this can make it challenging to "follow along at home," I have two reasons for this decision:

- I'm working on them currently, and I enjoy being able to do two things at once.
- Focusing on projects like these, as opposed to a single project made up for the book, gives you the chance to see how these ideas work in the real world, with all the frustrations and moments of unexpected joy that happen in real projects.

For most examples, we'll be using my portfolio site, *http://tzk-design.com*, as a model. This project is currently in the process of being redesigned as I refocus my studio, and it gives me a chance to walk you through the actual process of planning, sketching, creating layouts, and theming for a relatively simple site.

I am developing the second project, Urban Homesteaders Unite (UHU), with Tricia Okin of Papercut (Brooklyn, NY).[1] The site was originally conceived as part of Tricia's MFA thesis (as such, layouts had already been created), and I've been working with her to expand on that original idea and turn it into reality.

The goal of UHU is to connect urban homesteaders (e.g., people who are into gardening, food preservation, and other city-hippie pursuits) through home-based events, blog posts, and connecting with other homesteaders in their neighborhood. This lets me get into deeper areas of Drupal trickiness such as Views relationships and working with user profiles in Drupal 7 (cue evil laughing). You'll see some particularly interesting examples of this in Part IV.

Through these projects, I can show you a typical Drupal design process—from creating the project brief to ideation and sketches to prototyping and applying our look and feel to the site's theme.

Before we jump into the deep end, we'll start with some Drupal basics, for those of you who are just starting to learn Drupal. In the next section, we'll learn some key definitions you'll need to know to work with Drupal, understand how to break up the work required to make Drupal sites happen, and talk about the different phases that go into a typical Drupal project.

---

1. *http://papercutny.com*

Conventions Used in This Book

The following typographical conventions are used in this book:

Italic

> Indicates new terms, URLs, email addresses, filenames, and file extensions.

`Constant width`

> Used for program listings, as well as within paragraphs to refer to program elements such as variable or function names, databases, data types, environment variables, statements, and keywords.

`Constant width bold`

> Shows commands or other text that should be typed literally by the user.

`Constant width italic`

> Shows text that should be replaced with user-supplied values or by values determined by context.

 This icon signifies a tip, suggestion, or general note.

 This icon indicates a warning or caution.

Using Code Examples

This book is here to help you get your job done. In general, you may use the code in this book in your programs and documentation. You do not need to contact us for permission unless you're reproducing a significant portion of the code. For example, writing a program that uses several chunks of code from this book does not require permission. Selling or distributing a CD-ROM of examples from O'Reilly books does require permission. Answering a question by citing this book and quoting example code does not require permission. Incorporating a significant amount of example code from this book into your product's documentation does require permission.

We appreciate, but do not require, attribution. An attribution usually includes the title, author, publisher, and ISBN. For example: "*Drupal for Designers* by Dani Nordin (O'Reilly). Copyright 2012 Dani Nordin, 978-1-449-32504-6."

If you feel your use of code examples falls outside fair use or the permission given above, feel free to contact us at *permissions@oreilly.com*.

Safari® Books Online

Safari Books Online (*www.safaribooksonline.com*) is an on-demand digital library that delivers expert content in both book and video form from the world's leading authors in technology and business.

Technology professionals, software developers, web designers, and business and creative professionals use Safari Books Online as their primary resource for research, problem solving, learning, and certification training.

Safari Books Online offers a range of product mixes and pricing programs for organizations, government agencies, and individuals. Subscribers have access to thousands of books, training videos, and prepublication manuscripts in one fully searchable database from publishers like O'Reilly Media, Prentice Hall Professional, Addison-Wesley Professional, Microsoft Press, Sams, Que, Peachpit Press, Focal Press, Cisco Press, John Wiley & Sons, Syngress, Morgan Kaufmann, IBM Redbooks, Packt, Adobe Press, FT Press, Apress, Manning, New Riders, McGraw-Hill, Jones & Bartlett, Course Technology, and dozens more. For more information about Safari Books Online, please visit us online.

How to Contact Us

Please address comments and questions concerning this book to the publisher:

O'Reilly Media, Inc.
1005 Gravenstein Highway North
Sebastopol, CA 95472
800-998-9938 (in the United States or Canada)
707-829-0515 (international or local)
707-829-0104 (fax)

We have a web page for this book, where we list errata, examples, and any additional information. You can access this page at:

http://oreil.ly/drupal_designers

To comment or ask technical questions about this book, send email to:

bookquestions@oreilly.com

For more information about our books, courses, conferences, and news, see our website at *http://www.oreilly.com*.

Find us on Facebook: *http://facebook.com/oreilly*

Follow us on Twitter: *http://twitter.com/oreillymedia*

Watch us on YouTube: *http://www.youtube.com/oreillymedia*

Acknowledgments

The following folks helped me in various capacities while I wrote this book:

My intrepid editors, Julie Steele and Meghan Blanchette, gave me the opportunity to write the book and helped me make sense of O'Reilly's lengthy style guide. Thanks also to Laurel Ruma for introducing me to Julie so that I could actually sell this crazy idea.

Todd Nienkerk of Four Kitchens (*http://fourkitchens.com*) helped me understand how the ideas I've used in really tiny teams apply to the work of larger teams. His feedback as a reviewer (as indicated by the many times I quote him throughout this text) was invaluable.

Ben Buckman of New Leaf Digital (*http://newleafdigital.com*) was kind enough to lend a developer's eye to the text—including kindly nudging me about my consistent misuse of *Master* and *Origin* in the Git chapter. He, Ben Melançon, Stéphane Corlosquet of Agaric (*http://agaric.com/*), and Moshe Weitzman of Acquia, among many others at meetups and Drupal Camps/Cons, have been exceptionally generous in sharing their knowledge of Drupal development basics with me.

Jenifer Tidwell, a local UI designer in Massachusetts, was kind enough to review the book and provide perspective from a designer who doesn't know Drupal. If you haven't read her book *Designing Interfaces* (*http://shop.oreilly.com/product/0636920000556 .do*), published by O'Reilly, you should.

I'd also like to thank various colleagues and professional acquaintances, in and out of the Drupal community, who were kind enough to let me interview them for this series: Ben Buckman; Greg Segall of OnePica; Richard Banfield of Fresh Tilled Soil; David Rondeau of InContext Design; and Todd Nienkerk, Jason Pamental, Amy Seals, Mike Rohde, Ryan Parsley, Leisa Reichelt, and Andrew Burcin.

Finally, I want to thank my husband, Nick Malyska, for being the most supportive partner I could hope for, and without whose encouragement I wouldn't have been able to take the time I needed to make this book work.

About the Author

Dani Nordin is an independent user experience researcher and designer specializing in smart, human-friendly design for forward-thinking brands and organizations on the Web. Her projects have ranged from branding and positioning small businesses to redesigning the architecture of content-heavy websites to understanding how busy grad students organize their course workflow and designing online interactions to make the process easier. She discovered design purely by accident as a theatre student at Rhode Island College in 1995, and has been doing some combination of design, public speaking, and writing ever since.

She is a regular feature at Boston's Drupal meetup and is a regular speaker at Boston's Design for Drupal Camp. In 2011 she was one of several contributors to *The Definitive Guide to Drupal 7*, published by Apress, and she wrote three guides for O'Reilly's *Drupal for Designers* series; *Drupal for Designers*, which combines the three guides with new content, is her fifth book. You can check out some of her work at *http://tzk-design.com (http://tzk-design.com/)*.

She lives in Watertown, Massachusetts, with her husband Nick, and Persephone, a 14-pound ~~giant ball of black furry love~~ cat. Both are infinite sources of comedic gold.

About the Reviewers

For nearly two decades, *Jenifer Tidwell* has been designing and building user interfaces for a variety of industry verticals. She has experience in designing both desktop and web applications, and currently designs and develops websites for small businesses. She recently worked on redesigning the interface for Google Books. Before that, as a user interface designer at The MathWorks, she was instrumental in a redesign of the charting and visualization UI of MATLAB, which is used by researchers, students, and engineers worldwide to develop cars, planes, proteins, and theories about the universe. She blogs about UI patterns and other design-related topics at *http://designinginterfaces.com/blog*.

Todd Ross Nienkerk, Four Kitchens cofounder, has been involved in the web design and publishing industries since 1996. As an active member of the Drupal community, he regularly speaks at Drupal events and participates in code sprints all over the world. As a member of the Drupal.org (*http://drupal.org*) Redesign Team, he helped spearhead the effort to redesign Drupal.org (*http://drupal.org*) and communicate a fresher, more effective Drupal brand. He is also a member of the Drupal Documentation Team and has chaired tracks for DrupalCon Copenhagen 2010, DrupalCon Chicago 2011, DrupalCon Denver 2012, and DrupalCon Munich 2012. He is currently serving as the DrupalCon global chair for all design, user experience, and theming tracks.

Ben Buckman started programming with the BASIC page in a kids' magazine, and has been building websites since 1995. In college he studied political philosophy and worked as a web developer. Today his shop, New Leaf Digital (*http://newleafdigital.com*), specializes in development and assistance for nondevelopers with the Drupal content management system, and development with the Node.js platform. He has also ridden a motorcycle across 35 U.S. states, loves to sail, and is a cofounder of Antiques-NearMe.com (*http://antiquesnearme.com*). He currently lives in Buenos Aires.

Tricia Okin is a designer who has been based and working in Brooklyn, New York, since 2001, and founded Papercut in 2004. She resurrected Papercut in early 2009 after realizing she wanted to make good work with tangibility and purpose. She also realized she couldn't and would rather not do it alone in a design vacuum. From there, she called on the best resources she could find and mustered up a gang of wily collaborators with as much passion for being their own bosses as she has.

CHAPTER 1

Some Things to Remember About Working with Drupal

A Quick and Dirty Guide to DrupalSpeak

If you're just starting off with Drupal, one of the hardest things to figure out is what people are saying when they discuss Drupal terms. What is a node? What do you mean by taxonomy? The following list is a quick and dirty guide to DrupalSpeak, which is my tongue-in-cheek way of describing Drupal's unique jargon. It includes the most common terms you'll find people using when they talk about Drupal.

Drupal core (or core Drupal)
> The actual Drupal files that you downloaded from *http://drupal.org*. "Drupal core" is also used to talk about any functionality that is native to Drupal, as opposed to contributed modules.

Contrib
> Modules or themes that you install after you install Drupal core.

Module
> A plug-in that adds functionality to your site. Out of the box, Drupal provides a strong framework, but the point of the framework is to add functionality to it using modules. The website at *http://drupal.org/project/modules* has a list of all the modules that have been contributed by the Drupal community, sorted by most popular.

Theme
> The templates that control the look and feel of a Drupal site. Drupal core comes with several themes that are very useful for site administration and prototyping; however, custom themes should always reside in your *sites/all/themes* folder and not in the core themes folder, located at *themes* among your core Drupal files.

Custom

Modules or themes that you create from scratch for a particular site or use case and that reside outside of contrib modules. Modules can be created from scratch, or they can be created using Features (a module that you'll learn about in Chapter 18).

sites/all

A folder within your Drupal installation that contains all the files, including any contrib modules or themes, which are being used to customize your site.

 Any module, theme, or other customization that you create for your site should always reside in *sites/all*, in a folder labeled *modules* or *themes*, depending on the nature of the customization. Always.

Hacking core

Refers to the act of making customizations directly to Drupal core files, modules, and so on, instead of putting your customizations into *sites/all*. This is a bad idea for several key reasons, the most important of which is that every time you upgrade Drupal's core files (which could be several times over the lifetime of a site), any customizations you've made to core Drupal files, along with any modules or themes you've stored in the core *modules* or *themes* folder, will be replaced with the new core files.

Node

A single piece of content. This could be a news item, event listing, simple page, blog entry—you name it. Nodes can also have custom fields, which are useful for all sorts of things. Think of a node in the same way you would a page on a website or a record in an address book.

Content type

The type of node you're creating. One of Drupal's best features is its support of multiple content types, each of which can be sorted out and displayed by any number of criteria. For example, in a basic corporate site you might have the following content types: blog post, basic page, event, news item, and testimonial. Each of these content types can be sorted out and organized, using the Views module, to create the Blog section, Events page, News Room, and so on. Best of all, your client can easily update the Events page simply by adding a new event. Drupal will do all the work of sorting out the Events page and archiving old events.

View

An organized list of individual pieces of content that you create within the site, using the Views module. This allows you to display content related to taxonomy or content type, such as a "view" of blog posts versus a "view" of events.

Field

Elements of data that can be attached to a node or other Drupal entities. Fields are one of the best things about creating content in Drupal. Using fields, you can attach images or files to content, create extra descriptors (such as a date for an event or a subheading for an article), or even reference other nodes. While in previous versions of Drupal you needed to download a contrib module (Content Construction Kit or CCK) to add extra fields to a content type, Drupal core (as of Drupal 7) allows for a number of field formats, but certain formats—such as images, file uploads, or video—require you to install contrib modules. Chapter 13 provides a brief list of contrib modules that can extend the power and usefulness of fields.

Block

A small piece of reusable content such as a sidebar menu, advertising banner, or callout box. Blocks can be created by a view or other contributed modules, or they can be created by hand in Drupal's Blocks administration menu. The beauty of blocks is the flexibility of display—you can set up blocks to display based on any criteria that you set. This is especially helpful on home pages, for example, or for displaying a menu that's only relevant to a specific section of a website.

Taxonomy

Content categories. At its most basic level, you can think of taxonomy as tags for content (such as blog entries). The true power of taxonomy, however, lies in organizing large quantities of content by terms an audience might search for. For example, a recipe site can use taxonomy to organize recipes by several criteria—type of recipe (dessert, dinner, etc.), ingredients (as tags), and custom indicators (vegetarian, vegan, gluten-free, low-carb, etc.). In building the site, you could then use Views to allow users to search by or filter recipes by any one (or several) of these criteria.

Users, roles, and permissions

People or organizations that have visited, or registered, on your site. The key to working with users lies in roles; Drupal allows you to create unique roles for anything that might need to happen on your site, and set permissions for each role depending on what that role might need to do. For example, if you're creating a magazine-type site with multiple authors, you might want to create a role called "author" that gives the user permission to access, create, and edit his or her own content, but nobody else's. You might also create a role called "editor" that gives the user access to edit, modify, and publish or unpublish any author's content.

Base theme

A set of theme files, usually downloaded from Drupal.org (*http://drupal.org*) and stored in *sites/all/themes*, which sets the structure for your Drupal theme. Generally, a base theme should only set up defaults, such as page structure, grids, and some very basic typography; customizations beyond those defaults should be set up in a child theme, stored in *sites/all/themes/<client_name>*. The purpose of the base theme is to have a consistent set of files and standards that you can use for every project; the child theme holds all the project-specific CSS, jQuery, and so on.

Child theme

A set of theme files, stored separately in *sites/all/<client_name>* and built off of the base theme chosen for your project, which hold all project-specific customizations for your site. A discussion of base themes and child themes is available in Chapter 16.

Themers

The lovely folks in the Drupal community (which may include you, dear reader) who apply design elements to Drupal theme templates. This could include simple CSS and HTML, but often also includes more complex things such as PHP, jQuery, AJAX, and other frontend development tools. It also involves choosing the right base theme for your project and building a child theme that will contain customizations, and may involve creating specific functions in *template.php* for your theme. Advanced themers may also create their own base themes or build a custom theme for every project.

Template files (*.tpl.php)

Individual PHP files that Drupal uses for template generation. Most Drupal themes will have, at the very least, a *tpl.php* file for blocks, nodes, and pages. Once you get the hang of working with *tpl.php* files, you can create custom templates for anything from a specific piece of content or specific content types to the output of a specific view. You can also adjust the major *.tpl* files for your theme to create lovelier, more semantic code (e.g., getting rid of extraneous `<div class="container-inner">` tags).

Template.php

The PHP file, located in every theme's project folder, that contains all theme hooks, functions, and preprocessors used by your site's theme. In some base themes, you may need to create override functions in your child theme's *template.php* file to set up key variables, such as grid sizes or menu items.

Theme hooks/preprocessors

Bits of PHP code that you can use to override specific settings in your template files, such as how code is rendered, how menus are laid out, and other customizations. Some Drupal themers find using theme hooks and preprocessors much more efficient for cleaning up Drupal code, particularly when they want to customize code for a number of different content types, or for specific taxonomy categories. Rather than creating a custom *tpl.php* file for each different category or content type, you can create a function in *template.php* that sets up the code parameters depending on which content type you're rendering. For the most part, we won't talk about theme hooks in this book; however, they're quite useful to know as you move forward in Drupal. Konstantin Kafer and Emma Jane Hogbin's *Front End Drupal* (Prentice Hall) is a great resource for anything you'd want to know about theme hooks, although the current edition (as of this writing) is still focused on Drupal 6. Check out *http://www.frontenddrupal.com/* for more information on that book, and for a bunch of interesting tutorials on advanced Drupal theming. The chapter on theming written by Jacine Luisi for *The Definitive*

Guide to Drupal 7 (Apress) also contains a lot of great information about theme functions. Full disclosure: I'm one of the authors of that book.

Discussing Drupal with Clients

When discussing Drupal with clients, the biggest mistake you can make is starting to talk to them about blocks and nodes and views, and other DrupalSpeak. While some clients actually do understand these concepts, in my experience the majority of them don't, and frankly, it's not their job to know it. I've had this argument with many a well-meaning Drupaller who insists that "educating" the client about Drupal terminology is actually useful, but I see the same result every time someone tries: start speaking to a client about taxonomy and views, and watch his or her eyes glaze over.

My favorite way to talk to clients about Drupal is to start with the concept of a news page or blog home page (see Figure 1-1). Each individual post is its own piece of content, with its own fields, categories, and tags, and Drupal's job is to organize that content on the page for you. The client's job (or that of the client's copywriter) is to give you those individual pieces of content, with all their various fields, categories, and tags, so that you can put them into the system and set up rules for how they're organized.

Organizing Your Files

As noted earlier, any customizations to your site (modules, themes, etc.) should reside in your *sites/all* or *sites/default* folder. There are many reasons for this, but the most important one is for ease of upgrading your site. When upgrading Drupal core, you're essentially replacing all the files in your Drupal installation with the newest version of the files, and updating the site's database to reflect the new files. By keeping all your customizations in the *sites* folder, you lessen the risk that all your files will be replaced once you update. Another handy facet of using the *sites* folder to hold all your customizations is ease of editing; by keeping everything in one place, there's less to hunt through when you're looking to change a file.

By default, you should keep all your customizations in *sites/all*. If you're dealing with a single site, it's just as easy to keep things in *sites/default*, but if you ever get into creating multisite installations (which is way beyond the scope of this book), being in the habit of keeping everything in *sites/all* will serve you well. You also want to organize your code according to what it does; for example, themes should go into *sites/all/themes*, modules in *sites/all/modules*, and so forth. This is because Drupal actually looks for themes in a folder called "themes," modules in a folder called "modules," and so on. If you don't have things stored in the appropriate folder, everything goes to heck

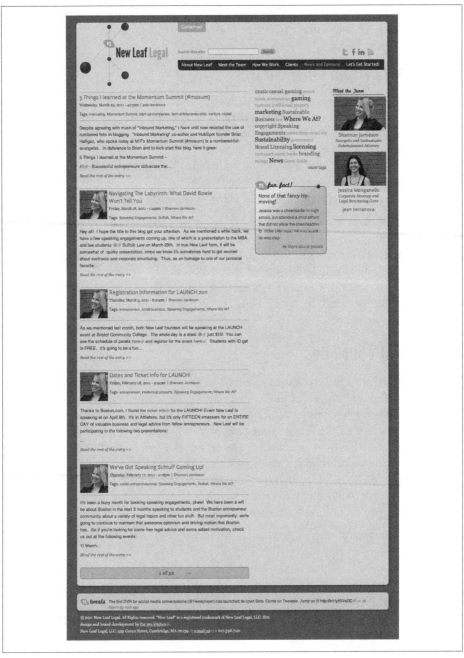

*Figure 1-1. A sample blog page (like this one, from a site I created for New Leaf Legal (http://
newleaflegal.com)) is a great way to start explaining the concept of nodes, taxonomy, views, and
blocks to your clients. Just don't call them that.*

Life Cycle of a Drupal Project

A good project plan for Drupal starts with the client. How much do they know about Drupal? Did they specifically request it, or was it something you suggested to them as you heard their list of requirements? This is surprisingly important information. For clients who are new to Drupal or just learning about it, you need to do a bit more handholding in order to get them on board with the process. Designing for content management systems is very different from designing for Flash or with straight HTML; it's remarkably common that designers new to Drupal realize too late that the brilliant layout they designed won't go into Drupal without a serious fight.

I typically divide Drupal projects into six distinct phases:

Phase 1: Discovery

> During discovery, we learn as much as we can about the client, the project, and the project's objectives. This is also where we start to create a map of the functionality we need to implement, any resources we'll need to bring in, and so on.

Phase 2: User experience (UX) and architecture

> This is where we take a deep dive into the lives, personalities, and other factors that define the humans who will need to deal with this project on a daily basis—both the end users who visit the site, and the clients who will end up managing the content once the project is finished. Deliverables for this phase may include wireframes, user flows, personas, and site maps. I may hold workshops with the client to brainstorm issues of information architecture and content strategy, or conduct rounds of user interviews with individuals who fit the client's target user base.

Phase 3: Prototyping

> During prototyping, which is usually done just prior to starting the functional implementation phase, we start testing some of the hypotheses and user flows that came out of the user experience phase. For simple sites, the prototyping and functional implementation phases go together; for more complex user flows, or for projects in which you're wrangling a ton of content, the prototyping phase is essential to making sure something you want to create will work the way you want it to in Drupal. The key distinction between the prototyping phase and the functional implementation phase is which components of the site plan you're working on; while the functional implementation phase focuses on how the entire site will be built, the prototyping phase often focuses on one or two key pieces of the user's journey through the site—for example, a shopping cart, or an area that requires a treatment unique from the rest of the site.

Phase 4: Functional implementation

> During this phase, the focus is on creating the functionality we described in the user experience phase, and ironing out any areas where the scope of the site may need to be adjusted due to budget constraints or the results of user testing. For smaller sites, there's a good chance that you'll be doing this work on your own, and many solo site builders can create great things with little outside help.

However, if you're not currently on a Drupal team, be advised: get to know some developers, and pay them to do things for you when you're in a rut with something. A good developer is a Drupal designer's best friend.

Phase 5: Visual design and theming

Notice, please, that visual design—here defined as the colors, fonts, images, and other branding elements that define the look and feel of a given site—comes fifth in this list. There are many reasons for this, most of which you'll find in this book. The most important reason, however, is that bringing visual design into the picture too early in a Drupal project—or in any significant project, for that matter—is a recipe for disaster. Part of your job as a Drupal designer is to keep clients focused on what's important—and what's important is how this site will serve their business objectives and their brand. While visual design is an important component of the site's value, it's just one piece of a much larger whole. Worse yet, it's also the piece that clients will most often fixate on, to the detriment of more important issues, such as whether a user actually needs 50 pages of content in order to make a purchasing decision. The best way to explain this to clients is that the discovery and user experience phases—*which are still part of the design process, by the way*—set up the experience you're creating for the user, and establish content priorities. The visual design and theming phase makes sure the experience you design in those early phases meshes with the client's brand and messaging.

Phase 6: Testing and launch

Always test before launch. And after launch. And again after the client has had a chance to muck around with the site. There are a few steps to the launch phase. First, you're moving your code from a development server to a staging server (the server that holds your site before the world gets to see it), and making sure parts of it didn't break in transit. Once everything is good, you'll move things from staging to production (where the site will ultimately live), and test again to make sure things didn't get lost in transit. For this process, it's incredibly useful to have developers on your team.

For most projects, I also like to include a seventh phase that helps consolidate everything we've learned from working on the project:

Phase 7: Wrap-up meeting/documentation

In the wrap-up meeting, you sit down with the client and discuss what worked well in the project, and what could have gone better. It's also a useful time to document the knowledge you gained through the project, either in an internal wiki for your team, or on Drupal.org (*http://drupal.org*), where it can benefit the Drupal community.

Figure 1-2 provides a quick visual breakdown of how a typical Drupal project works.

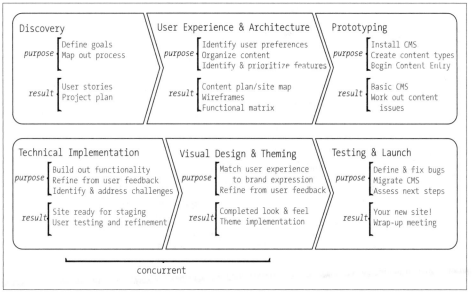

Figure 1-2. Typical project life cycle for a Drupal site.

Implementation Plans: Breaking Up Your Work

Another important issue to consider when talking to project stakeholders, and creating project plans, is how you categorize and prioritize your workflow. Since much of what you're doing in Drupal is managing content and/or creating specific functionality, it's vital to think, and speak, in terms of specific chunks of content or functionality that you have to create.

For example, Figure 1-3 shows the start of a functional matrix for Urban Homesteaders Unite (UHU), a project currently in process.

By setting up your work in chunks of content instead of discrete task types, you eliminate the confusion that comes with making a statement such as "On the week of the 14th, we're going to be setting up content types." While this can be perfectly fine if you only have a couple of content types to put together, any site that's larger than a few pages is likely to have enough complexity that each section of content or functionality will require its own content types, views, wireframes, and even custom page templates or modules—all of which will evolve during the course of the project.

By setting up the project plan with a list of very specific activities that will be done according to the tasks that must be accomplished on the site, you set a reasonable expectation with your client on what they'll be able to see at the end of a given period of time. Breaking down the tasks in order of importance also helps the development team get an idea of what the key user priorities are.

	A	B	C	D
1		Date	Task	Task Notes
2		**Task: Create and Post Events**		
3			Create "Event" Content Type	Events will likely be imported from Eventbrite; need to add Category and Neighborhood taxonomy before publishing.
4			"Event Types" taxonomy	Butchery, Urban Farming, Crafts, "Bikes, Bees & More", Cooking/Baking/Drinks, Canning & Preserving, DIY, Eco Home/Lifestyle
5			"Neighborhood" taxonomy	
6			"Location" taxonomy	Somerville/Cambridge, Brooklyn
7			Test Eventbrite RSS integration	
8			Document steps for Eventbrite registration	
9			Configure Eventbrite RSS feeds	Need to look at Feeds module documentation; how to figure out mapping?
10			Set up "event host" role	Permissions: post and edit events; access, create new Events feeds from Event brite.
11			Create documentation page for posting events.	Step 1: Sign up for Drupal account. Step 2: Sign up for Eventbrite. Step 3. Create your first event. Step 4. Go to "My Events" and copy the RSS URL from that page. Step 5. Create new Events Feed with the Eventbrite URL.
12		**Task: Post Videos or Blogs**		
13			Research on Video content type modules	What's the best option for 7? Do we want to stick with Youtube and Vimeo, or allow video uploads?
14			Set up "contributor" role	Permissions to post and edit their own events and blogs
15			Populate with sample content	
16			Views: Create Video feed.	
17		**Task: Search Events**		
18			Module: install Apache Solr	
19			Views: Create view of events by location	

Figure 1-3. Functional matrix for Urban Homesteaders Unite. Note the specificity of tasks: create a single taxonomy vocabulary or content type, rather than "all" content types.

Most importantly, setting up project plans by user tasks gives you the freedom to do whatever needs to be done to finish that specific task without having to waste time loading a bunch of milestones into Basecamp (or the project management tool of your choice) that the client doesn't really need to see.

And Now We Are Six

Now that we have an idea of how a Drupal project will play out, it's time to go a bit deeper into what each phase looks like. In Part I we focus on the discovery and UX phases, which help get everyone in the team (both you and the client) on the same page.

Discovery and User Experience

CHAPTER 2

Setting the Stage—Discovery and User Experience

In this chapter we talk about one of the most important pieces of the Drupal puzzle, and the one that new site builders often neglect. The discovery process helps us gain an understanding of the client, the objectives of the project, and some of the functional issues we might have to contend with; the user experience process helps us frame the interactions that will need to take place through the website, and helps everyone on the team agree on what we'll actually be creating.

Discovery: Breaking Down the Project Goals

Every project, from the most basic promotional site to the most complex online community, should start with a solid discovery process. During discovery, you're looking to accomplish two things:

- Find out everything you possibly can about the client, their business goals, and why they want to invest in this project.
- Create a set of documentation for the project that you can point to down the line to defend your design choices, and to help manage the inevitable "just one more thing … " conversations.

Every designer and team has a different process for discovery. Some like to have a quick meeting, sum it up with a few bullet points, and jump right into visual design concepts. Others need to take a deeper dive, and gather as much information as possible before doing anything other than very quick pencil sketches. I prefer the latter approach. It not only helps me orient myself to the client's needs more effectively, but it also gives me a well of information to draw from if I need to bring the client back to the same page down the road.

Project Discovery

I tend to break the discovery process into two distinct phases. The pre-estimate discovery phase (discussed in Part VI) gives you a chance to uncover the client's goals, establish some early functional priorities, and figure out how much work will be involved in creating their site, so you can provide a fair estimate of costs. During the project discovery phase, which happens after the project kicks off, you'll add to that knowledge and wade deeper into the client's business goals, competitive landscape, and other factors that will contribute to the design challenge. The goal of the project discovery process is twofold:

- To get a better understanding of the design challenge you're facing
- To put together a series of documents that will guide the design process, and which the client can agree to and sign off

Getting clients to sign off on your assumptions is, arguably, the most important part of the discovery process. Whatever your personal opinion of user personas and other types of design documentation, the most important purpose they serve is to give you something to reference in the inevitable event that you have to defend a design decision you've made, or redirect a conversation away from "Is it really going to be that shade of blue?"

For example, several years ago I did an ecommerce site for a client who was starting a business selling eco-friendly computer accessories and supplies. After moving through my standard discovery process and presenting the logo options I had put together, the client agreed on a specific logo option and we were ready to move into the next phase of the project. The next day, however, after discussing the logo with a couple of his colleagues, the client came back to tell me that something about the logo "didn't quite feel right."

Because we had established the client's business goals, audience profile, and other requirements in the Project Planner, the client and I were able to keep our conversation about the logo focused on the message we were communicating (i.e., what this business is and who it serves), rather than on subjective preferences (i.e., whether he likes a particular font). By the end of the conversation, we had moved from having to redesign the logo completely to realizing that a couple of minor tweaks would integrate the design more effectively.

This is one of the most valuable aspects of design documents. Not only do they help you frame your design decisions, but also you can defend those decisions and more effectively deflect stakeholder requests that will derail the design or throw your production schedule into disarray.

User Experience: Framing the Design Challenge

While the initial discovery phase sets up the client's objectives and perceptions of their audience, the UX phase focuses on gaining a deeper understanding of the site's intended users, and works on further framing the design challenge you're facing for the client and the development team. You can think of it as a second step to the discovery phase; this is where you start putting together all the documentation that will guide the team's development needs, settle issues of content organization and hierarchy, and work through questions and iterations with the client prior to spending time developing things in Drupal.

The tangible deliverables of this phase may vary from team to team, but they often include things like:

- User personas or scenarios
- An outline or matrix of functional requirements
- Sketches of screen designs or user flows
- Wireframes, which can be annotated to include functional requirements
- Paper or digital prototypes
- Content strategy documents, including a breakdown of site content, content types, and categories
- Breakdowns of the site's user roles (editor, member, etc.) and what content they have permission to access, edit, and so on

The goal of this phase, which can take anywhere from a couple of days to a few months, is for the client and the development team to fully understand who the site's users are and why they are coming to the site. Additionally, and most importantly, the goal is to identify areas of the project where budget or project scope might need tweaking, and head off any confusion that might occur down the road.

Getting Your Hands Dirty with UX

Being a user experience designer in the Drupal community can be challenging. In many of the conversations I've had with designers and Drupal teams across the world, UX deliverables are combined with project management activities, which can lead to a loss of focus on UX as the project moves forward and attention moves to time and resource management. Additionally, as the term *user experience* becomes more firmly established as an essential component of the web design puzzle, the question of what the term actually means has become a topic of debate—and the Drupal community is certainly not an exception to this.

For the record, when I talk about *user experience*, I define it as:

- A set of design principles that focuses on learning about the actual people using a site in a *qualitative*, rather than a *quantitative*, way. Numbers can be useful for segmenting markets and planning a campaign; good user experience requires balancing quantitative measurements with observing real people, and seeing beyond statistics.
- A set of design principles that balances the needs of a business with the needs of its customers in a way that encourages a positive experience for everyone involved.
- An activity that every member of the project team—from the official UX designer to project stakeholders—is responsible for, and that is best achieved by working collectively toward a common goal.

I do not, however, define *user experience* as:

- Creating a stack of wireframes or site maps alone in a cubicle and throwing it "over the wall" to the development team
- Creating and running usability tests
- Creating a set of "personas" based on who you think your customers are without doing any kind of research, prototyping, or testing to back up your assumptions
- Depending on frontend developers who can do usability testing or know a handful of UI "best practices" to handle all the UX aspects of your project

While these concepts are certainly important *components* of good user experience design, there's a distinct danger in considering any of them as being synonymous with a well-rounded UX practice.

Despite the challenges in defining the term, user experience designers are starting to make their mark on the Drupal community. A growing number of user-focused design firms are starting to embrace Drupal for projects, and the Drupal 7 redesign saw a huge number of usability improvements, led by UK-based designers Leisa Reichelt (*http://www.disambiguity.com/*) and Mark Boulton (*http://www.markboulton.co.uk/*), among many others. While there are still many improvements to be made, the fact that design and user experience are key components in the Drupal 8 project (see *http://drupal.org/community-initiatives/drupal-core/usability*) suggests that this issue is finally starting to gain traction among the Drupal community.

From the Trenches: Amy Seals, UI Architect

Amy Seals (*http://www.projectsend.com/*) is a UI architect from Boulder, Colorado, who works with Standing Cloud, a tech startup.

Dani: How do you find your time split up between UX and project management tasks?

Amy: In theory, it should be sort of half UX and half project management, but I spend a lot of time on the Drupal side, doing the overall strategy. Day to day, on a technical level, I end up in project management.

Dani: Which do you prefer?

Amy: I prefer the overall strategy. Watching something develop, reacting to users, and anticipating their needs is what I prefer to focus on.

Dani: How successful have you been at selling the idea of UX design to your clients?

Amy: In my experience, it seems the more complex the technology, the more willing a client is to trust your judgment about what needs to be done. Back in the early days, everybody knew what a website was, and there were these preconceived notions of how a website should work and what's to be expected. With Drupal, there's so much complexity and capability that clients seem to look for more guidance. But they also want to see results, so it's kind of a catch-22 in terms of how complex the system is and what you can deliver within a reasonable time period.

Dani: Have you found any challenges with rapid iteration or implementation with Drupal, or clients having unreasonable expectations in terms of when things will be ready?

Amy: Right now our development cycle is about two weeks, because we are using Agile, but [at] other places I've been there's a tendency to forget that Drupal is very flexible and very customizable, and you know—it is the Web. So we'd have these really long development cycles, and everybody would be really focused on these minute details that may or may not impact the overall user experience yet. There is a tendency towards trying to get things perfect, without really understanding what that is or whether it can be done.

Dani: I think there is also a tendency for some clients to focus on incredibly minute details, and it's hard for them to recognize that minor aesthetic details make little difference to their user.

Amy: Clients get overwhelmed with big-picture stuff, so they focus on very small details; if you can show them something like wireframes, for instance, or a user flow for a piece of technology, they can look at that, and think about it, and you can build on that instead of trying to constantly release these finished pieces—or having the idea that you need a finished project in order to get client buy-in.

From a client perspective, I understand the desire for something that's more "finished"—you're committing a lot of time and money, and you want to make sure that what you get is what you need. If you don't see it until the end, it's a little scary.

Dani: What kind of documentation do you build into a design cycle?

Amy: It depends on the project, and the client, and depending on the client, what stage of a project you're in. Wireframes are a given for me, but if [I'm] starting something from the ground up, I tend to actually deliver UI pieces, whether it's in Photoshop or something else.

If [I] have a project that's already underway and [I] have a look and feel set, I try to avoid touching the visual design, because it's more important for clients to get in and see how it's going to work and to understand functionality and how a user will use it, as opposed to spending time on visual elements trying to duplicate what's already there.

For complicated functions—like if [I] have a process that's ongoing, whether it's an account creation or something else—I tend to do user flows as well, even before I wireframe, so that ... the client [and I] can make sure [I've] covered all the pieces of that process. So [I] can say, "OK, here's the action at this time, here's how you can tell it's progressing and what pieces are required." From a project management standpoint, it helps [to] map out the project as well. The flows can help you map out what additional pieces you'll require to deliver the product, and make sure you have the resources to do it.

Dani: I also think it's important to be mindful of what the client needs to know versus what you or the developers need to know. When I'm looking at a wireframe, I need to know, "This is coming from a view of these content types, this is a block, and so on." The client doesn't need to know that. I find that half the panic attacks I see clients going through come from somebody talking to them about all of these very Drupal-specific things.

Amy: It's almost like you define your technical requirements for developers, but then you have to translate that for your customers.

Dani: You become multilingual in a certain way. You have to bring a bunch of people who don't necessarily speak the same language into the room together and say, "OK, this is what we're doing."

Amy: There is a tendency with complex systems for some people to say, "Let us take care of the details; we're experts." We don't understand that the client understands their users and who they're trying to talk to, and they need to be accountable for the product from a very detailed point of view. They may not be worried about whether or not this page is delivered with Views or whatever, but they need to understand at a base level how things might work, because ultimately it's their product, and if they don't understand what it is, how it's working at a basic level, and what to expect, I think that creates a lot of extra noise as well.

The client understands his or her customers, so there's a middle ground, where you're a translator—but you also have to be a filter. The client is going to tell you a lot of things, so you have to decide, as a UX person, which are the most critical to convey through the interface to the user? You're bridging the gap between a business, its customers, and the development team, and that sometimes can be a very big bridge.

Dani: What have been the biggest challenges for you in bringing UX to your team?

Amy: Educating people on user experience, and helping them understand what goes into that role. You're not just concerned with what this page says; it's how you're saying it and how that's reflected elsewhere in the site. It's how that user is going to go from here to here to here, and what they're going to expect when they click something.

Dani: How do you think Drupal changes the process of UX, if at all?

Amy: I think that because I tend to break things up into pieces—site flows and personas, or pain points and that sort of thing—Drupal helps with that because it's very much an evolving product. There's all these modules, and things you can do, and you can really mold it and shape the experience. Because of that flexibility, you have to be able to break it into smaller pieces. If you're implementing a new module, for example, there are various pieces at play, so it's easier to explain to a client that they're not going to be able to see instant implementation, because there's so much more to it than just turning something on.

Drupal also helps create the expectation that a website is not a fixed thing either. You get it out there, you mold it, and you shape it, and it changes as your needs and your strategy change. Drupal is very flexible and open, which makes it easier to drive that message home.

Dani: With Drupal, you have to get into a space where you are now talking about discrete sections of the site almost as a specific chunk of functionality. In order to engage a very rapid, iterative, and, indeed, Agile, process, you need to understand that you can't have a project plan that says, "On the week of the 14th we're going to do all the content types for the site." I've seen project plans that were like that, where on the week of the 14th we were going to do all the content types and on the week of the 20th we're going to do all the views. In reality, content types and views often get created together for specific areas of the site throughout the life cycle of the project—and they often get updated and tweaked throughout the implementation process as new issues are brought up.

Amy: It's integrated, so you can't break it up like you're used to doing traditionally—you know, "We're going to build something manually to update the content with PHP, so we can self-contain this little project and you never have to think about the rest of the site." Drupal really forces you to think about the site holistically every time you do something. That's fantastic from a UX standpoint. It does make managing pieces of a project much more complex, but it's a great self-check for managing that entire user experience, and managing it over time.

Dani: What tools do you use for wireframes and other UX deliverables?

Amy: I use Illustrator for user flows and wireframes. There are a couple of online components and bits of software that I've been playing with. I've been doing user flows and information architecture for a really long time in Illustrator, so it's kind of hard to move away from that. I have everything templated, so it's very fast for me to reuse the same components. Regardless of the tool you're using, I find that if you have things templated, the process is very fast.

Dani: What do you think is your role in the Drupal community, or rather the role of UX in the Drupal community?

Amy: I see it as, for lack of a better word, advocacy. I'm not a coder. I don't know how many UX people, if they specialize in that, are coders by nature, so I think our biggest role is getting out there and advocating for the use of the product—being able to articulate why it works and how it works and being a translator between the two worlds.

Bringing UX Design to an Embedded Team

If you're a designer who wants to bring UX principles into your next project, whether it's for a small project or for a larger team with multiple stakeholders, here's some advice from my experience working with a variety of clients and design teams. If you find you're really interested in this stuff, check out the resources at the end of this section for a list of articles and books I've found useful.

Study the Organization You're Working With

Working in any kind of organization requires a certain taste for politics. As designers, we get this already; we're used to having our work critiqued, and dealing with comments that we find, *ahem*, unhelpful. The trick to selling stakeholders on user experience design is, like visual design, in understanding its value to the organization and being able to back that up with hard facts. Speaking the language of the client also helps. This is where documentation that includes a clear set of project goals and key messaging points comes in especially handy. If you can point to a specific objective that your approach will help meet, you're well on your way to selling the idea.

Just as important as figuring out how to sell the idea of UX design to your clients is realizing when the client is a lost cause. In *Undercover User Experience Design* (New Riders Press), authors Cennydd Bowles and James Box offer some important red flags to watch out for when broaching the subject of user experience:

Design disinterest
> "Many organizations simply don't care about design, or see it as an expensive luxury rather than a strategic investment."[1] We've all met clients like this; they might focus on engineering more than design, or they might focus on what their competitors are doing to the point where they become little more than a "me too" business. If you can convince them of the value of your approach, supplementing your work with case studies from similar organizations that have been successful with this approach, you can help them make the switch into a design-forward company.

"Cash cows"
> If the company has a certain product, or area of the site, that generates huge amounts of revenue, no matter how poorly designed, expect a fight when you suggest changes. If you're still trying to introduce the concept of UX design to the company, you're better off leaving these areas alone unless you can prove your work will have a positive effect on the revenue stream for that product.

Enormous expectations and difficult deadlines
> "Sky-high expectations can cause disappointment, paralyzing fear of failure, and poor decisions."[2] Combining too-high expectations with unreasonable deadlines for delivery is a recipe for failure. If you run into this type of situation, the most important thing to do is to understand what's underneath these expectations, and see if you can shift the focus toward something that's more reasonable. If stakeholders aren't willing to budge, it's time to move on.

---

1. Bowles, Cennydd, and James Box. 2010. *Undercover User Experience Design* (New Riders Press), p. 20.

2. Ibid, p. 21.

In addition to these red flags, it's important to look at the organizational structure and decision-making process within the company. How many stakeholders are you dealing with? What's the approval process like? Are there any places where you can find an easy win, or does it look like this will be a struggle from start to finish? One of the interesting parts of UX design is running into clients who still don't understand what UX design is or how it can help their business, even if they believe they need it. As such, be prepared for stakeholders who will bring up strong objections to the approach you're trying to take, or managers who say they don't want to "waste time" on personas, user flows, or other common tasks associated with UX work. Also, be prepared to meet people who get UX and UI design confused, and who think of UX as playing around with Fireworks and jQuery, with a bit of usability testing thrown in. In time, you'll get better at figuring out which clients you can help and which will be an uphill battle.

It's Not About Looks

This is a tricky subject, coming from the world of visual design as I (and many of you, presumably) do. But if there's one truth I must impress upon you, it is this: user experience design is not about how something looks; it's about how it works. Is good UX design pretty? Often, yes. But is pretty design good UX? You'd be surprised how often it isn't.

Good UX design must balance the needs of the person visiting the site with the business objectives of the client who owns the site. This means that in order to truly create good UX—and I've found this to be true of effective visual design as well—you must be able to speak to the client's business goals, and to the path the user will need to take in order to help the client achieve those goals. This often means that, in the beginning stages of a user-centered design process, aesthetic issues (colors, fonts, etc.) will take a backseat to more pragmatic issues of sensible layout, information architecture, and functional requirements. It also might mean you make visual compromises that you really aren't happy with, if it makes the user's job easier. Thankfully, this is rare—but it does, and will, happen.

The Drupal Designer's UX and Design Toolkit

While every designer has his or her own set of preferred applications and supplies for everyday design and prototyping work, certain tools just seem to be particularly useful when working in Drupal. The following is the toolkit that I use for most of my work.

Balsamiq Mockups[3]

Balsamiq is a relatively small, but robust, Adobe Air application that helps you create individual pages of UI mockups incredibly quickly. The program itself contains many of the standard elements you'd expect in a web mockup (text boxes, headlines, video or image comps, etc.), but it's all done in a simple, cartoonish style that helps clients and the design team focus on what's important in the early stages of a project: content organization and hierarchy. Fusion by Top Notch Themes also put together a handy mockup of Drupal-specific components, which you can download here:

http://fusiondrupalthemes.com/story/100325/easier-wireframing-drupal-components -balsamiq-mockups

I've used this mockup's components to create some of the examples in this book. Figure 2-1 shows the entire set.

In the Resources section of this book's website,[4] I've also uploaded a copy of this document (as a *.bmml* file). For those using the 960 Grid System (960.gs) to more efficiently iterate wireframes and design mockups (see Chapter 6 for more information), the master download from 960.gs contains Balsamiq mockup elements for 12-, 16-, and 24-column layouts.

Fireworks[5]

Many designers prefer to use Photoshop or Illustrator to mock up screen layouts. Although both of these can be very useful (I used Illustrator for years before switching to Fireworks), Fireworks has both of them beat, for a few key reasons:

Ability to share layers among pages
> A key component of the multiple-pages feature of Fireworks is the ability to share layers (think Photoshop or Illustrator Layers) among several pages in your file. So your header, which is consistent from page to page, can be set up as a single layer, and then shared to every page in your document. Change that header once, and every page is changed. Genius! You can also export individual layers as an image, which is useful for logos, backgrounds, and other elements that you need to transfer from design comp to an image in your theme.

Ability to include multiple pages in one layout
> With Fireworks, you can include multiple pages for the same site in one layout. You can also share layers among different pages. Why is this valuable? Consider this: in most design projects, you might have several pages that you need to lay out

---

3. *http://balsamiq.com/products/mockups*

4. *http://drupalfordesignersbook.com/resources*

5. *http://www.adobe.com/products/fireworks.html*

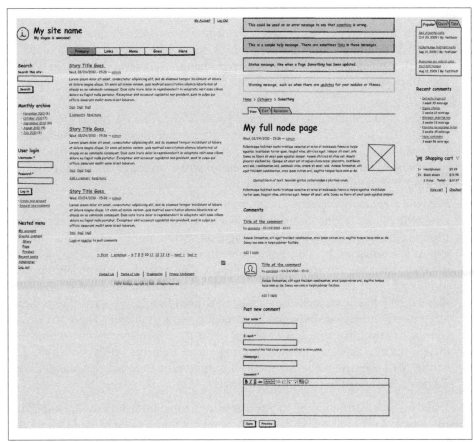

Figure 2-1. A set of standard Drupal components, for your rapid wireframing needs, courtesy of the fine folks at Fusion by Top Notch Themes.

for a given design. However, certain elements (such as your grid, or your navigation menu) don't necessarily change from page to page. If you created all of these layouts in Photoshop or Illustrator and had to make changes to the navigation, you'd have to modify *each of those files in turn*. With Fireworks, you can change one layer in your file, export it to PDF, and automatically see your changes across all the documents.

PDF export capability with clickable goodness

Speaking of multiple pages, you can export your entire document as a multipage PDF and use the Web Layer feature in Fireworks to create clickable hotspots to navigate to other pages, show rollover states, and more. The bonus? All of this can be exported into your PDF—meaning that your client can click around the PDF as though it is a prototype of their website.

Symbols

Symbols are how Fireworks collects elements that are standard in a given document. The beauty of working with symbols is that you can create a symbol, place it, and then quickly edit it when your design changes; wherever the original symbol appears in your document, it is replaced with the edited version.

Styles

If you're used to InDesign, you already know what styles are. Styles are a way of creating reusable visual elements in your design, including setting up standards for fonts and colors. If you alter or change a style, everything you applied that style to will change as well. This is especially useful when working with the greyboxing method, which I'll explain in Chapter 5.

Ability to use the same application for wireframing and design

One of the best reasons for using Fireworks is that you can use it for everything from wireframes to prototyping to design, all within the same file. You can also export individual layers to images from within Fireworks, which can save a bunch of time in theming, when compared to the usual process of slicing up large layouts in Photoshop or Illustrator. The fact that Fireworks handles vector images (like Illustrator)—but treats them as raster images (like Photoshop)—also makes it easier to tweak individual shapes without risking a loss of fidelity. There is a caveat to this, however; because Fireworks makes it so easy to incorporate design elements, it's also very easy to start putting visual elements into your wireframes before the project is ready for them. It's important to avoid that compulsion, particularly during the UX phase of a project.

Much like the set of Drupal components that were created for Balsamiq Mockups (discussed earlier), you can also find Fireworks templates for commonly used Drupal elements, courtesy of San Francisco's Chapter Three. In the Resources section of this book's website, you'll find both the Chapter Three Fireworks template and the Greybox template. You can also learn about the Fireworks templates here:

http://www.chapterthree.com/blog/nica_lorber/design_drupal_template_approach

Axure RP[6]

Axure is a program for creating wireframes, user flows, and prototypes for various types of web and software projects. While not inexpensive (as of this writing, a personal license costs slightly less than $600), it is one of the most well-documented, easy-to-learn, and efficient wireframing tools I've ever used. With Axure, you can wireframe all the major pages of your site map within a single file, quickly create links to other pages within that file, and annotate key elements with things the production team will need to know (e.g., which elements will require custom development, or what fields

---

6. *http://axure.com/*

they'll need to include in a content type). You can also use Axure's extensive widgets libraries (available on the site's Download page) to prototype all sorts of dynamic functionality, such as star ratings, pop-up windows, lightboxes, and other fun stuff.

But the best part of working with Axure is that once you're done, you can export the entire file as a working, clickable HTML prototype that you can upload and discuss with clients, with the click of a single button in the top toolbar. While you can also do some of this in Fireworks (using features such as states, hotspots, and symbols), the process is significantly faster in Axure, and Fireworks doesn't have support for subpages, which Axure does. What's more, the annotation tools allow you to explain how each piece of a given layout is supposed to work, giving important insight to the development team. In addition, it exports all your wireframes, with annotations—again, with the click of a single button—into a functional specification in Word. For busy development teams, the ability to create both a working prototype and a functional specification within the same file is a huge timesaver.

CHAPTER 3

User Experience— Techniques for Drupal

The methods and documentation you use for UX work will vary based on the project. For some clients you'll find yourself doing elaborate user personas and backing them up with weeks of research; for others a quick and dirty approach—in which you use existing information on customers to create a persona that you test as you prototype—is more than appropriate. The point of UX documentation is *to always do* some, *but to only do the things that make sense for the project.*

This chapter highlights some methods that I've found helpful. Many of them are borrowed from traditional UX methodologies; however, most of them have been adapted in one way or another for my Drupal workflow. Over time, you'll find a method that works for you. If anything, the key to creating UX documentation is to find a balance between an efficient workflow for you and creating something that effectively communicates the desired outcome of the project.

User Personas

A good user persona describes a specific person (or type of person) who uses your site, and focuses on documenting the reasons that type of user wants to visit the site, including specific tasks he or she wants to achieve. Every team does this differently, but there are a few components that make a persona valuable in the design process:

It involves real data
> If you don't have access to actual client interviews or surveys, talk to your client about their clients, and get some real data about what they need from the site. Note that this is very different from asking users what they want to see; your goal is to gauge specific tasks they need to perform, in order to generate ideas about what will help them accomplish those tasks easily.

It helps in mapping the site's functional or content areas to specific user needs
> The point of a persona isn't to tell a nice story about Judy the housewife; it's to make sure everything you're putting into a given site maps to a specific user need. This makes personas particularly valuable for working with stakeholders who come to you with long lists of complex requirements that don't meet specific user needs.

It helps the design and production team understand what they need to build
> A set of well-thought-out personas can clarify the overall direction for a site, answer questions about new things that come up, and keep the team on track. Good personas can also inform several other areas of design documentation, including visual design, functional specifications, and wireframes.

For most sites, you will have anywhere from one to four personas for different user segments. For example, a simple corporate site might have one persona for the target customer, another for the media, and another for others in the industry. If your client has broken up their target customers into different market segments, you may have a persona for each of them, or use your personas to demonstrate the commonality among a set of market segments.

Figure 3-1 shows a sample persona for a fictional site for holistic moms.

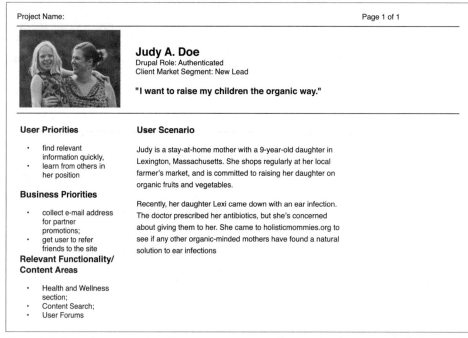

Figure 3-1. A sample persona. Note that it points to content/functionality this user might find especially useful. This is a great way to show stakeholders which functionality to prioritize.

When building personas, the important thing to remember is that your focus should be not on *who they are*, but on *what they are there to do* and *what components of the site will help them do that*. For example, an online banking website could have any number of user demographics, ranging from 20 year-old college students to retirees. A persona for this application, then, may focus on specific user tasks, rather than age/income demographics. This is useful in the beginning of the project, when you're just getting into user research, and even more so later in the project, when you have to defend your design decisions to the client.

From the Trenches: Richard Banfield, Fresh Tilled Soil

Fresh Tilled Soil is a UI firm that is based in Waltham, Massachusetts, and specializes in high-end application and UI design for startups. Richard Banfield, CEO, is a proponent of Lean Startup methodology. In the Lean world, similar to Agile, design starts with a set of user stories and behavior flows, put together quickly as hypotheses to test in the real world. The focus of Lean methods is to get something out and in front of people right away, to gain knowledge from real users, and to iterate frequently based on this new knowledge.

Dani: In terms of Fresh Tilled Soil's process, what types of documentation do you use? How do you keep the client focused on the right topic?

Richard: Let's think about all the documentation. There's the Scope of Work, which tells the client what you've agreed to do with them. Any change to that must be accompanied by a Change Order. This is kind of litigious stuff, or basic project management, but the Scope of Work may also include the development of personas, or the development of behavioral paths, or flows, or things like that.

Beyond the Scope of Work are the physical instruments you plan around: for example, a schedule that shows what we can achieve within the timeline. That's driven, in our world, somewhat by Agile, mostly by Lean, and that's about getting a Minimum Viable Product by a certain date. So if the client says, "I want to launch on the 25th of June," you say, "What can be done within that time that's going to move the needle?" Beyond that, it's "What are the flows we need to deal with that will allow us to achieve the behavioral goals that we have set forth for this particular set of audience members?"

We tend to develop flows instead of personas. That's not to say personas are irrelevant; if you are going to talk about those personas, you need to understand what behavior is associated with that persona, and is that behavior horizontally achievable across lots of different personas?

The documentation, then, is the schedule of what we're going to be able to do in a given period of time, and a set of flows. What are the various flows that are going to happen in order for a user to transition from being a stranger to being someone who is interacting with this project in the manner in which it was designed? Our documentation could outline five to seven different flows: here's what happens when this person is just browsing the Internet and comes across your site; here's what happens when they see your display banner; here's what happens when a friend refers them; here's what happens when they see you, but don't come back for six months and then come back again. Now that worries less about the persona, and more about the behavior.

User Flows

A user flow is a visual framework that describes the specific journey a user takes from point A to point B. For example, say you want to understand (or describe to a client) the decision process a user might take for creating an account. What's the primary incentive? How does he or she ultimately make the decision? What are the intermediate steps? A user flow can help you walk the client (or yourself) through the process visually.

I find user flows most helpful when framing a specific design challenge; for example, how a user might decide to make a purchase, or the decision process that leads someone to sign up for an account. The important thing to remember about any type of user flow is that it can sometimes be more useful to you and the development team than it is to the client; if you decide to present a user flow to a client, make sure you present it as a tool for helping you understand the design challenge, and not as a possible design solution.

I tend to start my user flows with pencil and paper (see Figure 3-2), and gradually move them into a program such as Axure (my personal favorite), OmniGraffle (see Figure 3-3), or Keynote. If you're an Axure RP user, you can annotate the flows you create in the program and export them along with your wireframes as part of the prototype or functional specification.

Mind Mapping

Mind mapping is a relatively quick and simple way to get a lot of ideas out on the table in one big brain dump, and to take a high-level view to recognize the patterns. Whether you're creating the map in software (see Figure 3-4), throwing up and rearranging sticky notes on a wall, or sketching it out with pen and paper, the point of a mind map is to generate as many ideas as you can around a specific issue, and then to step back and recognize the patterns that pop up.

I find mind mapping to be most effective when the objectives for a project are fuzzy or the client has trouble articulating them. By laying everything out in a visual format—either on a whiteboard or with a pile of sticky notes—you can often get the client to recognize their own patterns, or the deeper problems beneath the surface problem they're usually trying to solve. They're also very effective for outlining user characteristics; I use mind maps often to find common threads in the clients I work with—for example, when I'm working on my marketing plan (see Figure 3-4).

The best thing about mind maps is that they're quick; good software will often allow you to very quickly create and link thoughts to one another. In many cases you can

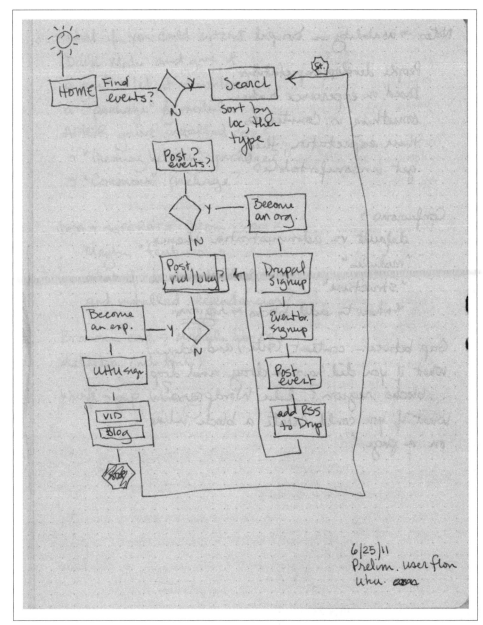

Figure 3-2. User flow sketch for Urban Homesteaders Unite (UHU).

even create a mind map during a conversation with a client, and convert the result into a set of bullet points for a project plan. For computer-based maps, I like MindNode for Mac (*http://www.mindnode.com/mindnode/professional/*) or Mindjet MindManager for PC and Mac (*http://www.mindjet.com/mindmanager-mac*). MindNode's basic version

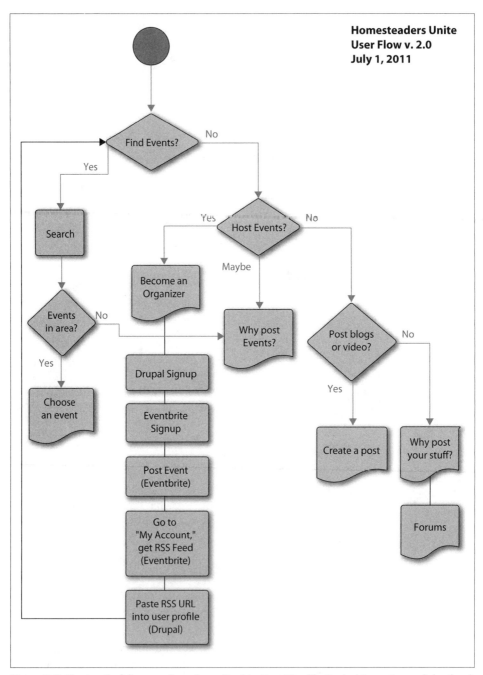

Homesteaders Unite
User Flow v. 2.0
July 1, 2011

Figure 3-3. Version 2 of the same flow, formalized in OmniGraffle. Both this version and the sketch in Figure 3-2 were shown to and discussed with the design team.

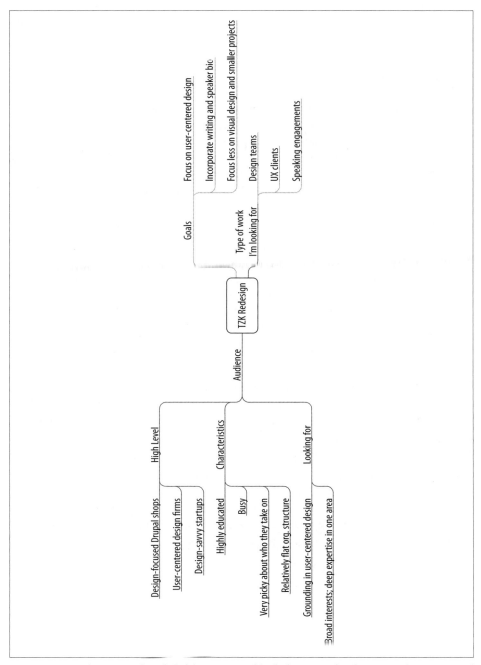

Figure 3-4. Mind maps can be a helpful way to quickly flesh out an idea for a site. This is an initial map for my professional site redesign (in progress).

is free and has many of the fundamental features you might need for efficient mind mapping; MindManager is pricier, but I find the interface and templates much more efficient to work with.

Functional Breakdowns

A functional breakdown is pretty much what it sounds like: it breaks down the functionality you're creating into manageable chunks. For simple sites this could be sections of content, such as the blog or the Events page; for more complex sites it could be the steps involved in creating a shopping cart or a particular widget. The key is to break up the site's implementation into chunks that are easy for stakeholders to recognize and for your team to focus on at once. It also helps with identifying Minimum Viable Product, a fancy Agile/Lean programming term that means "the most basic level of functionality we can start testing that will still be relevant to the user's goals."

 Minimum Viable Product is not about trying to work less, but about giving clients a return on their investment by getting them usable code as quickly as possible. This approach also has significant benefits for strategic UX; getting usable code into the world more quickly gives you a better opportunity to have real users interacting with your site quickly. This gives you valuable data that will help you continually improve the user experience of your site.

With Drupal, this concept becomes especially important; setting your bar for Minimum Viable Product too high can lead to exceptionally long development cycles, which drives clients crazy; setting it too low can result in a site that always looks half-finished.

For functional breakdowns, I may start with a spreadsheet, in Excel or Google Docs, and I list subtasks underneath a larger main task/set of functionality. Alternatively, if I'm using Basecamp, I'll create a discrete to-do list for each major task and use that list to hold all the subtasks related to the task. If I've spent some time wireframing, annotating, and creating a prototype in Axure, I'll look through my annotations and add them to my functional breakdown as discrete development tasks, which the development team can then add to the task management system of their choice.

On a very simple site, a functional breakdown might start like this:

- Task: Standalone pages
  — About Us
      — Get content from client
  — Contact Form
      — Install Webform
      — Get list of required info from client

- —Services
    - —Get content from client
- —Testimonials
    - —New content type, or standalone page?
    - —Get content from client
- Task: Create blog
    - —Get potential categories from client
    - —Create "tags" vocabulary
    - —Get sample entries from client (3–5)
    - —Create "blog" content type
    - —Create "blog" Views display: block, page
    - —How will usernames/author info be displayed?
    - —How will images be handled?
    - —Who's going to be creating these blog entries?

On top of these basic elements, I may use extra space/columns to relate functionality to its relevance for specific user personas/scenarios that we've identified, and for the complexity it will require to build. This is important for more complex implementations; if your client wants a component that's going to be especially tricky to build, but your user research indicates that users don't really find it valuable to their activities on the site, seeing the contrast between user needs and the resources required to build nonessential functionality can often help clients reprioritize in the right direction.

Screen Sketches and Wireframes

Wireframes can be created in a variety of different software programs; OmniGraffle and Axure are favorites among most UX designers I know, as is Balsamiq Mockups, and even Adobe Illustrator. Regardless of what program they end up in, however, wireframes should always start with pencil and paper sketches. The benefit to starting on paper is flexibility; when you're first designing an interface, quantity is much more important than quality. My initial sketches, done in pencil, are a mess more often than not. I use them primarily to work out issues of content placement, calls to action, and other basic "Why are we here?" issues. As I refine my ideas and things start to make sense, the sketches (still in pencil) start getting more refined as well, and eventually I can put them into a format that makes sense to someone other than me.

Over the years, I've created wireframes in each of the programs listed in Chapter 2, and I've found that each has its uses. Balsamiq is great for quickly documenting a conversation for someone who's about to start working on a page; in less than 10 minutes, I can throw together a page that reflects exactly what I'm thinking and send it off to a developer who can work on it. Fireworks is good for creating wireframes with very high visual fidelity that can easily be adapted to incorporate look-and-feel elements, which is useful if you're dealing with a very quick timeline and you'll need to jump into the visual design phase quickly after wireframing. Using Fireworks, you can start off with basic elements during the information architecture phase, then update your layout to include major visual elements in the same file you started with—and export those visual elements as images for the site's theme layer.

For more complex wireframing needs, particularly those that involve a ton of wireframes or are meant to test potentially complex interactions, I greatly prefer Axure. For one, it's fast; Axure's huge collection of libraries makes it easy to find widgets that perform the functions you need, and like Fireworks, you can include multiple pages in the same file, and share layers (called "masters") among different pages. Even more importantly, you can also create user flows directly in Axure, alongside the wireframes; annotate the wireframes to note important development considerations, functional requirements, or other tasks; and export your entire file as either a clickable HTML prototype or a fully functional specification, which can then be handed off to the project manager to flow into the project plan.

Content Strategy Documents

Content strategy documents can include anything from a simple spreadsheet with an inventory of current content to an in-depth analysis of content types, user roles, and a comprehensive site map. Since working with content can be one of the most complex and time-consuming aspects of working with Drupal (no, really), it's vital that you take time to understand the actual content you're working with and how it all fits together in the user experience. The various and sundry awesomenesses involved in content strategy are too many to get into here; however, should you want to explore the topic more deeply, check out Kristina Halvorson and Melissa Rach's *Content Strategy for the Web* (New Riders Press).

Low-Fidelity Prototypes

A low-fi prototype gives you all the basic functionality you're looking for in the finished product, using dummy content and without visual embellishments. You can build your prototypes directly in HTML, CSS, and jQuery, or export them from a program such as Axure or Fireworks. The purpose of the prototype is to quickly communicate the ideas that will guide design decisions and to get something that can be tested with real users, without having to put extensive development hours into ideas that will eventually be tabled.

It is important to note that a prototype is not, nor should it ever be, considered working code; although you can certainly prototype directly in Drupal, the time it takes to get a prototype in testable condition can be excessive when you're just hashing out ideas. Doing the prototype in a program such as Axure allows you to work through the concepts, discuss them with clients, and iterate your ideas in far less time than you would need to do the same thing in Drupal. For example, on a recent project that involved the creation of several different content types, each with complex relationships to one another, 35 hours were spent putting together a prototype in Drupal, and only one-third of the overall concept was represented in the prototype. When I switched from prototyping in Drupal to Axure, I was able to create a complete working prototype and functional specification, with all major concepts represented, as well as annotations and interaction, in about five hours.

Functional Specifications

Functional specifications can take different forms, depending on whom you ask. They can be straight text, with a list of functional needs broken down into discrete chunks, each starting with a statement such as "The system will ... ." Or they can be annotated wireframes, with each functional requirement listed in a table and numbered according to the annotations on the wireframes. Of the two, I find the latter most useful, and the development teams I've worked with seem to prefer them as well. As I build my wireframes/prototypes in Axure, I annotate as I go; this helps me keep track of the ideas behind specific decisions, and keeps everything related to the project in a single document. Once we've reached final approval of the wireframes, I reorganize my annotations so that they fall in a logical progression (left to right from the top of the page to the bottom), and export the entire file into a Word specification. I'll then add some front matter to the specification (e.g., a list of project goals and personas) and send it to the client.

In addition to helping the development team see exactly what a specific task entails, having wireframes directly in the specification also makes it easier to bid out projects, as external teams have found it much easier to connect the written specifications with a visual reference in the wireframe.

Paper Prototypes

While prototyping in the browser is useful when you're starting to imagine how a certain function or section of a site might pan out, it's also a lot of work. If you're not sure about a given bit of design logic, or how a particular piece of the user flow will work out, it could take a lot of time and energy to try to prototype the interaction in Drupal—and if you end up realizing the solution you've created has usability problems, or is best done another way, it can be frustrating to "throw away" all the work you did in Drupal.

One way to deal with this uncertainty is with paper prototypes. Paper gives you the flexibility to move things around when they don't work, as well as a way to try out complex interactions without having to throw a bunch of time into code. It also has the benefit of being extremely portable, and it lets you try out ideas on the fly. By showing a paper prototype to a user and having him or her show you how a given task would be completed, you get quick access to potential usability problems that crop up in your designs. Most importantly, once you discover those problems, *you can get more information about why the problems occurred, and make changes to your prototype on the fly*.

This is the single most important point about paper prototyping. While a usability test involving a piece of software or a website that has already been built can reveal usability issues that you have to tackle later, paper prototypes let you find the mistakes and fix them *in front of the user*. Each time you fix something, you get a little bit closer to something that works; and you save yourself a whole lot of headaches and code when it comes time to build things.

The level of fidelity in a paper prototype can range from printouts of screen layouts or wireframes to hand-drawn interfaces. No matter what level of fidelity you end up with, the point is to get something a user can start interacting with, and be able to show the user the interactions that are taking place while he or she is doing them.

When to Use a Paper Prototype

While paper prototypes could conceivably be used for any application, including a corporate website, they tend to be most useful when the interaction you're trying to create for a user has a bit of complexity to it. Examples include:

- Shopping carts
- Sites in which content categorization is a primary part of the navigation (e.g., higher-education websites, or ecommerce applications)
- Sites that require some type of form entry (login screens, checkout screens, etc.)

Working with a mobile layout (whether you're making a website or an application) is an especially good application of paper prototypes; since the experience of a mobile site may need to be more concentrated than that of a desktop site, paper prototypes can help you to identify which tasks or information is most important to users in that context, and where the frustration patterns come in.

Creating a Paper Prototype

The best place to start is the sketches you've already made—whether they're done in a notebook or in the wireframing program of your choice. In a YouTube example of a paper prototype test from Blue Duck Labs[1] for a kids' educational website, the examples are mocked up from digitally created wireframes; in another example, from South African UX designer Werner Puchert,[2] each aspect of the prototype is sketched by hand.

---

1. *http://youtu.be/9wQkLthhHKA*
2. *http://youtu.be/y4Wwnt9KIjg*

What you decide depends on where you are in the project and what you're comfortable with. At the least, the prototype should have:

A place to start
> This could be the home page, or it could be a specific section of the site you're focusing on.

Somewhere to go
> Each paper prototype should be focused on a specific set of tasks, so make sure your prototype includes each screen related to that task.

An indication of what happens when you go there
> This is the most important part. In a paper prototype, you're trying to assess the interaction that's happening, and make sure users understand how it is meant to work. Most importantly, users should be able to understand how it works without you having to tell them.

That last point is one of the key benefits of keeping paper prototypes low-fidelity. If, for example, a user clicks on a button you weren't expecting the user to click on, you should be able to show the interaction that will happen when the button is clicked. If you're sticking with low-fi prototypes, it's much easier to sketch out the interaction on a new piece of paper or a sticky note than it is to anticipate every possible interaction in a given flow for the purposes of a prototype—or worse, to try to make a quick mockup of a new screen in code while the user is waiting. That way leads to chaos.

Walking Through the Prototype

It's hard to demonstrate in words exactly how to walk through the prototype with a potential user. In an interview with David Rondeau of InContext Design (see sidebar), he walks through the process his team uses for working with paper prototypes; however, the following videos can give you a good visual demonstration of a variety of paper prototyping techniques:

- "Animating paper prototypes," a blog post plus video from UK designer Chris Neale (*http://e102.co.uk/?p=3*)
- Example usability test from Blue Duck Labs (*http://youtu.be/9wQkLthhHKA*)
- Low-Fi Web Prototype II, by Werner Puchert (*http://youtu.be/y4Wwnt9KIjg*)
- A few examples from Drupal UX designer Roy Scholten:
    - *http://www.youtube.com/user/royscholten#p/u/1/7VOkLzD3yDs*
    - *http://www.youtube.com/user/royscholten#p/u/10/Yn0ZgKf74xM*
    - *http://www.youtube.com/user/royscholten#p/u/9/Z0UZkkvDTCM*

From the Trenches: David Rondeau, InContext Design

David Rondeau is the Design Chair at InContext Design,[3] a user experience design firm based in Concord, Massachusetts. InContext Design created the Contextual Design process, which is taught at universities around the world. Paper prototypes are a significant part of the Contextual Design process, meaning that David and his colleagues use them as part of every project.

Dani: Why do paper prototypes work so well for you?

David: Paper prototypes are critical for allowing you to validate the structure, basic functions, and flow of your design, before having to code anything. It works because it's paper, so it's easy to make. There's not a ton of time and overhead involved; people argue that they can do HTML just as fast, but I don't believe it. Anytime you start using a specific digital tool, you start getting bogged down in details.

Dani: Walk me through the Contextual Design process.

David: In a typical project, we might go out and do 12–30 interviews with people, who are the users of whatever kind of product it is that we're creating. We consolidate the data, put it up on a wall, and then do what we call "walking the wall." We'll walk along the wall, looking at all this data, for a couple of hours, to prime our brains so we understand the user's problems—what they do, what works for them, what doesn't work for them. Then we have our brainstorming session, which we call "visioning."

In visioning, we tell the story of what the future would be, based on what we now know. It's wide, it's broad, and we come up with all kinds of cool things that will support the user in ways that haven't been done yet. Once we have that vision, that's when the second half of the project starts.

That's part of the process of using paper prototypes. You have a bunch of ideas, grounded in data. Even with all that data, and with clients in the room who understand the domain, you're still never going to get everything right. I've been doing design for 20 years, this type of design for 11, and I have yet to see a perfect first-round paper prototype. There's always something that's not quite right.

Dani: I think that's one of the things that make paper prototypes so useful. When you jump straight into code, or even Fireworks, you're tempted not to "waste" the time you just spent.

David: It's not something you feel like you can just throw away. If you've ever read Bill Buxton's book, *Sketching User Experiences*, this is one of the key things he talks about. What makes something a sketch is that it can be thrown away. Paper prototypes, then, are sketches that you have the user do their work in.

Dani: I have heard the argument that users don't get paper prototypes. These folks believe the only way you can really show an interaction is to show users something that looks the way it's going to look.

3. *http://www.incontextdesign.com*

David: I've been doing paper prototypes for 11 years, and I can tell you that they work. If someone's suggesting that they don't, that often means a) they don't understand how to use them, or b) they're trying to test the wrong level of interaction design.

The point of the prototype isn't just to validate your ideas; it's to come back with a prototype that's been changed to support the user's work practice. In interviews, a user might say, "Oh, I need it to do this thing," and we didn't put it in the design. Draw some buttons on the prototype, add another piece of paper, and put it in front of the user and say, "OK—let's try to use this." Once you've committed something to code, even in the early stages, it's too much work to change it. The user isn't going to sit there and wait for you to make changes to HTML.

It's all about being the most efficient and using your time wisely. If you think about design, you don't start designing the look of the buttons right away. You have to understand what the system is supposed to do—what are the core functions, what are the key places that you're supposed to go to, and how do you move between those places? Now you have an idea; now let's go see if this idea actually works for the people that I want to buy this thing.

Dani: What does the testing process look like?

David: It's a two-hour interview. Usually two people go into it. One person runs the interview/prototype, and the other takes notes, since it's too hard to do both at the same time. We go directly to the person's place of work because their office is where they do all their work, it's where they might have cheat sheets, notes, people they may consult to help them get their work done—things you'd never find out if you met them in a Starbucks. They also need to have their computer, because they may need to access their work so they can reference things, and so on.

We go in and ask questions for the first 15 minutes or so. What's their work? What do they do? Mind you, these are usually people that we've already interviewed in our initial research. We already understand their "work"; what we're looking for is hooks—real instances of work they just finished or need to do—so we can have them redo that work in the prototype.

Once we find those hooks, we'll stop and introduce them to the paper prototype. We'll give them a brief intro to the prototype, but we don't give specific details or show them how to use it. We'll say something like, "OK, you were talking about this specific piece of work [the hook] that you do; how would you do that here?" Then we give them a marker or a pen and tell them, "This is your new mouse; this is your new keyboard," and tell them that they can "click" wherever they want on the paper, and then we'll show you what happens.

Dani: Are there any pitfalls to testing the prototype with users?

David: One of the key things you don't want to do is what we call a "demo," which is more like putting it in front of someone and showing them what it does—"Isn't my baby beautiful? Don't you love it?" If you do that, you can't be sure they will give you an honest answer. If you get them grounded in a real case of their actual work that they've done or that they need to do, then you can talk to them about why they need something. You get the why, not just the what.

Often, we'll be going through the paper prototype, and they'll see some other piece of information or functionality and they'll say, "Oh, what does that do?" We'll say, "I don't know; why don't you click on it and we'll find out." They click on it and say, "I could use that." We could just capture that in a note as a validation of one of our concepts—but it's not really a validation because we don't understand why they want it. So we always ask why, or better yet, offer a hypothesis to the user and let them react to it. If you're wrong they'll tell you, and if you're right you'll be able to tell right away.

If you say, "Oh—do you need that for this kind of a thing?" [the user may say], "Uh ... yeah ... " and you ask, "When was the last time you did that?" and they say, "I don't know ... six months ago, maybe?" that's really a "no." But if they say, "I did that twice last week," we'll ask more questions. "What did you need? What did you do?" You want to give them the ability to tell you, but you can't ask too many really open-ended questions, because the users—being nice people—want to please you, so they'll make stuff up if they think that's what you want to hear.

Non-HTML Digital Prototypes

While paper prototypes are useful when you're working with users face to face, sometimes that's not an option. How do you rapidly create a prototype you can test remotely without having to jump into Drupal development?

Enter an entire world of digital prototyping software. With these applications, once you get over the initial learning curve you can create hotspots in your layouts, link them to other pages in your prototype, and mimic a wide range of responses to user inputs. You can test the prototypes in person, or use screen sharing/recording software such as Silverback (*http://silverbackapp.com/*) to test your work with people from their own computers.

If you're already using Adobe Fireworks to create your wireframes or design layouts (see Chapter 7), you can incorporate hotspots in your Fireworks layouts to link areas of the layout with other pages in your layout, and export the file as a clickable prototype. Axure RP, discussed in Chapter 2, is another great option for quickly creating prototypes you can post online and test with clients and potential users. Other options for clickable prototypes include:

- Justinmind,[4] another multiplatform desktop option. Justinmind and Axure both come with a hefty price tag: $495–$600.
- App Sketcher,[5] another desktop choice, with a price tag of less than $200.

---

4. *http://www.justinmind.com/*

5. *http://www.appsketcher.com/*

- HotGloo,[6] a web-based service available for a monthly subscription depending on how much you use the service.
- Pencil Project,[7] a plug-in for Firefox that will let you build prototypes from within the browser itself. It's also one of the few free options for digital prototyping I've come across.

HTML or Drupal Prototypes

If you're the type of person who prefers to "design in the browser," another option is to prototype your solutions directly in HTML and CSS, or go directly into Drupal. There are certainly times when this option is preferable to using other methods; for example, I may go straight to Drupal when I have complex content relationships to work out, or when I've sketched out a particularly complex solution I want to make sure can actually be built in Drupal. However, note that prototyping directly in Drupal or HTML can complicate the process very early in the game, and it's easy to get stuck focusing on what can be done rather than what *should* be done, in order to move through the process faster. In my experience, better design comes from sketching and moving to a prototype on paper or in Axure, and iterating on that prototype until the team feels confident that the solution we've designed is ready to move into development. This helps the entire process move along more quickly, and avoids time spent redoing solutions that don't turn out well in Drupal. We'll discuss prototyping in code more comprehensively in Part IV.

UX Techniques and Drupal: Some Practical Issues

Most of the techniques I've laid out here could work for any web project. How, you might be asking, would they be different in Drupal?

The main differences you'll see working with these documents in Drupal are the pieces of the design puzzle you're building and how they fit together. The Drupal framework has certain things baked into it—for example, the concept of views or blocks—and these can inform many of your deliverables in ways that aren't necessarily true for other systems. At the same time, it's important to remember that the purpose of deliverables is to communicate; while your developers would probably understand intuitively that content on a particular wireframe would be coming from some Drupal module or field, inserting this logic into client-facing deliverables can cause confusion.

For this reason, some designers use a layered approach to client-facing UX deliverables. In a persona, for example, you might include the user's Drupal role (which determines the permissions he or she has on your site) under the name, but you might also include

---

6. *https://www.hotgloo.com/*

7. *http://pencil.evolus.vn/en-US/Home.aspx*

the user's assumed market segment to help the client understand whom the persona represents. In a wireframe, you might stick to a more basic boxes-and-labels approach for showing the client, but you might have a separate "annotations" layer that shows the implementation team where specific content is coming from within Drupal.

A Further Note on Documents

The type and amount of design documentation you produce will likely depend on the project, the client, and how they communicate. At a minimum, most projects will include any combination of the following:

- A project brief that establishes the site's communication goals and functional priorities, and establishes standards for sign-off and approvals. You'll find a long-form project planner in Section 8; for a short-form project plan (useful for quick projects, or projects that build on work you've done before for the same client), see Chapter 4.

- A set of user personas or scenarios that offer specific profiles of the site's intended users, mapped to specific goals and tasks they need to accomplish. These can be full personas, such as those mapped out earlier in this chapter; you'll also find a short, one-paragraph persona example in Chapter 4.

- A preliminary site map that outlines the content we expect to see on the site and begins to establish a hierarchy for organizing it.

- A functional breakdown or specification that outlines specific tasks, functions, and so on that the site needs to "do." Preferably, tasks are prioritized according to both their relevance to the user personas and flows we've described, and the budget required to implement them.

- Any number of user flows or concept drawings that help the design team understand how a user will interact with what we're creating.

All but the last set of documents I share and discuss directly with clients, and require them to approve before moving on. User flows and concept drawings, although extremely helpful for solving user experience problems, often prove to be more important for me than for the client.

CHAPTER 4

Putting It in Practice—A Short-Form Project Brief

If you've taken a look at the project brief in Section 8, you've already seen the kind of information that goes into a long form project brief, which is good for working with brand-new clients and projects. But what if you're doing a quick, simple site for yourself, or a redesign of a site you've built one or more times before? In this case, you might want to create an abbreviated brief that focuses on just a few key items. For a short-form brief, you want to capture the following information:

Project goals

What are the goals of this new site or redesign? If you have information from the last time the site was designed, have any of those goals changed?

Personas/audience research

Who is the site looking to reach? Is it the same audience as the first time it was designed, or are you looking to tap into new markets? If personas exist from the last time the site was designed, how well do they align with what you know now?

Information architecture/content strategy

How will the site map need to change, if at all? What major sections of content will you need, and how much of that content do you have? How will the content be organized or tagged? This is where you can plan to spend the most time; in particular, pay attention to descriptive pages such as the "about" or "services" pages. How well does the current copy reflect the new audience and project goals? Don't forget major chunks of content such as blogs, project lists, and so on—what kinds of content will you share? What topics will that content be organized around? Is there current content that should be scrapped, or new content that should be developed? Develop a plan around getting the content organized, written, and into the new site.

New features or technologies

Are there any new features (slideshows, widgets, etc.) that you want to add to the site? Some may require adding and configuring new modules; others may require custom development.

Major release upgrades or content migration

Will the site require upgrading Drupal from one major release to another (e.g., Drupal 6 to Drupal 7), or migrating content from another technology, such as Joomla or WordPress (gasp!), into Drupal? Each of these will present some challenges and may require either rebuilding the site entirely or bringing in a developer to help with major upgrades.

Theme structure and CSS

How is the current theme structured? Are you comfortable with the base theme, or does it make sense to start over? This can be particularly problematic when working with sites that implement themes with many custom *.tpl* files; if the underlying base theme is poorly constructed (I'm looking at you, Garland), you could be in for a world of hurt when bringing the new theme into some logical order.

Real-World Example: The TZK Project Plan

To give you an example of how this works, let's look at a redesign for my business site, *http://tzk-design.com* (the old site is shown in Figure 4-1).

About four years ago, I redesigned this site to illustrate my focus on branding and web design for independent food companies and social entrepreneurs. Over the past year and a half, my focus has shifted to user experience research and design for complex Drupal implementations, as well as independent research and writing projects. This means a few things:

- My audience has changed.
- My project list should focus more on UX and writing work and less on site building and print design.
- My blog should also focus more on UX and less on things related to the food industry.

Also, the original site was built in Drupal 6, which means I'll have to worry about upgrading to Drupal 7, or possibly just scrapping what I have and building the whole thing in Drupal 7 instead. Most importantly, much of the marketing copy on my site will have to be rewritten to reflect both my new focus and the fact that my studio is a solo practice, rather than a team of independents as it had been.

Let's see what this looks like in the form of a project brief.

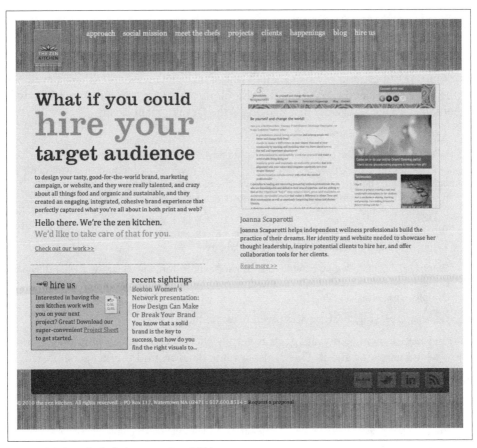

Figure 4-1. http://tzk-design.com circa 2011.

Step 1: Identify the Project Goals

A good list of project goals should be no more than about three bullet points, each representing the most important things you want to accomplish with your project. For this project, I have three main goals:

- To update the site's content and visuals to reflect my new focus on UX and research
- To better communicate my skills and the value I bring to teams
- To share my research (where possible) with the UX and design community by writing and doing speaking engagements

Now that I have my goals in mind, it's time to move on to personas.

Step 2: Identify the Audience

Back when this was designed, the audience I was looking for consisted primarily of entrepreneurs and small-business owners. Now I work mainly with teams who are working on Drupal projects, and generally one of the team members (either a developer or the project manager) is handling the task of introducing me to the person who will eventually hire me. Thus, my first persona is the Development Team:

> The Development Team
>
> *Who they are:* The Development Team is looking for a UX professional to help them understand the needs of their project's users. They are looking for someone who can quickly ideate and prototype based on research, and work with stakeholders to finalize functional requirements so that the developers can focus on writing code for products people want to use.
>
> *What will win them:* Understanding how the process works. Being able to fit UX into Agile development cycles. Knowing my availability.
>
> *What I need them to know:* How I work. What I expect from my clients and what they can expect from me. Emphasis on social innovation, progressive brands, and solving complex design issues.
>
> *Content focus:* Project list, services page, contact form.

Another key element to my site goals is getting the word out that I'm available and I know what I'm talking about. Thus, I also want to build around another persona, which I'm going to call the Sharer:

> The Sharer
>
> *Who they are:* Sharers scour the Web for interesting content and share it with their followers. They're active on sites like Twitter and G+. They may search under tags like #ux, #leanux, #agileux, #drupal, or #ixd.
>
> *What will win them:* Having interesting stuff to say. Making it easy to share posts among different networks.
>
> *What I need them to know:* How I think. That I want them to share my stuff with attribution.
>
> *Content focus:* Blog, presentations, "about me."

You may notice that these personas are much briefer than the more formal personas you saw in Chapter 3. There's a purpose to this; since this is a project I know inside and out, I want the personas to focus on documenting a brief understanding of whom I'm dealing with and how I'm going to meet their needs. Additionally, since this brief is mostly for my benefit (read: I don't have to show this to other people), I can get away with the basics.

Step 3: Focus on the Information Architecture and Content Strategy

The most recent redesign of the site featured some areas that were very successful for the audience I was trying to reach—for example, the Project List and much of the marketing copy. However, other areas have fallen by the wayside as my attention has been focused on other things. The site's blog hasn't been updated in a long time, and some areas, such as the recipe section (because, remember, my previous market was food companies), really haven't done much except sit there like boring, text-heavy lumps. For the new site, looking back on my goals and the personas I've created, I want to focus the content around a few primary areas:

Descriptive content
> A brief bio along with my CV/résumé, notes on the kinds of services I offer, and a list of clients.

Projects
> A list of projects, prioritized by the kinds of projects I want to get. Each section on the Projects page will have about three projects in each category, which will randomly cycle through a list of projects I've picked for the site. I don't want to completely ignore my years in visual design, so I'll organize them thusly:

> - UX research and design
> - Visual design and branding
> - Writing

The blog
> Focused around recent news, discussion of issues, methods, and ideas related to UX and interaction design, as well as current research I'm doing. All content will be easily shareable via buttons at the bottom of each entry. The focus will be on Twitter and Google+, but I wonder if there's a way to also send an entry to Instapaper or Readability through Drupal—or if that's even really necessary? Entries will be organized mainly with tags (to make remote entry easier); however, the main topics will be:

> - User experience
> - User research
> - Integrating UX with Lean and Agile development cycles
> - Bits of Drupal knowledge I pick up along the way
> - Other web design topics (responsive, mobile first, etc.) as they come up
> - Announcements (new work, events, etc.)

Speaking

Both events I'm speaking at, and notes/SlideShare presentations from selected speaking engagements. I need to find a way to separate the two (probably by date) so that upcoming events are always first on the list, and events that have SlideShare presentations attached will be in a sidebar or something similar. This content, like the blog entries, should also be sharable.

Contact/hire

Contact/screening form for new inquiries. I need to make sure I include a request for the reason they're contacting me (e.g., "I'd like to work with you on a UX project," "I'd like you to speak at our event," "I'd like to talk to you about your research," etc.), as well as an approximate timeline and budget.

Now that I have a general idea of what content will be on the site and how it will be organized (which I can add to and amend as I get deeper into the project), it's time to start looking at any additional features or technologies I want to add to enhance the site.

Step 4: Identify New Features or Technologies You Want to Include

Although I want to keep the overall look and feel simple and clean, there are a few things I know I'll have to add:

Responsive design

The current site's theme is based on the NineSixty base theme (*http://drupal.org/ project/ninesixty*); as such, it was easy to theme and customize, but it wasn't set up to be responsive. My ideal clients are likely to be tech-savvy executives and developers, and this means many of them may be checking out my work on their phones at any given time. From a theming level, this is relatively easy to accomplish using the Square Grid theme (*http://drupal.org/project/squaregrid*), which involves a different grid system but a lovely responsive-ready design; however, it will require thinking carefully about things from a content organization and display level.

SlideShare presentations and Vimeo/YouTube support

Currently, the site uses EmField (*http://drupal.org/project/emfield*) and Video Filter (*http://drupal.org/project/video_filter*) to handle SlideShare embedding; however, those are both Drupal 6 modules, and the new site will be in Drupal 7. I have to start investigating add-ons to the Media module (*http://drupal.org/project/media*).

Sharing capability on certain node types

I want to be able to let users share content (particularly slideshows and blog posts) easily once they're finished reading the page or viewing the content; for that, I'm going to have to research some good and simple sharing modules that are easy to theme and don't bring in a pile of excess code.

Aside from these things, I want the focus to be on the content of the site, not on fancy features or things that buzz and move. Now it's time to look at the last two things I need to worry about: upgrading from Drupal 6 to Drupal 7, and updating the base theme.

Step 5: Upgrade, or Start from Scratch?

The current site is built in Drupal 6 and has a lot of older content in it that isn't necessarily relevant to the work I do now. While it would make sense in many cases to do a major release upgrade (i.e., upgrading from Drupal 6 to Drupal 7), I've decided to start from scratch with Drupal 7 because, frankly, the site doesn't have much content to port over, and a lot of the content that will be there has to be created; thus, rebuilding it from scratch isn't going to be a huge deal.

If, however, I had a ton of content, particularly blog entries, that I wanted to save and give people access to over time, I would definitely try to do a major release upgrade instead of building from scratch. Upgrading will preserve the content and the URLs, and will ensure that people who have bookmarked entries on my site don't end up lost in a cyberspace wasteland when they try to revisit the site. This does involve a number of complications, though, and will likely require me to bring in a developer on the project. Although it would be totally worth it for a larger project, it's not worth it for this one.

Now that I have that settled, I have to consider the theme layer.

Step 6: Figure Out Theming and CSS Issues

The last thing I need to look at is the site's theme layer. Given the fact that the current base theme is a) set up for Drupal 6 and b) not set up to be responsive, it's time to look at a new base theme. After going back and forth between Omega (*http://drupal.org/project/omega*) and Square Grid (*http://drupal.org/project/squaregrid*), I've decided to go with Square Grid. It's light, flexible, and easy to customize (although it does require just a little bit of *template.php*), and I prefer the ease of updating the grid with a few values in *template.php*, one thing that drew me to NineSixty.

Switching themes will mean I have to redo much of my CSS, but since I'll be using LESS to theme this (discussed in Chapter 17), which I wasn't using when I last did the site, I would have had to do that anyway. Fortunately, I still have the files from my existing theme, which I can borrow from to create this one, once I have some designs set. See Chapter 7 to see how that goes.

Go Deeper: User Experience and Project Management

Books

Bowles, Cennydd, and James Box. 2011. *Undercover User Experience Design*. New York: New Riders Press.

Brown, Dan. 2006. *Communicating Design, 2nd Edition*. New York: New Riders Press.

Brown, Sunni, Dave Gray, and James Macanufo. 2010. *Gamestorming: A playbook for innovators, rulebreakers, and changemakers*. Sebastopol, CA: O'Reilly.

Buxton, Bill. 2007. *Sketching User Experiences: Getting the design right and the right design*. San Francisco: Morgan Kaufmann.

Krug, Steve. 2005. *Don't Make Me Think: A common sense approach to web usability, 2nd Edition*. New York: New Riders Press.

Norman, Don. 2011. *Living with Complexity*. Cambridge, MA: MIT Press.

Unger, Russ, and Carolyn Chandler. 2012. *A Project Guide to UX Design: For user experience designers in the field or in the making, 2nd Edition*. Berkeley, CA: New Riders Press.

Websites

52 weeks of UX. A blog about the process of designing for real people, published weekly. *http://52weeksofux.com*.

UX Magazine. A constantly updated magazine about varied topics of user experience design. *http://uxmag.com*.

UX Matters. Another online magazine about user experience, although not as pretty as UX Magazine. *http://uxmatters.com*.

Smashing Magazine's UX Design category. Regularly updated with great articles from designers around the world. *http://uxdesign.smashingmagazine.com/*.

PART II

Sketching, Visual Design, and Layout

CHAPTER 5

Sketch Many, Show One

When I create a logo design for a client, I'll often sketch many different options and then refine the three or four most effective options to show to the client. This approach works because the client feels they have a choice among several good options, but they aren't overwhelmed with decisions. It also works because they know I've carefully vetted each option and decided that any of them can work equally well.

Given this approach to branding work, it might make sense to give the client a few different options for their website's layout or information architecture, and to work with the client to choose the best option. In my experience, this approach fails for some very important reasons:

It keeps conversation focused on visuals, not content or organization of information
> I cannot emphasize this enough: the early stages of creating a website should be focused on content and communication priorities, not on visual ones. While visual communication is also an important part of the web design process, those conversations are best had after you've already established content and user experience priorities, and seen how real content flows through your site.

A website layout requires many more decisions than a logo design
> A logo, while essential to an effective brand, is a relatively small part of the overall identity of an organization. As such, the decision of which logo to choose is often a relatively quick one, and the client's focus is exclusively on this one image. With a web layout, there are many more variables to pay attention to. Is the font big enough for users to read? Does the navigation make sense? Have we covered everything that should (and shouldn't) be on this page? Throwing aesthetic decisions into the mix too early in the game prevents stakeholders from focusing on these other questions, which can hinder the user experience of the site.

For these reasons, and more, I recommend a "sketch many, show one" approach to both wireframes and design compos. With this approach, you sketch a bunch of different options for a web layout—usually the home page and at least two or three major interior pages—and pick the layouts that work best to refine and present to the client. A notable exception to this rule, which we'll discuss a bit later, involves the use of style tiles to present a few optional directions for key visual elements, such as fonts, colors, buttons, and paragraph/heading styles.

The "sketch many, show one" approach can be very successful, especially for clients who tend to focus on too many things at once. However, there's a caveat: whenever you present work in this fashion, it's important to reassure the client that you're showing them one approach based on what your research suggests will work best, and that this approach is open to change based on the client's objectives and preferences. Also, although clients have rarely needed it, I leave room in my contracts for a complete shift in direction, if the client feels strongly that the solution we've come up with doesn't fit their needs.

Some designers may bristle at the idea of only showing one layout option; however, I've found that this approach works well for a number of reasons:

- It keeps the conversation focused (which becomes more important as projects gain complexity).
- It moves you and the client through the process more efficiently, so you can move into prototyping more quickly.
- It shows confidence in your approach, which can give the client confidence in your team.

Perhaps most importantly, by presenting one design that can be iterated upon, you're making it easier on stakeholders and the production team by focusing everyone's efforts in one direction, rather than trying two or three directions to see which one fits. Additionally, when your process includes a solid UX phase prior to the visual design phase, showing one layout tells the client you've taken the time to get to know their brand.

A growing number of designers, including Milwaukee-based Mike Rohde (see the upcoming interview), have even started showing their early sketches to clients as a way to present truly low-fi wireframes and keep the discussion focused on user experience and not on visual design. In practice, I've found that the success of this approach often depends on the client and the rest of the project team. With some clients and developers, I can toss out a quick sketch in my notebook, show it to them, and they get it completely. With others, unless it's mocked up in a pixel-perfect Fireworks or Photoshop document, you spend more time defending your choice to sketch on paper than you do discussing potential design approaches.

Whether you build out your ideas in software or keep them strictly paper-based, the point of sketches is to come up with as many ideas as possible, get rid of the ones that don't work, pare it all down to the one or two best ideas you generated, and then talk those through with your stakeholders. Lately, I've been starting my sketches with the six-up templates from UX firm Adaptive Path[1] (see Figure 5-1) to help force myself to come up with more than a couple of options for a given page. Having to create six small

---

1. *http://www.adaptivepath.com/ideas/sketchboards-discover-better-faster-ux-solutions*

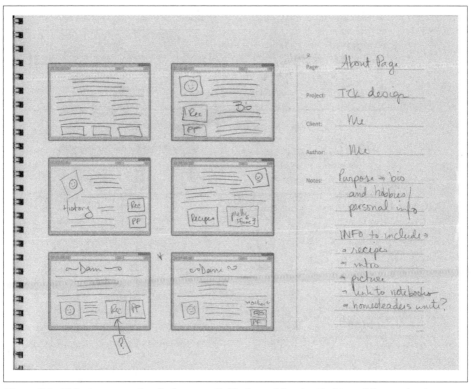

Figure 5-1. This six-screen sketch sheet, available from Adaptive Path's website, makes it easy to sketch multiple ideas for a page before refining the most effective concept.

sketches at a time helps move you past the obvious choices, and often I'll find that one of my later options works even better than my first instinct.

Once I've worked out a couple of ideas on the six-up template (or just created a bunch of thumbnails in my journal), I'll choose the one that seems to work best and work it into a larger sketch, either using a sheet from the Browser Sketch Pad from *http://uis tencils.com*, or mocking up a quick wireframe in Balsamiq Mockups (see Figure 5-2).

For projects that are more complex, or require moving beyond wireframes into a working prototype, I'll build things out directly in Axure, discuss and iterate with the team, and turn our final decisions into a functional specification for the developers to put into the project flow. Prototyping, whether I'm doing it myself or with a developer's help, also helps me work out areas of the content that may require special treatment, such as videos or content that needs to be formatted a certain way. I'll also use this opportunity to start collecting images, type treatments, and color options in a series of style tiles (discussed shortly), which I'll show to the client once we reach the visual design phase.

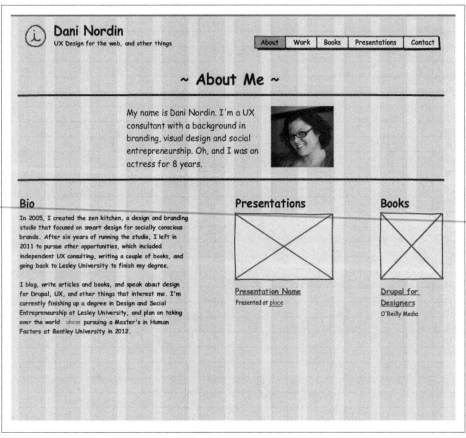

Figure 5-2. Using Balsamiq Mockups to refine one of the earlier pencil sketches. This mockup is based on a 12-column, 960-pixel grid, à la 960.gs.

From the Trenches: Mike Rohde, UI Designer and Illustrator

Mike Rohde is a UX/UI designer from Milwaukee who is known, among other things, as the illustrator for 37Signals' book *Rework* (Crown Business). As a designer who works on a variety of complex interaction challenges ranging from websites to multi-platform applications, Mike uses hand-drawn sketches extensively in his creative process, and considers them an essential component of client communication.

Dani: When you do interface work you show your clients hand-drawn sketches. How has that worked for you as you do UX work?

Mike: I've found that sketches work really well for helping to make a quick transition from [an] idea to a concept that the client can really get their head around. There's a level where you can [verbally] say, "Yes, it'll do this, and we can make it do that," and if they're not a web developer or even a designer, they often can't picture what that thing will look like when you describe it. In fact, it might become more confusing to them as they're trying to envision it. The other danger is if you describe it and they have one idea, then when you show it to them it's actually a different idea than what they had envisioned.

The challenge when you go straight to a finished project—let's say you invest a lot of time and energy creating a prototype, and you haven't gotten very good information or the client hasn't been as forthcoming as you'd like—is that you may have invested a lot of time and energy in creating a prototype that isn't going to work for the client, and you'll have to start over. Hand-drawn sketches provide something in between. You can do it to many different degrees; I've done everything from incredibly loose sketches that I've shown along with a little description and received approval on, to very detailed wireframe-type sketches.

One of the main things I've noticed about sketches is that clients aren't so afraid of them. One of the things that happens with wireframes, mockups, or prototypes—or anything that feels like it's at some level of "finished"—is that clients will sometimes feel that there's too much progress and they're afraid to say something. They won't say so directly, but they might feel like, "I can't really criticize it because they've already spent so much time on it." But that lack of up-front feedback ends up coming out in the end, and during development of the project we end up needing more changes, which are more expensive to implement. By giving them a sketch, you can let them feel like they can have some input because, you know, it's just a pencil sketch. I can criticize that—they'll just do another one, right?

Dani: *When you look at a wireframe that's been done in Fireworks, it's often easy for the client to offer critique like, "Oh, is that really going to be the font?" which doesn't move the project forward. I imagine that, with sketches, you can be really focused on "This is the hierarchy of information on this screen"—which is what you want to be talking about in the early stages.*

Mike: I think it comes down to setting expectations. Many times when I do sketch work, I'll work with Basecamp and upload a scan of a sketch that I've done, with a pretty detailed description of what they can expect to happen and what my thoughts are (see Figure 5-3 through Figure 5-5). If it's a combination of notes and a sketch itself, I'll very often include notes like "This will do that" with an arrow pointing to a button that will do such and such or so and so. But then I'll provide a description. And then when I speak to the client, I'll talk to them on the phone and point to parts of the sketch, and we can even go in and mark the sketch up during an in-person meeting.

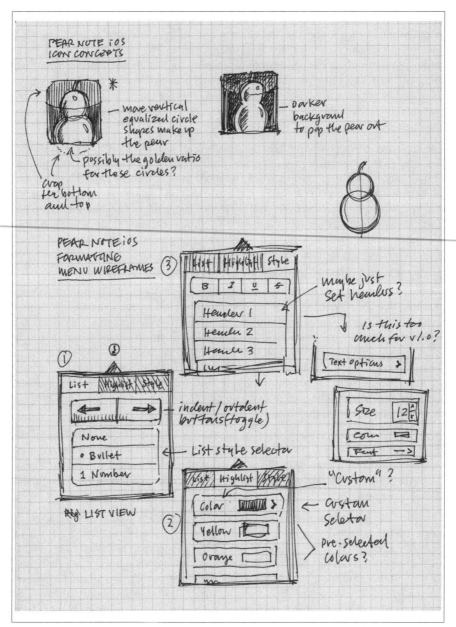

Figure 5-3. An early sketch concept wireframe for Pear Note on the iPad. Image credit: Mike Rohde, http://rohdesign.com.

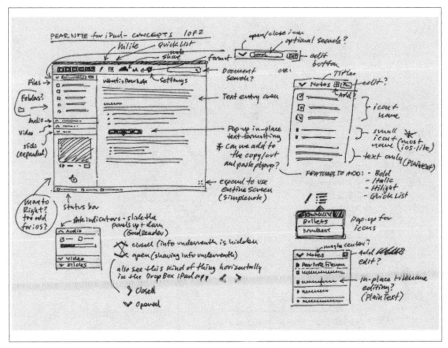

Figure 5-4. *Rough concept sketches for the Pear Note iPad icon and menus. These were created to explore some ideas with Chad (iPad developer) before jumping back to Photoshop for mockups. I explored all kinds of ideas and shared them with Chad. We discussed them further and then I created final mockups that Chad used for reference in the final development of the app. Image credit: Mike Rohde, http://rohdesign.com.*

What that does is brings them into the process of decision making and understanding. I think if I prepare them and say, "Look, this is a very high-level sketch of the idea that we're going for—we're not going to show fonts or colors or any of those things right now," it seems to work pretty well. Again, it's a question of setting expectations that happens with every kind of design we do.

As you can see, as with many things in Drupal there are many different ways to accomplish the same goal. Whether you show your clients hand-drawn wireframes or build them up in Fireworks or Axure, the point to remember is that a wireframe's purpose is to help the project team establish user experience and content priorities. Thus, it's important to keep wireframes as basic as humanly possible—you can deal with fonts and colors later

This, of course, doesn't mean you never have to think about fonts or colors. With style tiles (discussed next), you can collect all those visual elements that inevitably pop into your head during the early phases of a project.

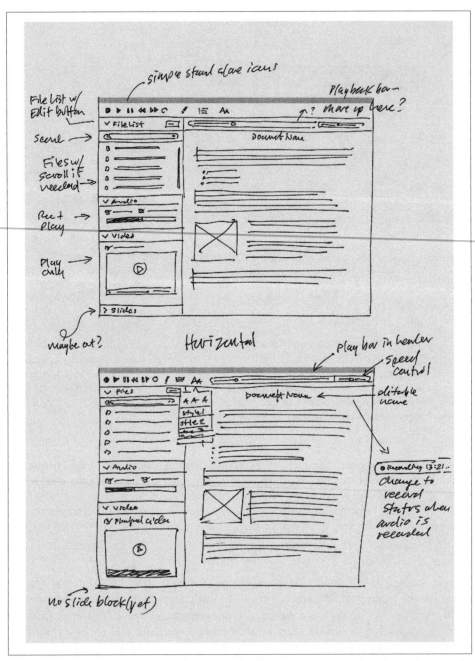

Figure 5-5. Two detailed wireframe-like concept sketches, used to explore ideas for working out the Pear Note for iPad interface details. In the end the app was simplified a bit from these sketches, focusing on core features for v1 (audio and text). Image credit: Mike Rohde, http://rohdesign.com.

Style Tiles: A Way to Explore Multiple Design Ideas

A style tile (sometimes called a *mood board*) is a simple collection of images, fonts, colors, and other inspiration to inform your design. The important difference between a sketch or layout concept and a style tile is its lack of structure; while a layout comp is meant to represent an entire page, a style tile is best kept simple. In a style tile, you collect specific elements (navigation options, headline and text treatments, etc.) that make sense for the project, shuffle them around, and see how they work. Style tiles are also meant to be works in progress; while the hope is that layout comps will only reach the client when they're in good enough condition that the client will sign off on them, a series of style tiles can be shown to a client at early stages of the project, to gauge aesthetic preferences and make sure you're on the same wavelength. They're also great for fleshing out ideas or keeping track of visual stories for future projects. For examples, see Figures 5-6 and 5-7.

As the figures show, this isn't a complete layout as much as a visual exploration of fonts, colors, and treatments for different areas of the site. When it comes down to theming the site, I might end up doing something entirely different, but at the very least, I'm developing a sense of the mood that I'm trying to create, and working out how the different types of images I will need to show will be displayed, how headlines should be treated, and so on.

You can create style tiles at any stage of a project. They're especially good for exploring ideas early on, while you're wireframing, as a way to collect your thoughts about visual solutions before you are ready to explore them with the client. The most important thing to note about them, particularly if you plan to discuss them with clients, is that *style tiles should not look like a web page.* Their purpose is to explore visual elements and treatments, not to create a layout for the website.

The benefit of showing style tiles instead of design layouts is similar to the benefit of starting a discussion with sketches instead of a more formalized wireframe:

They're fast
> A complete set of style tiles can take as little as one to three hours to put together, sometimes even less. They're also much easier and more efficient to iterate than full design comps; rather than fleshing out these ideas in full designs that then have to be iterated again and again, you can use style tiles to quickly identify a set of visual guidelines that will guide the overall look and feel of a site quickly and inexpensively. The quick turnaround on style tiles also makes them great for presenting and discussing multiple approaches to look and feel, for clients who really need the extra options.

They're modular
> Because you're using the style tiles to explore visual approaches rather than to set up a specific set of layouts for a given section of the site, style tiles can fit in very well with the modularity of the Drupal design process. In some cases, you can

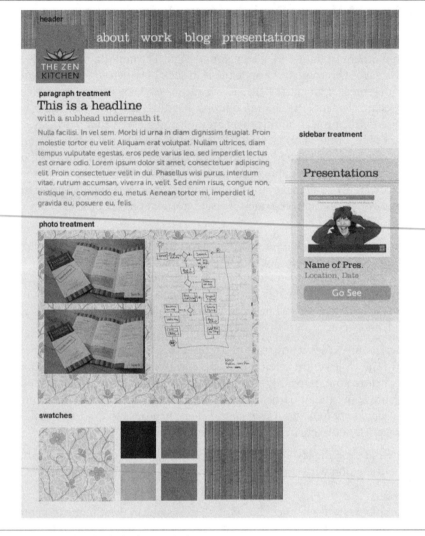

Figure 5-6. An initial style tile for http://tzk-design.com.

even start theming based on style tiles and wireframes instead of creating full layout comps.

They bring the client into the conversation, which increases their confidence in your approach and lets them see the design process happening in front of them

Having the client involved in the conversation early in the process helps them feel they have "ownership" of the design, which increases the likelihood that they'll approve the proposed design when you get to the point of theming the site.

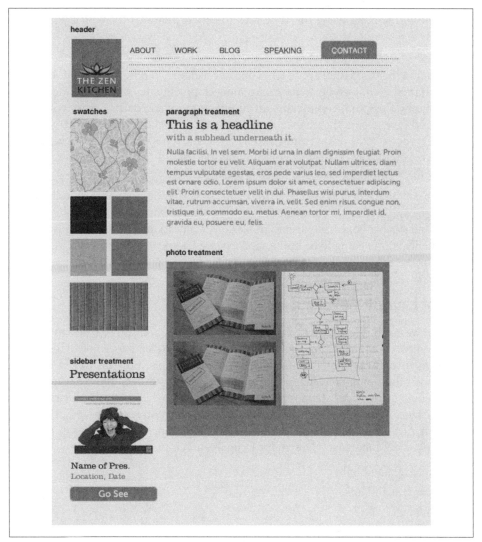

Figure 5-7. A second style tile, with a different feel to it.

They help keep the conversation focused

> By walking the client through a set of style tiles, rather than a complete layout, you can keep the conversation focused on aesthetics, rather than content and placement—which, ideally, will have already been settled by the time you've started discussing the style tiles.

What you're doing, in essence, is setting up a series of stylistic conventions to be used across the site's various elements. This has two benefits: 1) it helps you collect ideas for visual elements as they arise, often in the middle of other areas of design tasks; and

2) in some cases, it can help you save time in production by letting you go straight from wireframe to theming, using the style tiles to set conventions for your theme's key elements.

Once you've iterated your style tiles to the point where you and the client agree that you've found the best visual approach, you have a choice in how to proceed. If you've already started getting some content into a development site (which you ideally will have done by this point), you can start applying these standards across your site's theme, and give clients the chance to see how these visuals will play out with real content. If you're still working out issues with specific types of content or special areas of the site, you may want to start working the style tiles into full design comps, preferably with examples of real content from the client's site.

Whether you go to theming straight from your style tiles or you go from style tiles to full design comps, it's important not only to consider the basics, such as headers, paragraphs, and sidebar boxes, but also to think holistically about the types of content and functionality you're going to be building. Next, we'll look at some of the key elements you should be thinking about when designing for Drupal.

Design Layout: Covering All Your Bases

Once you've established a visual direction with style tiles and you're ready to get into design comps (or start theming), you must consider all the elements you will be dealing with in the process of theming a Drupal site. For example, how do you style block quotes and tables of data? What about pagers for list pages (i.e., the navigation that tells you how many pages are in a particular section and which page you're on in that section)? The following is a brief list of the elements you should consider when creating your style tiles or layout comps, adapted from San Francisco Drupal firm Chapter Three's excellent blog post, "Design for Drupal—a Template Approach":[2]

- Header text and links
- Footer text and links
- h1–h5 tags
- Body copy
- Links
- Unordered list items (bullets versus no bullets)
- Block quotes
- Image styles (sizes, scaling/cropping, etc.)
- Code snippets within text areas
- Admin tabs (the View/Edit/etc. tabs listed on node pages when users are logged in)

2. *http://www.chapterthree.com/blog/nica_lorber/design_drupal_template_approach*

- Secondary admin tabs (the links listed under admin tabs)
- Collapsible field sets and accordions (if applicable)
- Headers and typography for blocks
- "Read More" links/buttons
- Form elements and labels
- Tags, both within individual posts and in content listings
- Pagination for Views listings
- Data in pages
- Error/Status/Warning messages
- Help messages
- Blog post titles
- Author and post date information
- Page breadcrumbs

While you don't have to style every last element within a style tile, it's useful to keep these elements in the back of your mind while playing around with ideas. In fact, you may even consider doing two style tiles for a given project: one for front-facing pages (i.e., what the world sees) and another for client-facing pages (i.e., site editors, etc.).

Once you've gone over the style tiles with your client and you're confident that the visual approach you've decided on will work, it's time to start looking at the layout of your pages. As with the elements in the preceding list, the key is to make sure you've got your bases covered. While it's not necessary to create a design comp for every single page in your Drupal implementation, there are certain page formats that will show up over and over again in a typical Drupal site, and it's useful to set a visual standard for each of them. This list includes:

- Single node page, with one sidebar (remember, a node is an individual piece of content)
- Single node page, with two sidebars
- Single node page, with no sidebars
- Blog listing, with pagination
- Single blog entry, with comments
- User profile pages
- Pages showing everything for a single category or tag
- 404 (not found) and 403 (access denied) pages
- Groups pages (if applicable)
- Contact forms
- The home page

If you're working in Fireworks, the good news is that you can collect all of these pages into one document, discuss and iterate with the team, and export entire layers (similar to Photoshop layers) into images that can then be used in theming. If you want to get a head start on your design layouts, Chapter Three has created a multipage Fireworks file that you can download at *http://www.chapterthree.com/blog/nica_lorber/design_dru pal_template_approach*, and that has the following pages created:

- News/Blog page
- News/Blog page with sidebar
- Basic node page and typography
- Basic node page with sidebar
- News/Blog views
- Admin login with tabs
- Admin: collapsible boxes
- Admin: table
- Contact Us page
- Profile page
- Error message

While with Drupal 7 theming you may not need to worry about a couple of these pages, such as the admin areas, they're extremely useful for Drupal 6 projects, where the admin theme is often the same as the site's theme. However, when theming a Drupal 7 site, you should consider things such as admin links on individual pages, the site's login page, and profile pages, which don't use the Drupal admin theme. In Chapter 7 we'll walk through the process of creating a set of Fireworks layouts from scratch.

Greyboxing: An In-Between Option

Although it's tempting to go straight from wireframes to design layouts, some interactions are complex enough that it makes sense to take a step in between. Other times, you might find yourself dealing with a very tight deadline for a project and you need to move from wireframe to design more quickly than you would normally—but you still want to make sure the client's attention stays focused on content and information priorities before you jump straight into colors and fonts.

One alternative to going straight from wireframes to design is greyboxing, a process outlined by Chapter Three's Floor Van Herreweghe in her blog post, "Designing in the Grey,"[3] and in a recent presentation at Drupal Design Camp in Boston.[4] Greyboxing

---

3. *http://www.chapterthree.com/greyboxing*
4. *http://boston2011.design4drupal.org/sessions/art-wireframing-using-greybox-model-visualize-user -experience*

---

is, in essence, a middle step between wireframes (simple layouts with placeholders/blank boxes for content) and design layouts (which are often meant to represent the ultimate design of the site's pages). It gives you an opportunity to include some visual design elements while you're wireframing, but it also lets you move from wireframe to final design sooner than you would in a traditional wireframe-to-layout design process, which is useful for projects that require a very strict timeline.

The idea is that you already have a sense—through your sketches—of the page's content, as well as some different visual approaches for the page, which you incorporated into your style tiles. But you're not quite ready to take the leap into full-on design mode—for example, if there are content issues the client still needs to settle on. The important thing to note here is that *greyboxing does not replace sketching*; rather, it gives you an interim step in the process before you get to a complete design. For example, Figure 5-8 is an example of a greybox layout for the Events page of the Brooklyn Urban Homesteaders Unite site.

In projects with very tight deadlines, greyboxing can also be a way to go from sketches to a starting point for your layout while keeping the client's attention on content organization and flow rather than aesthetic preferences. In her session at Design for Drupal Camp,[4] Van Herreweghe used an example from a project that had only three weeks available for the entire design phase; going into greyboxing allowed her to quickly set a visual standard, and evolve that visual standard with colors, fonts, and so on as the layout moved closer to being finalized. This is another benefit to using Fireworks for the greyboxing process; by using the Styles feature (similar to InDesign's Styles palette) and layers that are shared among multiple pages, you can simply edit a style to change all instances of a given element within your document, and translate that change to multiple pages within the document, rather than changing it in a half-dozen individual Photoshop files. This means you can start with your greybox layout, iterate, and finalize the design for multiple pages, all by adjusting one file.

Another thing that can help you make your layout decisions more efficiently is working with a grid framework. In the next chapter we'll discuss two of my favorites: 960.gs and Square Grid.

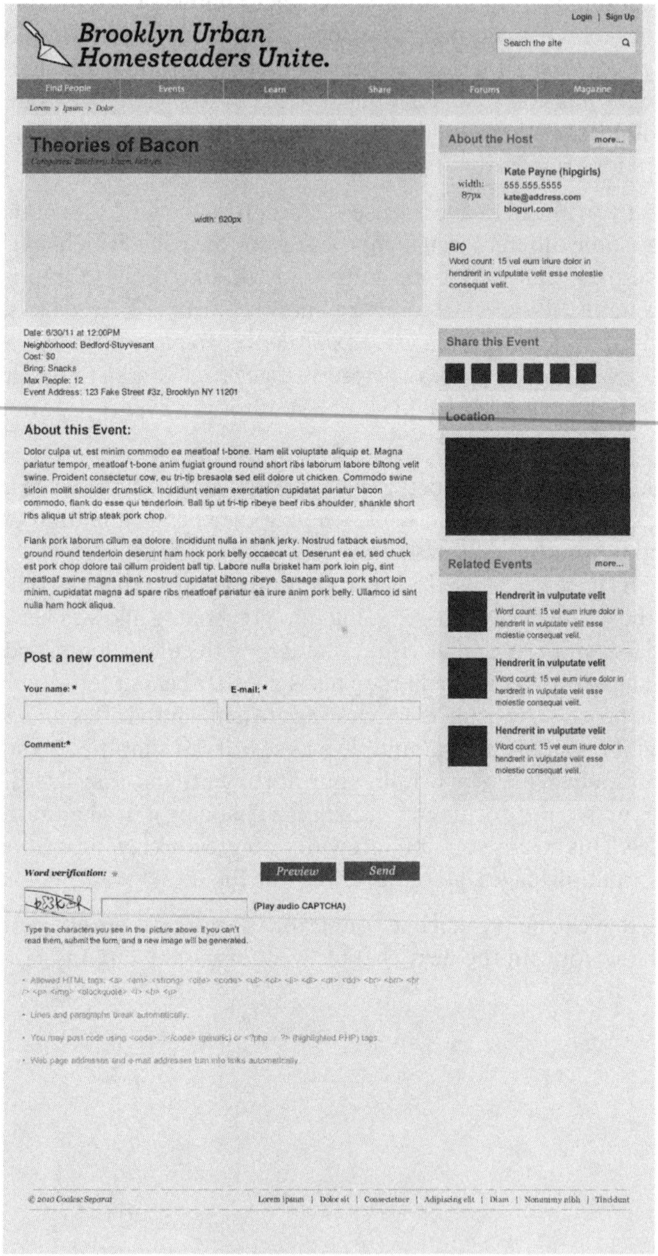

Figure 5-8. This Events page was laid out using the greyboxing technique. Note that some visual standards have already started to be set; images have placeholders connected to them, but everything is still in varying shades of grey.

CHAPTER 6

Working with Layout Grids

As you may have noticed from the series of semitransparent rectangles overlaying a few examples in this book, I use grid systems fairly often. Several different grid systems are available for websites, many of which were created for specific projects by developers who decided to give their work back to the design community. This chapter will focus on two that I've become a fan of: 960.gs and Square Grid.

The 960 Grid System (960.gs, see Figure 6-1), developed by Nathan Smith, focuses on a page width of 960 pixels, which makes it suitable for any monitor with a resolution of 1024 × 768 or higher. Three standard grids are available—12-column, 16-column, and a relatively new 24-column grid—and each column in the grid is set up with 10-pixel margins on each side to give your blocks plenty of room to breathe. The grid is incorporated into both the NineSixty (*http://drupal.org/project/ninesixty*) and Omega (*http://drupal.org/project/omega*) Drupal themes, and the 960 grid generator (*http://grids.heroku.com/*) allows you to create your own version of the 960 grid by setting up some initial grid values, which you can then add to a base theme of your choosing.

Square Grid (*http://thesquaregrid.com/*, see Figure 6-2), developed originally by Avraham Cornfeld, uses a total width of 994 pixels and is built on 35 columns, each 28 pixels wide, that you can combine in a wide variety of ways. This offers a bit more flexibility than 960.gs; grids are available in ranges of 2, 3, 4, 6, 12, and 18 columns, and you can set up the grid to use the Golden Ratio with two, three, or four columns, which makes design nerds very, very happy. The Square Grid theme by Laura Scott of PingV Creative (*http://drupal.org/project/squaregrid*) incorporates the Square Grid in a mobile-first, responsive-friendly theme that's lightweight, well documented, and remarkably simple to customize, although you will need to spend a little bit of time in *template.php* to customize the grid settings.

Why Use a Grid?

Grids have been a standard part of graphic design for decades. In addition to providing much-needed structure in a layout, grids also make information easier for users to

Figure 6-1. Nathan Smith's lovely 960.gs is a good starting place for working with grids in your web design. If you want to try your hand at a custom grid, it even includes a custom grid generator that will compile all the CSS for you.

process. When confronted with a layout—whether it's a printed brochure or a complex social media website—our eyes struggle first to instill some sort of order to what we're seeing. When we come across a chaotic layout we focus more on the misalignment than the message or content of the piece. Grids, then, give us the ability to create that order, and to make it easier for the people accessing our content to pay attention to what's important about the page. See Figure 6-3 for an example.

Additionally, and particularly in regard to layout for the Web, a grid system can enable you to create a set of known constraints that can help you to focus your design choices. As the logistics of implementing our solutions for the Web continue to increase in complexity, the structure provided by different grid systems gives you one less thing to worry about when implementing your layout.

This also means you can iterate on a design more quickly. Rather than thinking of elements on a page in terms of pixel widths, which can range from 100 pixels to 960

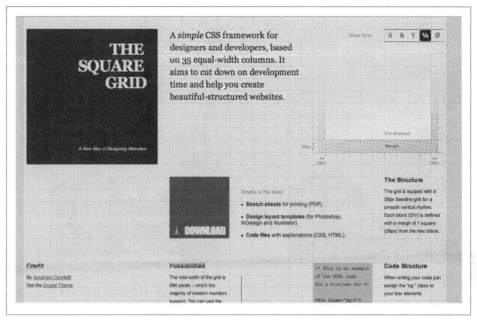

Figure 6-2. The Square Grid website has a full download for the Square Grid framework, including CSS, sketch sheets, and layout templates. You can also download a Square Grid base theme for Drupal 7 at http://drupal.org/project/squaregrid.

pixels or more, a grid system allows you to think of those elements in terms of how many columns they occupy. This is remarkably useful when it comes to efficiency; instead of kvetching about whether a sidebar should be 200 pixels or 234 pixels wide, for example, and spending your time worrying about padding and floating, you can simply change the sidebar's width from two columns to three columns.

Grids in Wireframing

Working with a grid system also makes wireframing more efficient. I find that a well-constructed grid even makes it easier for me to sketch my ideas; having a grid right there on the page lets me more easily consider issues of hierarchy, proportion, and overall layout without second-guessing myself. The classic 960 grid uses 12 or 16 columns; however, recently a 24-column grid was added, which was built into the Omega theme as a grid option. Square Grid offers a variety of grid options, and the website includes a "cheat sheet" that will let you quickly visualize how many columns you'll need in each section to achieve a desired layout.

When using 960, I prefer the 24-column layout; it has enough columns to be very flexible (e.g., you can have either three or four columns of content in a given region), but not so many that it's hard to figure out how many to use for a given element.

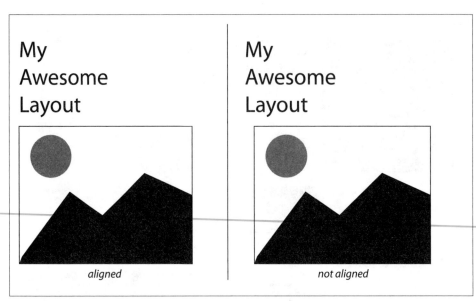

Figure 6-3. Elements that are even slightly misaligned can distract users.

Figure 6-4, a very early wireframe for my personal site, uses a 12-column grid. In Figure 6-5, I've revised the wireframe to use a 24-column grid.

Grids in Theming

Currently, the only base theme that incorporates Square Grid is the Square Grid theme, by Laura Scott (*http://drupal.org/project/squaregrid*). The Square Grid theme has the advantage of being extremely lightweight and very well documented, although you do have to use theme functions in template.php to set up custom grid values. If you prefer 960, several base themes are available for Drupal that have the 960.gs grid built right into them. Two of these themes, NineSixty (*http://drupal.org/project/ninesixty*) and Omega (*http://drupal.org/project/omega*), we'll discuss further in Chapter 16. For now, we'll focus on the following options (both of which are available for Drupal 7):

Panels 960.gs (http://drupal.org/project/panels_960gs)
> This is an HTML5-based theme that incorporates the 960 Grid System with Panels (*http://drupal.org/project/panels*), a module that allows you to create customized drag-and-drop layouts for multiple purposes. Panels is a module created by Earl Miles, the creator of Views. I haven't used this theme, as I don't tend to use Panels in my sites; however, for those who use Panels regularly, it seems like a great option.

Sky (http://drupal.org/project/sky)
> Developed by Jacine Luisi of Gravitek Labs, Sky isn't so much a base theme as it is a nice, simple theme with sensible defaults. It's also Color module-enabled,

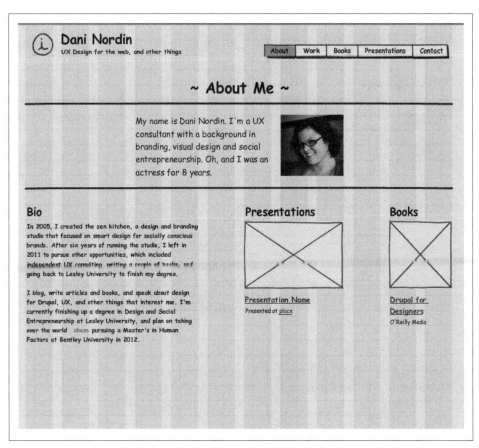

Figure 6-4. This quick wireframe for the About page of my website refresh uses a 12-column grid.

which means you can easily change the default color scheme of the theme in your site's Appearance settings. I used this theme for a project I worked on in early 2011; while many of the defaults seemed to be very sensible, I needed to override a large number of settings in order to customize it to the level I required for the project.

Aside from these, most base themes can be adjusted to incorporate the grid system of your choice. Simply download the appropriate files from the grid system's website, load the files into your subtheme, and add their names to the theme's *.info* file. Then sketch your layout using the grid, and incorporate those grid values as custom classes into your subtheme's template files, or use the Block Class module to add a custom grid value (represented as a class, such as `grid-2`) to a block in your theme. See Chapter 13 for a description of the Block Class module.

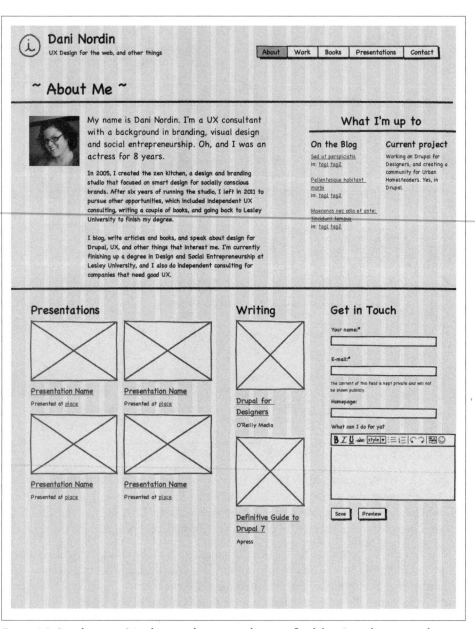

Figure 6-5. Switching to a 24-column grid gives me a bit more flexibility; I can fit more on the page, but still keep things organized.

Anatomy of a Grid Layout

The 960 Grid System (and many others) works like this. You start with your container width. The *container* contains your grid columns. Regardless of the number of columns (12, 16, or 24), inside each container `div` you'll have a series of `div`s, each with a certain column width, denoted by the class `grid-number`. So, for example, let's say I have a layout such as the one shown in Figure 6-6, with a 12-column grid: a content area of six columns and two sidebars of three columns each.

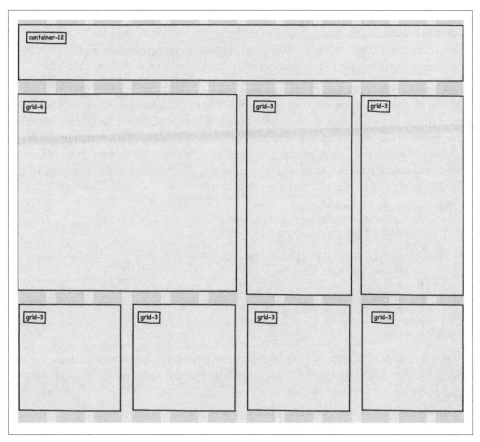

Figure 6-6. A sample grid-based layout, using a 12-column grid.

If I were building that out in code, it might look like this:

```
<div id="page" class="container-12">
    <div id="header" class="container-12">
    </div>
    <div id="middle" class="container-12">
        <div id="content" class="grid-6 alpha">
            <p>Some text goes here</p>
```

```
            </div>
            <div id="sidebar-first" class="grid-3">
                <p>some text goes here</p>
            </div>
            <div id="sidebar-second" class="grid-3">
                <p>some text goes here</p>
            </div>
        </div>
        <div id="footer" class="container-12">
            Etc. Etc. Etc.
        </div>
    </div>
```

As you can see, each horizontal section of the layout—header, middle, and footer—is given a `container` class, while each vertical section in the layout gets a `grid` class with a number corresponding to the number of columns I want the section to have.

In addition to the grid values, 960.gs also has push and pull classes that will apply negative or positive margins to a given layout; this can help you achieve a content-first layout (helping search engines and screen readers better deal with your site's content) while maintaining the aesthetic you want. For example, let's say I want that first sidebar to show up on the left side of the page instead of after the content area, but I still want to keep the sidebar's content showing up after the content area in the markup. In the "middle" section, I could adjust the markup thusly:

```
<div id="middle" class="container-12">
    <div id="content" class="grid-6 push-3">
        <p>Some text goes here</p>
    </div>
    <div id="sidebar-first" class="grid-3 pull-3">
        <p>some text goes here</p>
    </div>
    <div id="sidebar-second" class="grid-3">
        <p>some text goes here</p>
    </div>
</div>
```

There are also `prefix` and `suffix` classes for adding space between elements; for example, if I wanted to put some air in between the content area and the second sidebar, I could change the markup like this:

```
<div id="middle" class="container-12">
    <div id="content" class="grid-6 push-3 suffix-1">
        <p>Some text goes here</p>
    </div>
    <div id="sidebar-first" class="grid-3 pull-6">
        <p>some text goes here</p>
    </div>
    <div id="sidebar-second" class="grid-2">
        <p>some text goes here</p>
    </div>
</div>
```

It may sound a bit complicated, but as long as all the numbers in your grid add up to the width of your container, you're all set. Here's a quick checklist for doing the math:

1. `Push` and `pull` values should match the widths of the elements with which they're being swapped. If the content area in the preceding example (`grid-6`) needs to swap places with the first sidebar (`grid-3`), the sidebar should have a class of `pull-6` and the content area should have a class of `push-3`.

2. `Prefix` and `suffix` values add up to your column total. So, if you have a 12-column grid and your content area has a width of `grid-5` and a suffix of `suffix-1`, you have exactly six columns left in your grid. This is especially noticeable when you're dealing with longer pieces of content, or sidebars that require less room than you originally anticipated.

From the Trenches: Todd Nienkerk, Four Kitchens

Four Kitchens is a Drupal shop in Austin, Texas, that specializes in helping clients create large-scale websites. It also runs DrupalCamp Austin, a yearly Drupal event, and it co-created and co-maintains Pressflow, a specialized Drupal distribution optimized for large-scale implementations. Todd is a vocal advocate of grid systems, and gives presentations on the system at Drupal events around the United States.

Dani: Why do you love grids?

Todd: My own reason is the one that I perhaps don't hype enough in the talks I give about grid design, but it's a constraint that frees me. Just as a painter would first choose a palette, or limit the size of the canvas—you impose a limit on what you design, because then you can innovate within those constraints.

If you have not only a blank canvas, but a blank canvas of any size, or shape, or orientation, how do you even start, really? Whatever you're creating, you have to make that first decision. A grid is like that first decision. What's even better about it is that it's a first decision that's kind of already made for you; you don't have to feel like, "Oh, did I screw up?" You're rarely going to say, "I picked a width of 920 pixels for my website. I hope I don't regret this in a year."

Typesetting is a really good analogy for this kind of thing, because it's why grids were developed back in the day. You had to create grids to set your type, because you couldn't build actual typesetting machines for each book. You had to develop something that you could reuse from one book to another.

Using a grid allows you to say, "My content is going to be somewhere in this range," and now I have fewer decisions to make. Consider the paradox of choice; if you have too much choice, you're going to freeze up and maybe not make any decision whatsoever. But if you have a limited number of choices—for example, 12 columns to work with—you can configure them in a finite way, and it's easier to make decisions about that configuration. You can have 12 one-column spaces; you can have one 12-column space; you can have three 4-column spaces, and so on. It's actually freeing, because it limits your choices and you can propel the process forward. You get beyond that first [existential] stage of "What am I going to do with this giant blank canvas of infinity?" and create a starting point from which you can move forward.

Dani: Knowing I have a certain amount of structure also helps me come up with ideas more quickly, because I know the language of the grid. For example, I frequently create wireframes where I specify "grid-5," "grid-7," and so on. One of the things I love about grid systems is that, if a column suddenly appears way too wide, you can just move down a number on the grid class and it's done. Boom. Resized. You don't have to change exact pixel values in four different stylesheets, like you do with some themes.

Todd: Yes, the ease of use of a grid system—and I don't think this is exclusive to 960, but I think that 960 does it best in terms of setting the tone for this kind of thing—is that changing stuff, and visualizing the markup and CSS, is orders of magnitude simpler. It's no longer about "Is this 127 pixels?" or "What's my negative margin here?" It's a shortcut, or shorthand; if I'm working in a 16-column grid, I know that a single column is 40 pixels wide, and it has a margin-right and margin-left of 10 pixels. I know that academically. But when I'm in the zone, and I just need to move things around, and I need to rapidly iterate and prototype, I don't want to be thinking, "Why did my layout break? Why did this object flow to the next row?"

With the grid, I can simply look at the numbers and say, "All of these numbers add up to 12; I'm done." If I decide one thing is too wide, and I want to make it one column shorter, I just have to add a column somewhere else and I'm done. Thinking of widths in terms of columns, rather than pixels, is a huge timesaver. How often have we had to do a web design with a calculator next to us? Why not create the math up front, and never have to think about it again?

Working with Square Grid

Although the values are different with Square Grid, as are the names of the specific grid classes, using Square Grid is very similar to using the 960 grid. The major differences between the two are as follows:

- Square Grid uses a standard 28-pixel square for its columns, regardless of your layout. Thus, for a layout where all of your content is presented in three columns, you would need each column to have a width of 11 squares, represented with the class sg-11. The Square Grid website (*http://thesquaregrid.com/*) has a handy "cheat sheet" with a number of different options for grid layouts, including the grid values you'll need in order to accomplish the layout you want.

- Square Grid includes a baseline, and a 28-pixel margin on the bottom of your elements as well. This is decidedly different from the 960.gs theme, which is generally focused on left-to-right widths, although there is a baseline for text. This margin can work very well for content areas, but it's much less useful, for example, in headers, where you may want things a bit tighter.

Aside from these differences, which grid you choose may eventually come down to which base theme you prefer working with. In Chapter 16 we'll discuss the pros and cons of various base themes, including both Omega (which incorporates the 960 Grid System) and Square Grid (which incorporates the Square Grid framework). Both offer plenty of regions, which gives you plenty of options for placing your content, and the ability to support responsive, mobile-first layouts—with the help of some careful planning and a few well-placed media queries and JavaScript helpers.

But What About All These Presentational Classes? There Must Be a Better Way!

While both 960.gs and Square Grid offer a ton of flexibility and can make constructing a page more efficient, using grid systems can add a fair amount of code to your site—not only the CSS files that construct the grid, but also the presentational classes that are needed to set up page defaults (`grid-x` or `sg-x`, `push-x`, etc.). For those who pride themselves on fully semantic code (organized by hierarchy, presentation well separated from content, etc.), this can be a major annoyance. What if there was another option—an option that could set up a grid for you without all those annoying extra CSS classes?

Currently, there is one option: Susy.[1] Susy is billed as a way to make "unobtrusive grids for designers." It allows you to create custom grids using Compass and Sass[2] (command-line CSS tools), without any presentational classes cluttering your markup. While Susy looks very powerful, there are some caveats to its awesomeness:

It requires knowledge of the command line
> You'll need to install a Ruby gem in order to install the Susy plug-in; you'll also need the command line to start a new project and to compile your CSS once you've set up your definitions.

It requires knowledge of Compass and Sass
> Compass and Sass are, as mentioned earlier, command-line CSS tools. They are similar to LESS, which you will read about in Chapter 17, but instead of using client-side JavaScript (or the Less.app compiler) to compile your CSS, everything happens through the command line.

You need to do lots of math
> In order to plan out and define your grid, you'll need to do some advanced planning and set up the math.

I'm not saying that any of these things is a deal breaker; over the years I've actually gotten somewhat cozy with the command line. However, the power of Compass, Sass, and Susy comes with a pretty steep learning curve; every designer will have his or her

---

1. *http://susy.oddbird.net/*

2. *http://compass-style.org/*

own take as to how much of that learning curve he or she is willing (or has time) to take on. For those who are interested in using Compass but aren't ready for the command line just yet, a reasonably priced ($10) app that works with both Mac and Windows and will compile your Compass for you is available at *http://compass.handlino .com/*. I don't know if it also works with Susy, but it's worth a try.

The New CSS Grid Layout Module: The Future Is Now

With the growing popularity of grid systems for the Web, the future looks promising. An actual CSS Grid Layout module is, as of this writing, in editor's draft at the World Wide Web Consortium (W3C).[3] The CSS Grid Layout module will allow you to define a basic grid at the top of your CSS, and position your elements directly within the grid.

For example, let's go back to my layout and see how I'd construct that grid with this new module (see Figure 6-7).

The first thing I'd want to do is define the grid container. I'll call that #page in the CSS. Since most of the widths are actually grid-3 (in 960.gs terms), I can probably get away with doing four columns instead of 12. I'll also need three rows: one for the header, one for the middle, and one for the bottom.

```
#page {
    display: grid;
    grid-columns: 1fr 1fr 1fr 1fr;
    grid-rows: 130px auto auto;
}
```

The fr in the grid-columns is shorthand for "fractions"; it's a percentage of the overall grid.

This will set up the grid with four equal columns and three rows, all of which automatically size vertically. Now I want to start setting up the rest of the page. I'll start by styling the header:

```
#header {
    grid-column: 1; /* location of the element */
    grid-column-span: 4; /* width of the element, in column spans */
    grid-row: 1; /* location of the element */
}
```

From there, I'll work on the second row; I'll call the first element article, and the second sidebar-1 and sidebar-2:

```
#article { grid-column: 1; grid-column-span: 2; grid-row: 2; }
#sidebar-1 { grid-column: 3; grid-column-span: 1; grid-row: 2; }
#sidebar-2 { grid-column: 4; grid-column-span: 1; grid-row: 2; }
```

3. *http://dev.w3.org/csswg/css3-grid-align/*

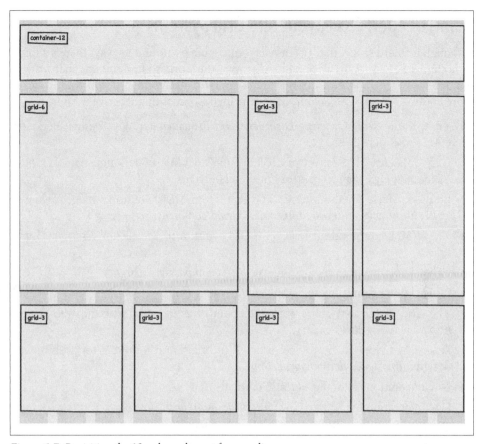

Figure 6-7. Revisiting the 12-column layout from earlier.

Finally, I'll work on the bottom section. I'll call these `postscript-1` through `post script-4`:

```
#postscript-1 { grid-column: 1; grid-column-span: 1; grid-row: 3; }
#postscript-2 { grid-column: 2; grid-column-span: 1; grid-row: 3; }
#postscript-3 { grid-column: 3; grid-column-span: 1; grid-row: 3; }
#postscript-4 { grid-column: 4; grid-column-span: 1; grid-row: 3; }
```

As you can see, this new module is fairly easy when compared to Susy, or even 960.gs and Square Grid—especially in terms of defining your grids and placing information. However, at the time of this writing, this specification is only available in the IE10 Platform Preview, which means you can't actually use it right now. It also means that, paradoxically, IE is ahead of the curve on something. I'll give you a moment to think about that.

Going Deeper: CSS Layout and Grid Systems

Although it's hard to feel that CSS as a layout engine has found its way, there's a lot to be hopeful for. People are working hard around the world to find options that work in multiple browsers, and new options are turning up all the time. If you want to learn more about grids and CSS layout, the following resources might prove useful:

- Vinh, Khoi. 2011. *Ordering Disorder: Grid Principles for Web Design*. Berkeley, CA: New Riders Press.
- Gasston, Peter. "The Future of CSS Layouts." .net Magazine. August 3, 2011; *http://www.netmagazine.com/features/future-css-layouts*.
- Boulton, Mark. "Rethinking CSS Grids." From Mark Boulton's blog, August 8, 2011; *http://www.markboulton.co.uk/journal/comments/rethinking-css-grids*.
- The W3C's editor's draft for CSS Grid Layout: *http://dev.w3.org/csswg/css3 grid-align/*.
- Official documentation on Compass: *http://compass-style.org/*.
- Official documentation on Sass: *http://sass-lang.com/*.
- The Grid System, an online resource about grids in both print and web design: *http://www.thegridsystem.org/*.
- Design by Grid, which provides articles, tutorials, and resources for grids in web design: *http://www.designbygrid.com/*.
- Documentation for 960.gs: *http://960.gs*.
- Documentation for Square Grid: *http://thesquaregrid.com/*.
- The Golden Grid System. I haven't played with this yet, but it looks very promising for responsive grid-based layout: *http://goldengridsystem.com/*.
- The 1140 grid, designed by Andy Taylor. This is another option for adaptive layout, which starts at 1140 pixels wide and reflows columns down to mobile: *http://cssgrid.net/*.

Now that we've learned a bit about grids and about working with Fireworks for layout, let's put some of these ideas into practice. In the next chapter we'll walk through the process of creating a custom Fireworks layout for a portfolio site redesign.

CHAPTER 7

Putting It in Practice—Setting Up Fireworks Templates for Drupal

While the Fireworks templates provided by Chapter Three[1] can be an excellent starting point for your layouts, you may find that having a predetermined set of styles and pages inhibits your creativity. Even if something's all in Helvetica and isn't meant to be a final layout, it can be easy to get caught up in other priorities and let the defaults do the heavy lifting. Additionally, while the templates provide a good set of default areas that you'll want to consider for 90% of your Drupal implementations, every project is unique enough that it generally makes sense to put some thought into how you want to set up your layouts rather than depending on what another design team has done.

In this chapter I'll outline a fairly simple process for creating your own custom layout in Fireworks. This tutorial assumes that you have a basic knowledge of how to use Fireworks; if you haven't used it before and need to learn it, Lynda.com (*http://lynda .com*)[2] has a Fireworks CS5 training course, and the *Adobe Classroom in a Book* series has an excellent book on Fireworks.[3] In addition, the book *Adobe Fireworks CS4 How-To's: 100 Essential Techniques*[4] deals with the previous version of Fireworks, but still provides an excellent introduction to using the software. If you are already familiar with Photoshop or Illustrator, the transition to Fireworks should be relatively smooth.

For the purposes of this overview, I'll focus on setting up a layout for tzk-design.com (*http://tzk-design.com*), my personal site. Since I've already set up style tiles (see Chapter 5) with some of my style conventions, we'll head straight to dressing things up, rather than taking a greyboxing approach (see Chapter 5). However, if you wanted to

---

1. Available at *http://www.chapterthree.com/blog/nica_lorber/design_drupal_template_approach* and *http:// www.chapterthree.com/greyboxing*.

2. *http://www.lynda.com/Fireworks-CS5-tutorials/essential-training/59962-2.html*

3. *http://www.amazon.com/Adobe-Fireworks-CS5-Classroom-Book/dp/0321704487*

4. *http://www.amazon.com/Adobe-Fireworks-CS4-How-Tos-Techniques/dp/0321562879/ref=sr_1_2?s= books&ie=UTF8&qid=1315255117&sr=1-2*

execute this quickly, you could leave the fonts and colors low-key until you're ready to finalize your designs; just be sure to create actual Fireworks styles for your elements, such as h1, paragraph tags, and other key typography elements, so that you can easily change them when you're ready to.

Step 1: Set Up the Grid

The first step to efficiently setting up a layout is to start with the basics. What are the primary content areas of the page? How will you deal with body text and headlines? What about links, lists, and so on? These are collected onto a sample page, and styles are set so that they can be reused elsewhere.

We'll start with the page grid. Since I'm using the Square Grid theme (*http://drupal.org/project/squaregrid*) to set up this site, I'll start with a layout grid, based on the Square Grid, that allows two-column, three-column, and four-column layouts. Each area of the grid is based on a 28-pixel-wide column, colored pink at 20% transparency, and placed with a 28-pixel gutter between each piece. That is a layer in my document called "35-column grid," which I'll place at the top of my layers and share with all other pages in my document. Figure 7-1 shows how my layout looks after I've set up the grid. Note that if you don't want to create all the boxes yourself, you can download a Fireworks template for the Square Grid, created by San Francisco interaction designer David Hogue, at *http://www.idux.com/2010/10/04/square-grid-template-for-fireworks/*.

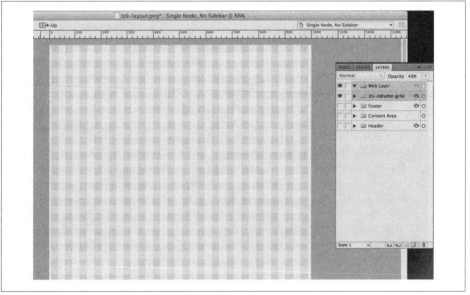

Figure 7-1. After setting up the 35-column grid, I already have a layer set up for the Fireworks template. The icon to the right of the layer title means the layer is shared among all pages.

Now that I have my grid set up, I need to lock the grid layer so that I can move around my document without accidentally moving my grid. After setting up multiple pages, I'll make sure the layer is shared with all my pages by right-clicking on the layer and choosing Share Layer To All Pages from the contextual menu (see Figure 7-2).

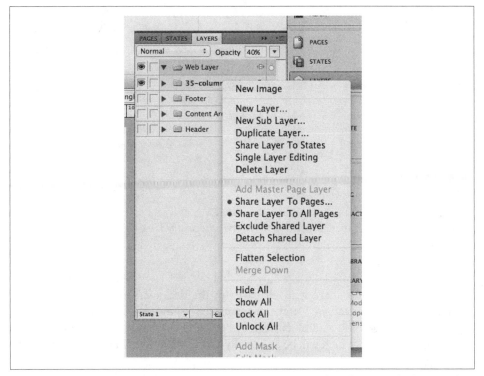

Figure 7-2. Sharing a layer with all your Fireworks pages saves you from having to do the same thing twice, and makes it easier to update global elements in your design.

Step 2: Set Up the Header

With my grid in place, it's time to think about how the navigation will be organized and set up some type defaults. For this, I'll create a new layer called "Header" and bring in my logo, the navigation links, and other elements. I can bring these in directly from my style tiles (see Chapter 5).

With the navigation elements, I also want to play around with the format of links, text, colors, and so on—but I want to be able to change them across the board when I make edits. For this, I'll convert the navigation elements to a symbol called "navigation" (by selecting the navigation elements, right-clicking, and selecting Convert to Symbol from the contextual menu). I'll also set up some styles for the navigation, including the type format for links in both the On and Off states, and a style for the background of the On state. Figure 7-3 shows what things look like when I'm done.

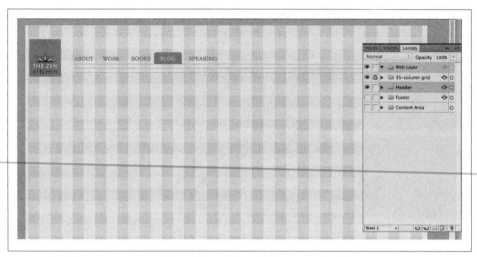

Figure 7-3. The new navigation, adapted from the style tiles created in Chapter 5.

With the navigation created, I make sure to label the new layer "Header" (so that I can find it easily later) and share it to all pages in the document. I'll also add a small "Available for new projects in:" status message (see Figure 7-4) in the upper-right corner, which I will bring in as a block when I build the site, and a bold "Contact Me" ribbon for the header, which will be a specially styled menu item in the top navigation.

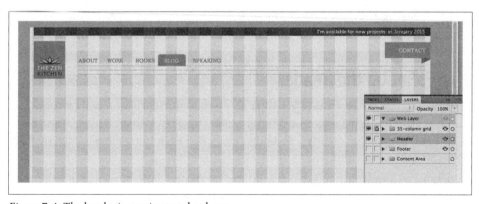

Figure 7-4. The header is starting to take shape.

Step 3: Create a Single Node Page Without a Sidebar

Now that I have the header in place, it's time to think about how the type will look. For this, I'll start with a single node page without a sidebar, which will give me an opportunity to figure out a variety of type defaults.

The focus of a single node page should be on the legibility of the page's content. I want to avoid a line that's too long, so I'm keeping my content area 21 squares wide, which takes up just less than two-thirds of the page (and is the same size as my content area in a layout with one sidebar, which I'll be using later). It's important to test out a few different types of copy that could appear in a given text sample, so I'm including a secondary heading, a pullout quote (which I'll convert into a symbol), and some sample body copy. I also want to make sure I plan for titles that might go long, so I'm setting my h1 as a two-line title to see how it looks. Finally, I save the style of each element in my sample copy in the Styles palette:

- h1 (the page title).
- p (the body copy).
- h2 (the secondary title underneath the first paragraph).
- block quote (the pullout quote). The entire block quote is pulled out from the main flow of the text and saved as a symbol.

Figure 7-5 shows what I've done so far.

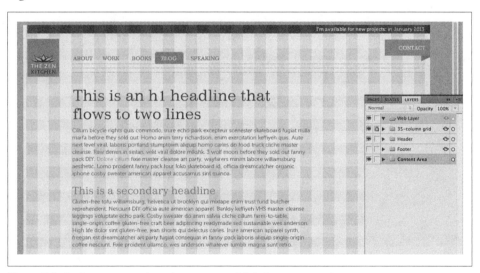

Figure 7-5. Setting up a sample node page to establish the content styles

Right now, I'm assuming this page has no sidebar; this means I'm going to end up with a lot of extra space on the right side of the content unless I come up with some sensible margins. Looking at the grid again, I see the logo is set as a two-column-wide image, so I move the content two squares to the right to align with the left edge of the navigation. I also make the content area wider, 14 squares instead of 12. While I'm at it, I create a footer for the page, repeating the three dotted lines I used below the navigation to create a balance to the page, and creating new styles called "footer p" and "footer a" for the footer text. Figure 7-6 shows where I've landed.

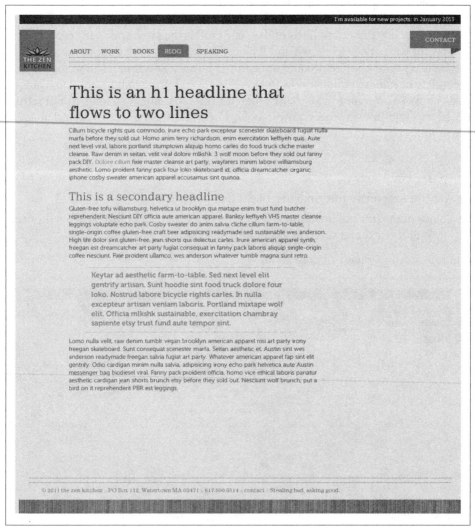

Figure 7-6. My finished node page.

Now that I have an idea of what a node page looks like without a sidebar, it's easy enough to duplicate this page and use it to create a second template with one sidebar, and another with two sidebars.

Step 4: Create Single Node Pages with One and Two Sidebars

The point of starting your template with a node page that doesn't have sidebars is this: *you will inevitably have a page like this somewhere on your site.* And many designers, well meaning as they are, end up forgetting this, and assuming there will be one or two sidebars on the page. As Drupal's default behavior reflows the text to fill the entire page when there are no sidebars, this results in these pages having long and drastically uncomfortable line lengths.

That being said, it's safe to assume that most pages will have at least one sidebar, and that the sidebars will contain different types of blocks, for example:

- A list of node titles or categories
- Static text or images
- A tag cloud or something similar
- Callout boxes, such as a contact form or customer testimonial

Therefore, while I'm working on my node pages, I should also take a look at how these different types of sidebar blocks will be styled, and how I'll set up both one-sidebar and two-sidebar layouts. I'll use my two-sidebar layout as my blog post page, and set up two sidebars. The first, which will have a width of 10 squares, will contain an "about the blog" description block and a list of tags, formatted as a tag cloud. The right sidebar, which will be four squares wide, will have a "recent posts" block and a "presentations" block, which will include thumbnails and titles of various presentations. This will also give me the opportunity to create defaults for other blocks that include images. Figure 7-7 shows the result.

Creating the sidebars gives me an opportunity to set up a few more styles, including "sidebar h2" (for block titles), "date callout" for the blog post date and presentation date, "tag cloud" for the links in the cloud, and "a" for links. Note the style names: each style's name is related to a piece of the theme that's going to be styled with CSS when we get to theming.

Another thing to note here is the placement of blocks: since I'm using Square Grid (*http://drupal.org/project/squaregrid*) as my base theme, viewing my layout on a smaller screen, such as a tablet in portrait mode or a smartphone screen, will cause the blocks to the right of my content area to float underneath the content in the order they appear. As such, I want to make sure the blocks are placed in order of importance: first the "about" section, then post tags, then recent entries, and finally presentations. As I build this site, my priorities may change, but for now, this looks good.

Once I have a two-sidebar page done, it's easy enough to do a single-sidebar page. I start by duplicating my two-sidebar layout and removing the right sidebar. Then I make the right sidebar just a little bit wider (13 squares), which will help it fill out more of the page. Figure 7-8 shows the single-sidebar layout.

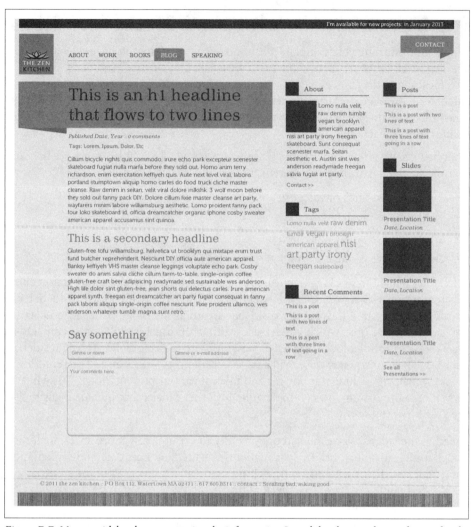

Figure 7-7. My two-sidebar layout contains the information I need, but leaves plenty of room for the blog post, which is the focus of the page.

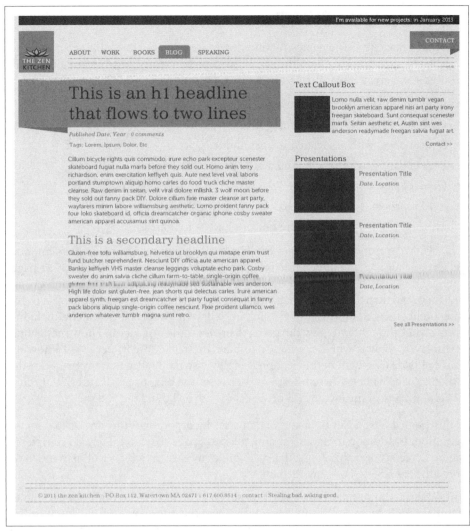

Figure 7-8. The one-sidebar layout is much less cramped compared to the two-sidebar layout, and is mostly useful when just a few things will appear on the page aside from content.

 One of the great things about working in Fireworks—although this is also true of Illustrator and Photoshop—is the ability to easily show and hide layers. In my Fireworks document, I can toggle my grid on to quickly size elements, and then toggle it off to see how the page looks.

Step 5: Create the Other Pages

Now that I have my basic page structure down, it's time to start looking at the other pages in my site. Working with the styles I've already created (and creating new ones as I need to), I create the following pages in my layout:

- Blog listing, with the sidebars as used in my two-sidebar layout
- Category page, based on the blog listing page
- Project page, with associated images and text
- Project listing, with images and a brief project description
- Contact page
- A 404 (page not found) and 403 (access denied) page
- The home page, with associated blocks and callout areas

This should cover most of the pages I will be setting up in my Drupal implementation, and give me more than enough to work with. Many of the pages will feed other pages —for example, my blog listing page will start with my two-sidebar layout, and change the listing, and then the category page will follow from that. However, the project pages, being highly focused on images/case studies, will require special treatment, including putting some thought into how I'm going to organize the projects and how they should be displayed. This is where it's handy to have the real content; because I know the content I'm dealing with in this section is highly visual, I realize that my needs for this particular page will be different from my needs for the blog pages. Figures 7-9 through 7-11 show a few of the layouts I'll be working with as I build out the site.

At this point I have a set of layouts I can start incorporating into my Drupal implementation. In addition to understanding the basic page structure, I've also started setting up some typographic styles that will guide my design, which will help me make more efficient CSS to code my theme.

With some design standards set and the pages laid out, it's time to think about building a Drupal site. Before we do that, however, we want to go beyond simply downloading Drupal and a few modules, creating a database, and installing. We want to learn how to set ourselves up for success and efficiency as Drupal designers and site builders. And that means learning a few developer tricks. In the next section, I'll show you how to set up your own local development environment, including setting up Drush, which will allow you to more efficiently download, install, and update modules, among other things, get a bit cozy on the command line, and set up version control using Git, the open source version control system. Are you scared yet? I didn't think you would be. Let's do this.

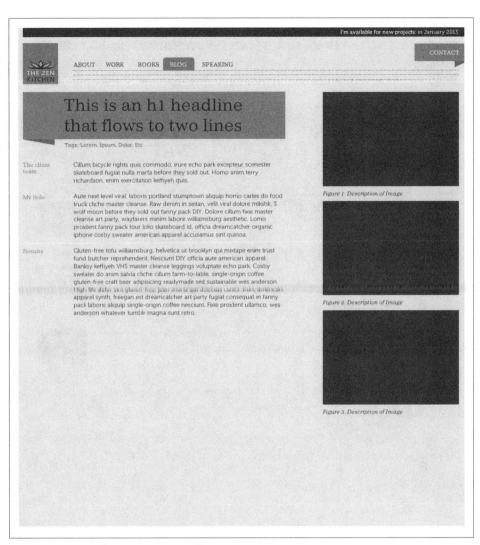

Figure 7-9. Project description page, with images.

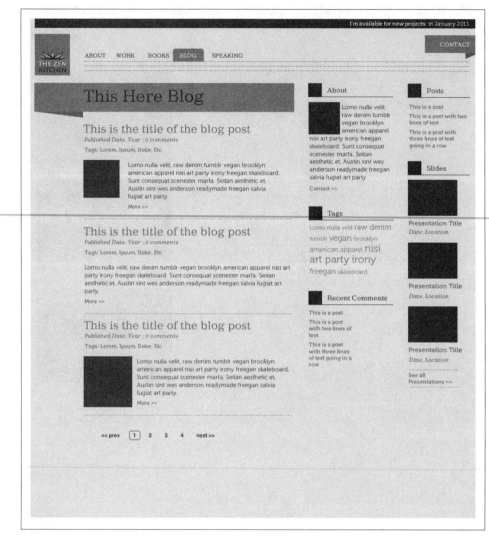

Figure 7-10. The blog listing, with pager.

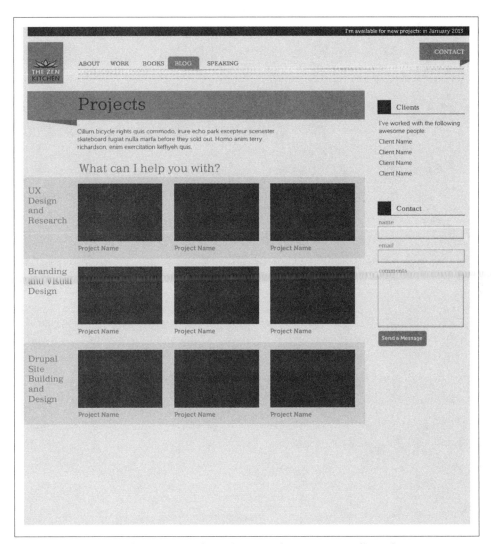

Figure 7-11. The project listing, grouped into the types of projects I typically work on.

PART III

Setting Up a Local Development Environment

CHAPTER 8

The Drupal Designer's Coding Toolkit

By the end of the section that follows, you'll understand basic command-line processes, know how to install a local development environment, including Drush and Git, and put all of this new information into practice by installing Drupal locally and using Drush to download key modules you'll need for a basic implementation.

Wait, What? Why?

I realize the idea of learning how to use the command line, or how to set up a local development environment, isn't as sexy as learning how to push the envelope of Drupal design. Trust me, I get it. But if there's one thing that prevents Drupal designers from pushing that envelope, it's this: *site building in Drupal isn't terribly efficient if you haven't figured out at least a few of these tricks.* Want to know why the same task that takes some developers only an hour or two takes some of us several hours of banging our heads against the computer? It's because they know how to quickly update or download modules, or how to use version control (hallelujah!) to protect themselves from bone-head mistakes.

The goal of this section isn't to show you everything you can possibly do to make development easier for you, or to provide a comprehensive guide to everything a given development tool can do; the list is entirely too long, and if you're anything like me, you'll get halfway down the list before you start wondering where your coffee is and forget you ever looked at it. My goal is simple: *to help you figure out how much of this stuff you need in order to speed up repetitive tasks in Drupal.* The rest you can figure out as you go—and you'll have more time for dealing with design challenges.

A Note for Windows Users

As you read through these pages, you might note that the instructions I provide are focused on the Mac platform. Although I don't want to ignore my friends on Windows, most of what I've learned about working with Drupal—particularly the command-line stuff—works more reliably on the Mac. Windows seems to add an annoying layer of complexity to most of the command-line stuff you'll see in these pages. Dear friends in the community have tried several times to work in Git and Drush on Windows, and nearly all have fought with their machines for hours on end to get their configurations running. This complexity has led many developers I know to forgo Windows altogether and get things done on the Mac or Ubuntu platform.

If you prefer Windows, however, you can use a program such as Cygwin[1] to create a Unix-like environment on your PC; or, if you're feeling adventurous, a program such as VirtualBox[2] will allow you to install a Linux distribution such as Ubuntu directly on your machine, which you can then use as a virtual machine to work on command-line stuff. If you plan to use Drush (see Chapter 9 for several reasons why you darn well should), there's actually a Drush for Windows installer, which you can download at *http://drush.org/drush_windows_installer*.

From the Trenches: Ben Buckman, Drupal Developer

Ben Buckman is a Drupal developer currently living in Buenos Aires, Argentina. His shop, New Leaf Digital,[3] specializes in helping Drupal teams solve tough development problems. He is also a cofounder of Antiques Near Me,[4] a web-based startup (built in Drupal!) that helps connect antiques collectors with shops and events near them.

Dani: You've always been very generous in terms of showing me how to do things in Drush, Git, and so on. What made you want to help me? Obviously, development stuff is your gig, so what's the benefit to passing this kind of knowledge along to nondevelopers?

Ben: There are probably many motivations; the most rational one being [that] it's a win-win. It's not a threat to me if designers know Git; in fact, it makes it easier to work with them. (As long as I keep learning new things, I'll always be 10 steps ahead of the people I'm teaching with the things I know better, and they'll be 10 steps ahead in the things they know better, and that makes for a good market/community/and so on.) Proprietary knowledge is shortsighted; there's plenty of work to go around. It also makes me a go-to resource for development questions, which has all sorts of practical benefits. If I said, "I know how to do that but I won't tell you," people would think I was a jerk and not want to work with me, and if no one knew that I knew anything, they wouldn't know to refer clients to me.

Dani: In terms of what you've shown me directly, you've gotten me started with Drush and Git, and I think I sort of ended up spiraling from there into learning Drush Make and Install Profiles. Are there any other developer-centric tools that you think designers could benefit from?

1. *http://www.cygwin.com/*

2. *http://www.virtualbox.org/*

3. *http://newleafdigital.com/*

4. *http://antiquesnearme.com/*

Ben: Learn other shell tools like `grep`, `find`, `tail -f`, piping, loops, and writing shell scripts, and the power is endless. You can dump text to your clipboard on a Mac by piping to `pbcopy`. You can have the terminal tell you via Growl when a DNS record has propagated. Or write a deployment script to push your code, SSH to the server, and pull it, that you call with one line. The Unix shell is like a pocket toolkit; once you know how each tool works (and they're usually simple on their own), you start to see all kinds of problems as easily solved with a few commands.

[Author's note: I have no idea what he just said.]

Other than that ... Firebug or the WebKit (Chrome/Safari) Inspector has made web development much easier. Everyone should know how to test CSS and JavaScript in the Inspector, so they don't have to keep saving-reloading-saving-reloading.

Dani: What do you think designers can gain from using these tools?

Ben: Efficiency ... proficiency ... . People should know the things they work with. We should all know the basics of how a car works, if we drive a car. Likewise, if we use a computer, or build things that work across networks of computers, we should know the basics of how they work. (And the Unix shell happens to be a good way of getting straight to the raw underbelly of all these systems.) Developers should know their way around a Photoshop file, and designers should know their way around Git and `bash` and some PHP, and we'll all understand each other better.

Dani: In terms of workflow management, I know that one of the things you like as a developer is being able to solve interesting problems in Drupal (or whatever technology you're using for the product). Where do you think the balance should lie? What's the ideal engagement for you—building the whole thing from scratch, or consulting during the early phases of a project and then helping the design team put together the more advanced functionality?

Ben: This is a good question, and I can't say I've found the perfect balance. I've covered a pretty wide range in the last few years. Lately I've been building some websites from start (static designs) to finish (site in production) and I don't usually enjoy those projects. The challenges (basic content architecture) are mostly repetitive, and the clients don't understand the difference between a good product and a bad one half the time. Too much of the emotional value of those projects depends on the quality of the client—a bad client makes those projects awful from start to finish, whereas a truly interesting project can be rewarding even if the client is unpleasant.

The ideal engagement for me is working with designers or site builders who hit a glass ceiling in their development skill sets and want a boost up, or developers who want another brain to help think out of the box. Everyone should know what they don't know and be able to reach out to people to fill those gaps. If I teach someone to fish on a project, they might not need me on the next project, but they'll very likely refer me to someone else who does. I like doing custom development on existing sites, or refactoring bad code (when the client understands what they're asking for). A client recently wanted functionality added to some existing but partially built modules to bridge Webform with contextual filters in Views, with the resulting code submitted as a patch for the community to use; I really like that kind of project. I also like doing investigative troubleshooting. Aside from client work (and a separate startup business I cofounded), I enjoy learning new platforms, and have been spending a lot of time lately immersed in Node.js.

Dani: In your mind, at what point in the project does it make sense to hire a developer, and at what point should a designer or site builder be able to figure things out on his own?

Ben: The point where your budget justifies hiring some additional help. ;) Actually, this is probably a better question for you to answer than me, since I'm on the other side of the equation. I know that I'd pay someone to teach me the inner workings of Varnish, because I've hit a wall with what I can learn by Googling. I'm often amazed [by] what nondevelopers can build with Drupal, but eventually, if you want something out of the box, you'll need to write some code, and most designers don't write modules. (Different side of the brain? I don't know.) Also, I've written about a trend in Drupal toward higher complexity, which brings more bugs, which means it's more likely you'll need a developer to troubleshoot something.

The Drupal Designer's Coding Toolkit

Every Drupal designer and developer has his or her own set of preferred applications for making his or her work easier; the following is a synopsis of applications that I use, and that many of my friends in the Drupal community prefer as well.

Coda[5]

Coda is a relatively inexpensive (less than $100) application for coding websites. Not only does it allow you to code your pages and upload them in the same screen, but it also can connect to Terminal on your remote server from within the application, which is useful when you're running shell commands, such as Drush or Git. Most importantly, Coda's Clips library allows you to keep commonly used code snippets in one place and insert them into your HTML simply by double-clicking. This is extraordinarily useful for theming, or creating custom modules.

If you're working with a team over the same network, you can also use Bonjour to collaborate with other Coda users in your team. Through the network, you can edit someone else's code (or let him or her edit yours), save the files, and watch the changes happen in front of you.

---

5. *http://panic.com/coda*

Less.app[6]

LESS (which you'll read about in more detail in Chapter 17) is a CSS framework that allows you to code CSS more efficiently. In addition to allowing you to set variables and "mixins" for colors, fonts, and so on directly in your stylesheets that can be inserted elsewhere in said stylesheets, it allows you to nest styles within one another. For example, a simple navigation menu might look like this:

```
ul#navigation { list-style: none; display: inline; }
ul#navigation > li { list-style: none; float: left; margin-right: 1em;
    border-right: 1px solid gray; }
ul#navigation > li a { padding: 3px 0; color: black; text-decoration: none;}
ul#navigation > li a:hover { color: white; background: black;
    text-decoration: underline; }
```

In LESS, you'd style it thusly:

```
ul#navigation {
    list-style: none; display: inline;

    > li {
        list-style: none;
        float: left;
        margin-right: 1em;
        border-right: 1px solid gray;
        padding: 3px 0;

        a {
            padding: 3px 0; color: black; text-decoration: none;
        }

        a:hover {
            color: white; background: black; text-decoration: underline;
        }
    }
}
```

This code will compile into the same code as the first example, but a) you get to save yourself some typing, and b) you get to keep all your code for a given element organized in one place. This is especially useful when working in Drupal, as often you'll find yourself customizing a much larger amount of CSS for any given area of a site—from a particular page, to a block, to the entire sidebar. You'll read more about the awesomeness that is LESS in Chapter 17.

Ordinarily, you would compile your LESS using a small JavaScript file either on your site's server or directly in your template files. While this is one way to do it, it forces a load on the server that you may not want, and it could mess you up if your user is in a browser that doesn't have JavaScript enabled. Yes, it does happen sometimes. This is where Less.app comes in. It's a tiny Mac application that sits open while you work,

6. *http://incident57.com/less*

and "watches" any folder that you put into it for changes to .less files. As you're working, every time you save the file, Less.app will compile your LESS for you into a .css file, allowing you to more efficiently see what you're doing. Figure 8-1 is a screenshot of the app, which is available at *http://incident57.com/less*.

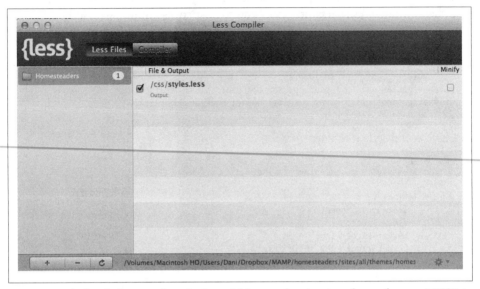

Figure 8-1. The handy Less.app "watches" any folder you drag into it and compiles your LESS into CSS as you work.

MAMP[7]

MAMP creates a virtual Apache server directly on your Mac. Using it, you can proto-type, build, and theme a Drupal site quickly on your local machine, without having to worry about FTP servers, or people accidentally seeing your half-finished work. If you're working independently, or your staging server is incredibly slow, the time sav-ings you get by working locally cannot be understated. Working locally is also a beau-tiful thing when you don't have Internet access or access is spotty; I once got a website halfway to launch on a plane ride.

Terminal

Terminal is a native application in Mac OS X that lets you run command-line prompts. If you're going to use Git or Drush, you will need to get cozy with Terminal.

---

7. *http://www.mamp.info*

Navicat[8]

Navicat is a Mac-based application to help you manage databases. While you can also use phpMyAdmin (which comes with MAMP), I like using Navicat because it's highly visually oriented, and you can connect—in one location—to databases not only on your local hosting environment, but also on other hosting environments, as long as you've set up a way to access the host remotely. As all hosting companies deal with remote access differently, make sure you check your hosting company's FAQs or support wiki for how to establish remote access, and whether your account includes shell access, which you'll need for both Drush and Git. With Dreamhost, which I use, it's generally as simple as entering into an "allowed hosts" field in the user's profile the IP address from which you're trying to access the host.

phpMyAdmin

If you don't need drag-and-drop functionality, or if you just need to handle a couple of quick things (such as creating a new database that Drupal will populate for you), you can also use phpMyAdmin, which comes automatically installed with MAMP. It's also installed on most hosting servers that support PHP; check with your hosting provider's control panel for how to get in and use the program.

Drush

Drush is a shell program you can install on any server with a Drupal installation, including your local development environment, which allows you to access several key tasks from the command line. Why do this? Because once you get the hang of it, it takes significantly less time to do many key tasks (such as syncing databases, installing or updating modules, and clearing caches). We'll go deeper into the awesomeness that is Drush in Chapter 9.

Git[9]

Git is a free, open source version control system. It allows you not only to keep separate versions of your work, but also to revert to an old version of your work should you make a change and everything breaks. This is particularly important when doing custom work, such as theming or building a custom module, or when upgrading modules, as relatively minor things can sometimes cause everything to go haywire in your Drupal installation. Check out Chapter 10 for more information on using and installing Git in your development environment.

8. *http://navicat.com*

9. *http://git-scm.com/*

Dropbox[10]

Dropbox allows you to manage files across the Internet using a folder on your desktop. The glory of Dropbox is that it's free (for up to 2 GB), it works on any platform, and it allows you to access your files on any machine that has Dropbox installed, or on the Web. I keep my MAMP site files in a folder within my Dropbox, which allows me to work on sites from wherever I happen to be, no matter which computer I'm working on. The one challenge to the Dropbox/MAMP combination is where databases are stored; although you can easily store your site files in a Dropbox folder, the database files exist on whatever machine you're on, which means you have to sync the databases from one machine to the other if you want to do work on a different machine. Although there are ways to sync the databases on the command line, my preferred method is to use the Backup and Migrate module for this task (*http://drupal.org/project/backup_mi grate*), which allows me to download a backup of one site's database and restore to my downloaded backup in the other site. The whole process takes about 5 to 15 minutes, depending on how long it takes you to switch machines.

Now that you have a sense of what tools you'll need to start building in Drupal, let's learn a little bit about the command line.

Working on the Command Line: Some Basic Commands

OK, folks, here we are: it's time to start looking at the command line. Back when I was a new and naïve Drupal designer, I fought passionately against the command line, arguing that Drupal should be easy enough that I shouldn't *need* to use Terminal to get things done. And technically, many aspects of Drupal are actually easy enough to get away without needing it. But, my friend, *easy* (or rather, "easy-ish") doesn't mean *efficient*. Since realizing this, I've made a point of learning just enough to get things done more quickly.

Here's why you should get familiar the command line:

It's quicker
> Many commands are just a few characters long and can get you to what you need to be doing in half the time compared to ordinary methods. When we get into Drush in the next chapter, you'll see this firsthand.

It makes you feel like a ninja
> Let's face it: even with all the wonderful usability enhancements that have been built into Drupal 7, working in Drupal can be intimidating for people who aren't developers by training. Being able to work in the command line, just a little bit, can be ridiculously gratifying.

---

10. *https://www.dropbox.com/*

It makes developers like you

While I've certainly annoyed my share of developers by constantly asking them questions about different command-line things, most of the developers I've spoken to genuinely appreciate someone who's willing to learn the basics. For one thing, it makes their jobs easier (no constant requests for minor things while they're trying to solve complex code issues); for another, it helps give you a common language.

Here's a quick primer on command-line things you should know. Use it in good health.

Some of these commands are a bit scary and can mess up your filesystem if you're not careful. Make sure you use these commands with caution, and keep backups of your work. Luckily, we'll be talking about file backups when we get to working with Git in Chapter 10.

Commands

~

This character (called a *tilde*) is your *HOME* folder. On a Mac, this usually points to Macintosh→HD→Users→<YOURNAME>.

cd

Use this command to navigate to a particular directory in your filesystem. If you want to navigate to your *MAMP* folder, for example (assuming that, like mine, it's located inside a Dropbox folder), you'd use the command cd ~/Dropbox/MAMP.

ls

This command will list the contents of any folder you're in.

mkdir

This command will make a directory in whatever folder you happen to be in.

mv [*FILENAME*] [*DESTINATION*]

This command will move the file you specify into the location you specify. It's also useful for renaming a file.

chmod

Use this command to modify permissions on a file or folder in a system. You can configure this command in a number of different ways, and frankly, it can be pretty confusing. With the exception of using it to make Drush executable when I install it on a server (see Chapter 9), I rarely use it.[11]

rm [*FILENAME*]

This command will remove any file you specify. Use this with *extreme caution*; removing files willy-nilly can mess up your system.

11. There is, however, a pretty decent rundown of this command on Wikipedia, should you be feeling brave today: *http://en.wikipedia.org/wiki/Chmod.*

```
rsync -a [SOURCE] [DESTINATION]
```
This command, one of my favorites, will sync two folders of your choice. It's easiest to use when the two folders you're syncing are in the same main folder; for example, if you have a staging site on a subdomain of your main site (e.g., Staging.site.com and Site.com), you could use the code `rsync -a staging.site.com/ site.com/` from your web root to sync the files—in far less time than you would need to copy them via FTP.

 When using the `rsync` command, make sure you include the trailing slashes in your URLs, which ensures that you're copying the *contents* of the folders and not the folders themselves.

That Wasn't So Bad, Was It?

Now that we've gotten that over with, it's time to start looking at Drush. Ready? I knew you would be.

CHAPTER 9

Installing Drush

Drush is the Drupal shell, a robust and mighty library of commands that are designed to make your life easier in Drupal. Among the many things you can do with Drush, some of the most exciting commands (from a designer/site builder's standpoint) are:

drush dl [*module_name*]

> This lets you download any module from Drupal.org (*http://drupal.org*). You can even download a string of modules by separating the machine names of the modules (i.e., the words that go after *drupal.org/project/* in the module's URL) with spaces.

drush en [*module_name*]

> This lets you enable any of the modules you just downloaded. Like dl, you can enable a string of modules by typing a space-separated list.

drush up

> This is my single favorite thing to use Drush for, and the reason that you, dear reader, *must learn Drush*. With this simple command, you can update all your modules and Drupal core in about five minutes, as opposed to the—ahem—considerably longer amount of time it takes to do it manually.

If you'd like to see a demonstration of the merits of using Drush versus installing modules manually, check out the video "More Beer, Less Effort" from Development Seed:

http://developmentseed.org/blog/2009/jun/19/drush-more-beer-less-effort/

Synopsis: installing a site and a pile of modules via Drush versus manually left our hero with an extra hour or more of time on his hands—plenty of time to celebrate with a refreshing beverage.

Installing Drush

Grab the Drush package from *http://drupal.org/project/drush*. You want to download the *tar.gz* file containing the latest recommended release (see Figure 9-1).

Drush

View Version control

Posted by moshe weitzman on *November 13, 2006 at 2:00am*

drush is a command line shell and scripting interface for Drupal, a veritable Swiss Army knife designed to make life easier for those of us who spend some of our working hours hacking away at the command prompt.

See http://drush.ws, the homepage for the drush project. It contains many important resources for drush users.

It is valid to use the latest '7.x' (or master) no matter what your version of Drupal is. Drush is independent of Drupal version :)

drush is not a module, and does not participate in the usage statistics system at drupal.org.

A list of modules that include Drush integration.

Beloved Windows users. Please use the All-versions-5.x-dev release. There is a convenient Drush installer for Windows available on drush.ws. The 4.x releases are not at all Windows compatible.

Drush was originally developed by Arto for Drupal 4.7 (this alpha code can still be found in the DRUPAL-4-7 branch). In May 2007, it was partly rewritten and redesigned for Drupal 5 by frando. The module is now maintained by Moshe Weitzman, Owen Barton, Adrian Rossouw, greg.1.anderson, jonhattan, and Mark Sonnabaum.

#D7CX: I pledge that Drush will have a full Drupal 7 release on the day that Drupal 7 is released.

Downloads

Recommended releases

Version	Downloads	Date	Links
7.x-4.4	tar.gz (247.08 KB) | zip (289.47 KB)	2011-Mar-14	Notes

Figure 9-1. The Drush project page. You can download the recommended release of any project by clicking the "tar.gz" link to the right of the version.

The website at *http://www.drush.org/resources* offers a bunch of resources related to Drush, including a handy Windows installer, for those readers who work on a PC.

Unpack the *tar.gz* file into your working folder. If you're developing locally, this could be the *Users/<USERNAME>* folder. If you're on a remote server (and you have shell access—this is important), you would unpack it into the directory *outside* the folder that holds the site's public files.

Drush works inside any directory that contains a working Drupal installation. If you've hosted multiple sites on the same server, you can install Drush once on the main server and use it by navigating (via the command `cd ~/path/to/directory`) to the directory that contains the site you want to work with.

Once you have Drush unpacked, you want to make the Drush file executable. You can do this by using the following code:

```
chmod u+x /path/to/drush
```

where */path/to/drush* is the location of your Drush folder (in my case, this is ~*/drush/ drush*). Once you've done that, you want to create an *alias* to Drush so that you can use the command outside of the actual Drush folder (e.g., your various Drupal installations). This is where things get interesting, but it's only for a moment.

Start by entering the following code:

```
nano ~/.bash_profile
```

This opens an old-school text editor that will allow you to create an alias to Drush, giving you the ability to run Drush commands from within any folder that contains a Drupal installation. There might be one or two lines of code here, but you don't need to worry about them. Scroll down and make sure you're on a new line at the end of the file, and add the following code:

```
alias drush='path/to/drush'
```

So, on my computer, it looks like Figure 9-2.

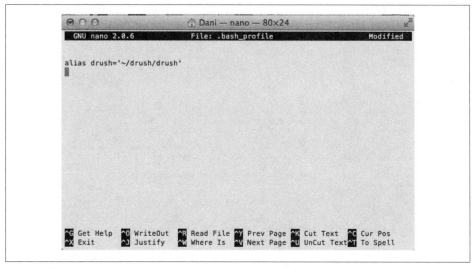

Figure 9-2. The .bash_profile file with our fancy new Drush alias.

Save the file using <control>-x, y (for yes), then press Enter.

If you're interested in learning just a bit more of the command line, Jenifer Tidwell, a UI designer from the Boston area, also suggests this one-line trick for adding a line to your .bash_profile. Be careful to enter the text *exactly as shown*, or you'll have to go into a text editor anyway.

```
% cat >> ~/.bash_profile alias drush='path/to/drush'
    # hit return
^D
    # hit CTRL + D
```

Once you've finished updating your `.bash_profile`, type in the following:

```
source .bash_profile
```

to reload your updated `.bash_profile`. Now, if you type **drush**, you should see something like Figure 9-3.

```
Danielles-MacBook-Air:~ Dani$ source .bash_profile
Danielles-MacBook-Air:~ Dani$ drush
Execute a drush command. Run `drush help [command]` to view command-specific
help.  Run `drush topic` to read even more documentation.

Global options (see `drush topic core-global-options` for the full list):
  -r <path>, --root=<path>         Drupal root directory to use
                                   (default: current directory)
  -l http://example.com,           URI of the drupal site to use (only
  --uri=http://example.com         needed in multisite environments)
  -v, --verbose                    Display extra information about the
                                   command.
  -d, --debug                      Display even more information,
                                   including internal messages.
  -y, --yes                        Assume 'yes' as answer to all
                                   prompts
  -n, --no                         Assume 'no' as answer to all prompts
  -s, --simulate                   Simulate all relevant actions (don't
                                   actually change the system)
  -p, --pipe                       Emit a compact representation of the
                                   command for scripting.
  -h, --help                       This help system.
  --version                        Show drush version.
  --php                            The absolute path to your PHP
                                   intepreter, if not 'php' in the
                                   path.


Core drush commands: (core)
  cache-clear (cc)       Clear a specific cache, or all drupal caches.
  core-cli (cli)         Enter a new shell optimized for drush use.
  core-cron (cron)       Run all cron hooks in all active modules for specified
                         site.
  core-rsync (rsync)     Rsync the Drupal tree to/from another server using ssh.
  core-status (status,   Provides a birds-eye view of the current Drupal
  st)                    installation, if any.
  core-topic (topic)     Read detailed documentation on a given topic.
  drupal-directory       Return path to a given module/theme directory.
  (dd)
  help                   Print this help message. See `drush help help` for more
                         options.
  image-flush            Flush all derived images for a given style.
  php-eval (eval, ev)    Evaluate arbitrary php code after bootstrapping Drupal
                         (if available).
  php-script (scr)       Run php script(s).
```

Figure 9-3. Look at all the things you can do!

Another Option: Creating a Symbolic Link to Drush

Todd Nienkerk of Four Kitchens (Austin, TX) also recommends this method for skipping the old-school text editors (nano, vim, etc.) by creating a symbolic link using the following command:

```
ln -s /PATH/TO/drush/drush /usr/local/bin/drush
```

Then close and reopen Terminal. Type **which drush** to verify that it's installed; if it gives you the path *usr/local/bin/drush*, you're done.

Note that the second "drush" in */PATH/TO/*drush/drush is *important*. In the example I've described, my literal command would be:

```
ln -s ~/drush/drush /usr/local/bin/drush
```

Now the Fun Begins

Now that you have Drush installed, there are all sorts of things you can do from the main folder of any working Drupal installation:

- Need to download and enable a module? Type **drush dl** *MODULE_NAME* where *MODULE_NAME* is what comes after drupal.org/project/ (*http://drupal.org/project/*) in the URL.
- Need to update some modules? Type **drush up**. What used to take a few hours if you had a lot of modules to update, now takes a minute or two.
- Want to clear the caches? Type **drush cc all**.
- Want to enable a new module? Type **drush en** *MODULE_NAME*.
- Need to synchronize your default database with the copy on your local machine? Type **drush sql-sync default localhost**.

It's just so beautiful!

Now that we've installed Drush, it's time to learn about the next tool in our "make my Drupal life easier" arsenal: Git, the open source version control system.

CHAPTER 10

Getting Started with Git

The reasons for using version control on your Drupal projects are several and various, and have only recently become clear to me, as I've started working with Drush and Git. Although adding version control to your workflow can be daunting at first, the benefits far outweigh the initial annoyances. Consider this.

- In a recent project, while attempting to theme complex navigation on a Drupal 7 prototype, I found myself messing things up in a bad, bad way, less than an hour before major stakeholders were supposed to look at the site. Because we were using Git, I was able to roll back to the former, not-messed-up menu while we focused on other priorities—without having to make a frantic phone call to our developer.

- When working with more than one person, version control allows you not only to figure out who made what changes to the code, but also to work on the same file at once without accidentally overwriting each other's changes.

- Finally, version control ensures that you have exactly the same files installed in all locations. This means you never have to worry that your local site is on a different version of a module than your server copy.

In this chapter we'll install Git in our local development environment, set up a local and remote repository for a basic Drupal implementation, and learn how to work Git into our Drupal workflow.

Master Versus Origin

Git allows multiple development tracks to be going on simultaneously, using a technique called *branching*. Branches could be used to separate work by multiple developers on a team, or to isolate work on specific bugs, or to separate development code from stable/production code. Working with branches is not necessary to get started with an effective version control workflow, however; so, for now, we'll assume all work is on the default branch, called "master." Where the word *master* appears in the Git commands to follow, you can substitute other branch names if you're using other branches.[1]

When working with Git, you'll primarily be working with a local copy, or "clone," of your repository (which we'll be calling *Master*) and pushing/pulling that copy to a remote copy, called *Origin*, hosted on a separate server. A repository, in version control terms, is a collection of all the files that Git is tracking for your particular project.

As you work, you add your changes to *stage*, a temporary space that tracks the files, using the command `git add [`*filename*`, `*foldername*`, or `-A` for all files]. When you're ready to finalize things, you commit your changes to the branch using the command `git commit -m "`*message goes here*`"`. If something gets messed up and you need to roll back your changes, you can use `git revert HEAD` to roll back the code to your last commit, or you can throw away everything you've just changed using the command `git reset –hard HEAD`, provided that you haven't yet committed your changes.

 Git will only let you roll back changes to either the most recent commit or a numbered commit that you specify. Therefore, *you should commit any change you may eventually want to roll back to, before you move on to the next bit of coding.*

Origin is your remote repository, where you push and pull all the working code for your project. This is generally a repository that is saved on GitHub or a similar Git-enabled hosting service.

Setting Up Git for Your Workflow

For a solo workflow, I'll typically start with three clones of the same repository:

- A remote *Origin*, hosted on GitHub.
- A local clone of the repository, hosted on my MAMP server.
- A second remote clone, hosted on a staging server with protected access. The staging server allows clients and collaborators to view the site's progress as it's happening, without affecting the production (i.e., live/launch) domain.

All of these repositories are *clones* of one another, which means they have the same files and data; pushing and pulling syncs the files among them. Most development workflows start this way; as you add collaborators, or move your code from staging to launch, each of these different environments will require its own clone of the main repository. Each collaborator on the team will push and pull to the main repository.

---

1. For more on branches, check out this great write-up on version control: *http://hoth.entp.com/output/git_for_designers.html*.

When I first started using Git, I was overwhelmed trying to figure out how everything worked. After a few sessions, however, I realized it was relatively easy to get the hang of Git. The basic workflow is as follows:

1. Create an empty repository on GitHub, which will become *Origin*.
2. Create a local directory for your installation and copy your files into it.
3. In *Terminal.app*, navigate to the new directory and initialize your new *Master*:

   ```
   git init;
   ```
4. Commit your files to *Master* by typing the following:

   ```
   git add -A
   git commit -m "first commit"
   ```
5. Add the remote *Origin* you just created on GitHub using the following command:

   ```
   git remote add origin https://github.com/username/repository-name.git;
   ```
6. Push the files to GitHub using the following:

   ```
   git push origin master
   ```

Next, we'll look at those steps in a bit more detail. Steps 1–4 cover installation, and you only need to do them once for each computer or server on which you're installing Git; the rest of the steps will help you set up the workflow for each project.

Step 1: Create an SSH Key

In order to push your first commit to the remote *Origin* you'll create in step 2, you need to create an SSH key for your account. This helps your computer connect securely to GitHub, and you only need to do it once for each computer from which you want to access the repository. The GitHub site has a pretty in-depth write-up of how to do this (see *http://help.github.com/mac-set-up-git/*); however, I'll give you the basic steps here:

1. In *Terminal.app*, navigate to your SSH directory using the following command:

   ```
   cd ~/.ssh
   ```
2. Check to see what's in the directory by using this command:

   ```
   ls
   ```

   This will list all the contents of the directory. If you see the filenames *id_rsa* and *id_rsa.pub*, those are your current SSH keys, and you can skip to step 5. If you don't see them, you want to create a new one.
3. To generate a new SSH key, enter the following code:

   ```
   ssh-keygen -t rsa -C your_email@youremail.com
   Enter file in which to save the key (/Users/your_user_directory/.ssh/id_rsa):
   ```

4. Now you need to enter a passphrase:

```
Enter passphrase (empty for no passphrase):<enter a passphrase>
Enter same passphrase again:<enter passphrase again>
```

This should give you a message such as this:

```
Your identification has been saved in /Users/your_user_directory/.ssh/id_rsa.
Your public key has been saved in /Users/your_user_directory/.ssh/id_rsa.pub.
The key fingerprint is:
01:0f:f4:3b:ca:85:d6:17:a1:7d:f0:68:9d:f0:a2:db user_name@username.com
```

5. You now want to add this key to your GitHub account. To do this, go into the Account Settings page and click on the SSH Public Keys tab (see Figure 10-1). Create a new key by clicking the "Add key" button.

Figure 10-1. Adding our SSH key to GitHub

Now you have to get the contents of your actual RSA key. If you have your Finder set up to show hidden files (this is usually not a good idea, as it's easy to accidentally delete things you need), you can navigate directly to the *.ssh* directory and open *id_rsa.pub* in a text editor such as TextWrangler to copy the key. I prefer using the command line. Assuming that you're still in the *~/.ssh* directory (if you aren't, use `cd ~/.ssh` to navigate there now) you can use the following code to spit out the key:

```
ls
```

This spits out the contents of the directory, which should be:

```
id_rsa    id_rsa.pub    known_hosts
```

From there, if you type the following code:

```
cat id_rsa.pub
```

it should spit out a long line of gobbledygook that starts with `ssh-rsa` and ends with your email address. Copy all of it with no lines or extra spaces and paste it into the text box on GitHub, then click "Add key." Go ahead; I'll wait.

Once you do that, you should be all set to push and pull to your GitHub account.

Step 2: Install Git

Installing Git is fairly straightforward, although it does require you to step into the command line.

To install Git, first you need to grab the installer. To do this, visit *http://git-scm.com* and download the installer appropriate to your OS. Find the icon that suits your operating system (see the box on the right in Figure 10-2), and use it to download the correct installer.

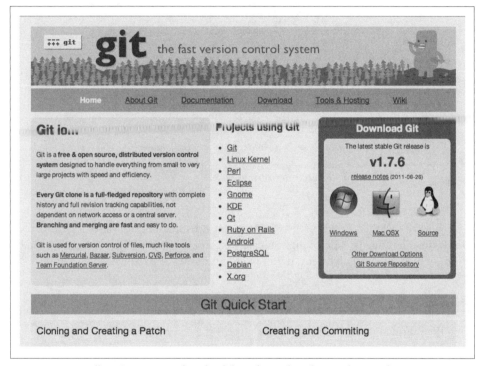

Figure 10-2. Installing Git. You can download the software by selecting the icon that represents your operating system.

Install the Git software using the instructions that come with the package you downloaded. Once it's installed, if you go into *Terminal.app* (on the Mac) and type **git**, you should see a whole bunch of commands in the window (see Figure 10-3). If that doesn't work, try quitting *Terminal.app* and reopening it.

```
Danielles-MacBook-Air:homesteaders Dani$ git
usage: git [--version] [--exec-path[=<path>]] [--html-path] [--man-path] [--info-p
ath]
           [-p|--paginate|--no-pager] [--no-replace-objects]
           [--bare] [--git-dir=<path>] [--work-tree=<path>]
           [-c name=value] [--help]
           <command> [<args>]

The most commonly used git commands are:
    add        Add file contents to the index
    bisect     Find by binary search the change that introduced a bug
    branch     List, create, or delete branches
    checkout   Checkout a branch or paths to the working tree
    clone      Clone a repository into a new directory
    commit     Record changes to the repository
    diff       Show changes between commits, commit and working tree, etc
    fetch      Download objects and refs from another repository
    grep       Print lines matching a pattern
    init       Create an empty git repository or reinitialize an existing one
    log        Show commit logs
    merge      Join two or more development histories together
    mv         Move or rename a file, a directory, or a symlink
    pull       Fetch from and merge with another repository or a local branch
    push       Update remote refs along with associated objects
    rebase     Forward-port local commits to the updated upstream head
    reset      Reset current HEAD to the specified state
    rm         Remove files from the working tree and from the index
    show       Show various types of objects
    status     Show the working tree status
    tag        Create, list, delete or verify a tag object signed with GPG

See 'git help <command>' for more information on a specific command.
```

Figure 10-3. The Git manual, as seen from Terminal.

Once you've installed Git, you also want to set up some configurations within your specific installation. This helps make it easier to see what's been checked out and in by whom, which is especially useful if you're collaborating with others.

Step 3: Set Up Your Git Configuration

Type the following into Terminal to navigate to the *.ssh* directory:

```
cd ~/.ssh
```

If you don't have an *.ssh* directory (which sometimes happens), you can create it:

```
mkdir ~/.ssh
chmod 700 ~/.ssh
```

The command mkdir creates the directory; chmod 700 ensures that only your user—that is, *you*—has access to that directory (important for the security of your system).

Type the following into your Terminal (within the *.ssh* folder) to set up your Git configuration:

```
git config --global user.name "First Last"
git config --global user.email "username@example.com"
git config --global color.ui true
git config --global color.status auto
git config --global color.branch auto
```

```
git config --global color.interactive auto
git config --global color.diff auto
```

If you then type the following into Terminal:

```
git config -l --global
```

you'll see your configuration settings. The preceding configuration gives Git records as to who made the commit that you've posted, and it gives you the ability to read the Git commands more easily by color-coding them.

Step 4: Set Up a GitHub Account

I use GitHub[2] to store my remote repositories. GitHub is fairly easy to set up, and it's reasonably priced (free if you make all your repositories public; $7 per month if you want to have up to five private repositories and a few collaborators—important for client work; additional plans are available as well). Once you have an account and sign in, the GitHub Dashboard (see Figure 10-4) has instructions on how to create a repository and do some other common things you'll need to do on GitHub. Go ahead, poke around; I'll wait.

Figure 10-4. The GitHub Bootcamp screen on your account dashboard. This will give you a quick overview of what you need to know.

Step 5: Create the Remote Repository

Once you have your account set up, the first step is to create a repository. For client projects, I keep my repositories private; I prefer not to have my code hanging around where other people can grab at it. To create a new repository, click on the New Repository button on your GitHub dashboard (see Figure 10-5).

2. *https://github.com/*

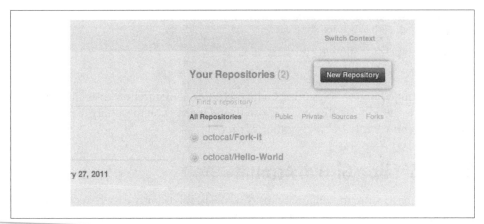

Figure 10-5. Creating a new repository. Image borrowed from http://help.github.com/create-a-repo/.

In the screen that follows (see Figure 10-6), give the repository a name and description, and choose whether you want it to be private or public.

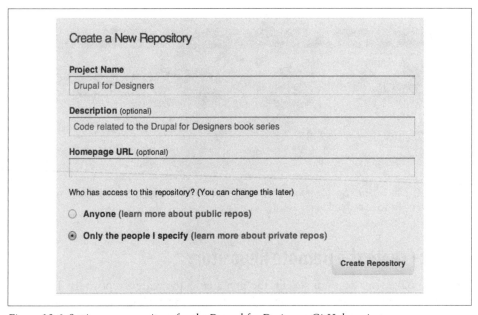

Figure 10-6. Setting up a repository for the Drupal for Designers GitHub project.

Step 6: Set Up the Local Repository

Once you have your repository set up on GitHub, you'll get a set of instructions on the next screen that walks you through the commands you need to create a local repository on your computer. This will help you set up Git so that your code can synchronize between your local and remote repositories.

To create your local repository, start by going into the folder that holds your Drupal installation. This, as you may recall, is done using the following code:

```
cd ~/path/to/d7-demo
```

Once you're there, use the following commands to start a local repository, make your first commit, add a remote repository, and push your files to the remote repository:

```
git init
git add -A
git commit -m 'first commit'
git remote add origin https://github.com/username/repository-name.git
git push origin master
```

Do all of those things in *Terminal.app*, using the values for your GitHub account name and the name of your repository. Once you've created your remote *Origin*, use the command `git pull` to pull down the changes on the remote server each time you start doing work, and `git push` to push the changes back once you're done.

So, What Happens on a Team?

The preceding instructions will help you set up a *Master* repository on your local machine, and push it to a remote *Origin* account. But what happens if you're working on a team? Or you want to have a version of the code on a staging server? This is where things get fun.

First Things First: The Git Workflow

Assuming that you're developing locally (you are developing locally, aren't you?), your workflow would look like this:

1. At the start of your coding session, you'd use the following code in *Terminal.app* to navigate to your project folder and pull the latest code from the repository:

   ```
   cd ~/PATH/TO/FOLDER
   git pull
   ```

2. As you work, you'd use this code to add your changes to Git for tracking and commit them to the *Master* repository:

   ```
   git add [FILENAME, DIRECTORY or -A]
   git commit -m "Description of Changes"
   ```

3. When you're finished, or ready to show your changes to the team, you'd do one last pull:

   ```
   git pull
   ```

... then push your changes back into the *Origin* repository by using the following code:

```
git push
```

4. If you have a second version of the repository hosted on a staging server, you'd then log in to the staging server via SSH and use `git pull` to pull the changes down into the staging server.

 Why pull before pushing? You may have noticed that in step 3, we pulled from *Origin* before we pushed back to it. This is important when you have more than one person working on a repository, and it's a good habit to get into. Pulling the code down syncs any changes that have been made by your other collaborators with the code you're working on; pushing the code adds all the changes back to *Origin*.

And There We Go

So now we've learned how to set up a local development environment, install Drush, and set up Git for our project. Next, we'll put all of this in practice, install MAMP, and set up a new Drupal site.

CHAPTER 11

Putting It in Practice—Setting Up a Local Development Environment and Installing Drupal

When I first started working in Drupal, I created all my sites on a staging URL (*http://newsite.tzk-design.com*) that lived on my studio website. Updating a module meant downloading the project from *http://drupal.org*, unpacking and uploading it to the staging URL, and then running updates manually on the server. Theming meant making changes to a file, uploading it to the server, and refreshing the page to see changes.

While this is a totally reasonable way to work, there were a few problems with it:

- Depending on my Internet connection or the size of a file, uploading files to a server took a significant amount of time—particularly when you add up the time spent tweaking little bits of CSS and checking the results.

- If I had no Internet connection (e.g., when traveling) or if the connection was spotty, I was screwed.

- Perhaps most importantly, everything I was doing could conceivably be found by someone else on the Web. This left me constantly worried that people—particularly clients—would end up randomly finding my half-finished work all over the Web. And while there were certainly ways to avoid that, such as HTTP authentication on the server,[1] that alone didn't solve the first two problems, which are much more annoying.

---

1 If you are using a remote staging server, one way to prevent your dev/staging environments from being seen is to edit the *.htaccess* file (included in Drupal) to require all visitors to use a password just to view the site. You can use this tool to create the text you need to paste into the top of *.htaccess*: *http://www.htaccesstools.com/htaccess-authentication/*. Then use this to generate the *.htpasswd* file that contains the username and password: *http://www.htaccesstools.com/htpasswd-generator/*. Of course, I didn't learn any of this until *after* I'd discovered how to work locally, but that's my issue, not yours.

When I finally figured out how to set up a local hosting environment on my laptop (thanks to a few wonderful friends in the Drupal community, including developer Ben Buckman, interviewed at the beginning of this section), I was delighted. Now I could develop sites more efficiently, from anywhere I happened to be. Of course, it also meant I was more likely to work while on vacation (ask me about the time I had to launch a website in the middle of a yoga retreat), but overall, it's been a lifesaver.

In this chapter we'll focus on creating a local development environment, and installing Drupal 7 in a temporary folder we can access from that environment. From there, we'll use Drush (which you already learned about in Chapter 9) to download and enable some modules. Before we start, however, we have to install MAMP.[2]

Step 1: Install MAMP

In order to set up a Drupal-friendly environment on your computer, you'll need an Apache server running PHP version 5 and MySQL on your laptop. If you're on a Mac, you can download MAMP at *http://mamp.info* for free[3] (see Figure 11-1).

Once your copy of MAMP has downloaded, you'll want to set up your computer to support development on your local server (which is called *localhost*).

Step 2: Set Up Your Local File Structure

Drupal's database and code depends on having a well-organized file structure. MAMP and its Windows and Linux counterparts essentially turn a single folder in your computer into a miniature development server. This means all the sites you develop in MAMP will be subfolders of that main folder (e.g., */MAMP/my-crazy-awesome-site*). Once you have MAMP installed, it's important to make sure you set the location of the main folder to something that makes sense for your filesystem, and to back up that folder regularly. I like to keep my MAMP folder in Dropbox (*http://getdropbox.com*), which allows me to sync my site files in the cloud and access them from any computer I'm on.

To start up MAMP and reset the main folder's location, follow these steps:

1. Click the MAMP icon in your dock. This will start up the MySQL server and PHP. You should see a screen like the one in Figure 11-2.

2. Ignore the browser window that it opens, and go back to the MAMP application. (If you want to turn off the Start screen, you can change it in your MAMP settings

---

2. If you want to try some other options, there's also XAMPP, which is open source and available for a host of systems, including Windows, OS X, and Ubuntu.

3. If you're on Windows, you can download WAMP at *http://www.wampserver.com*. If you're on Ubuntu, the Lullabots have put together a video on how to install a LAMP server on Ubuntu: *http://www.lullabot .com/videos/install-local-web-server-ubuntu*.

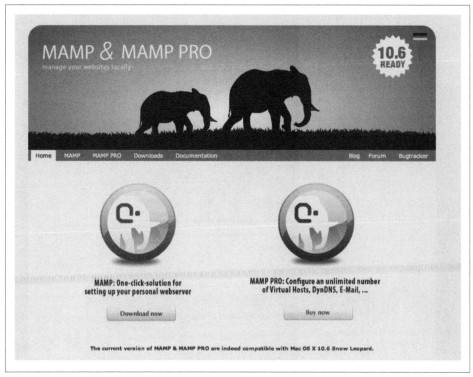

Figure 11-1. The MAMP home page. You want the version on the left.

by unchecking "Open start page at startup" from the Start/Stop tab in the Preferences screen.)

3. Choose Preferences from the menu on the right, and go to the Apache tab (Figure 11-3). Set the document root (which we'll call the "web root" going forward) to something that makes sense for your filesystem. As I mentioned earlier, I'm using Dropbox for my files.

When starting MAMP for the first time, you may get a dialog asking you if you want to use MAMP or MAMP Pro. If you get this dialog, choose MAMP instead of MAMP Pro. For most Drupal development, the free version of MAMP will be more than sufficient.

Dropbox, as mentioned in Chapter 2, is available at *http://getdropbox.com*, and it allows you to store up to 2 GB of data for free, which is synced over the Web. If you don't have a ton of large files to store, it's an easy way to keep your data available to you no matter what machine you're on. If you build sites using multiple machines, however, you also need to make sure you sync your databases among those machines; MAMP keeps the databases you create in the */Applications/MAMP/db/mysql* folder of the ma-

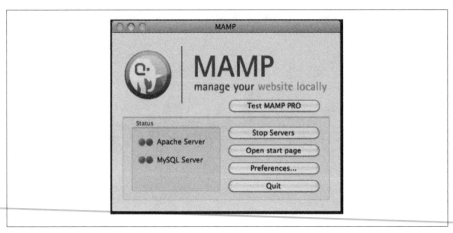

Figure 11-2. The MAMP application screen.

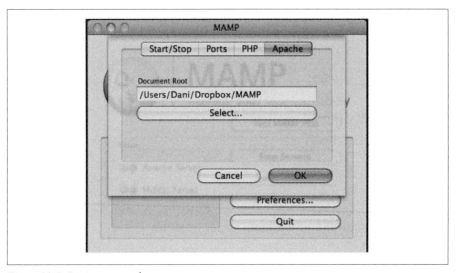

Figure 11-3. Setting up our document root.

chine you create them on, so you may have to export a file of the site's database using a module such as Backup and Migrate (*http://drupal.org/project/backup_migrate*), and import them into the database of the machine you're working on at the beginning of each session. Backup and Migrate lets you back up your site's database and import databases from other sources; it also includes Dropbox integration, which allows you to export the databases directly into Dropbox instead of on the FTP server.

Step 3: Set Up the Drupal Files

Drupal's core files are hosted as a project on Drupal.org (*http://drupal.org*) along with thousands of contributed modules (called "projects") that can extend the core functionality of Drupal. Start the installation process by downloading Drupal at *http://dru pal.org/project/drupal*. You want to download the *latest stable release* of Drupal 7.

Once you have these files downloaded, extract the Drupal folder into your MAMP directory and rename the folder to something that makes sense for your site. I like to name my site folders after the client, generally using a short code for them to save time when navigating to the site. For example, my portfolio site, *http://tzk-design.com*, is in my MAMP folder as */tzk*. For this demonstration, we'll use the folder name *d7-demo*.

> Any code you add to or customize for your Drupal site—whether it's modules, themes, or uploaded files—must go into the */sites/* folder, and *not into any of the core folders*, such as the core *sites* or *themes* folder. If you do not do this, all your hard work may be replaced the next time you upgrade. Seriously.[4]

Now that you've extracted Drupal and put it into your MAMP directory, navigate to the *sites* folder within your Drupal files. Any modules, themes, libraries, and so on that you use to customize this Drupal site should be downloaded into the *sites/all* folder, in folders named *modules*, *themes*, or *libraries*, depending on their purpose. If you're using Drush to download modules, Drush will create those folders within the *sites* folder for you if they don't exist. Because it's awesome.

Now, to develop locally, we want to create a *localhost* folder within *sites*, which will hold the database settings for our local Drupal installation. If you're already cozy with the command line, there are several ways you could set this up, including creating multiple local sites within the same Drupal installation; however, for our purposes, we can stick with creating a *localhost* folder.[5] Once you've created that folder, navigate into the *sites/default* folder and make a copy of the file called *default.settings.php*, move it into your *localhost* folder, and rename the file to *settings.php*. Leave it alone for now; you'll need it for what happens later.

---

4. All. Of. It.

5. If you plan to use the same Drupal distribution to host multiple sites (which is totally valid and possible), you'll need to learn how to create multiple local URLs.

You may notice that we're putting our Drupal configuration in a different folder than *sites/default*, which is the typical way of installing Drupal. We're doing this because leaving *sites/default* where it is for now is useful for minimizing confusion when you eventually publish the site to its final URL. Doing this, however, means that all the changes you make in your Drupal site will be stored in the *localhost* folder, and you will need to use `drush sql-sync localhost default` to sync the *localhost* database with the *default* database, which will require logging in to the staging server via SSH. You can also sync the local and remote databases using a program such as Navicat (see step 4), or by exporting the *localhost* database and importing it into the remote site—both of which you can do using the Backup and Migrate module (*http://drupal.org/project/backup_migrate*). As with most things in Drupal, there are about 372 ways to accomplish the same goal.

Step 4: Set Up the Drupal Database

Drupal stores all the information related to your site in a database. In order to install Drupal, you need to create this database on your local MySQL server.

You can create a database using phpMyAdmin, which is free and comes with MAMP (instructions on how to create the database using phpMyAdmin are available in the sidebar "Using phpMyAdmin"). If you prefer a more visually oriented way of dealing with databases, Navicat, available for purchase at *http://navicat.com*, is one of the best programs I've found. Although the premium software is on the pricey side (and you'll need it for copying or syncing databases on multiple servers, unless you use `drush sql-sync`—important when it's time to launch your site), you can download an inexpensive version called Navicat Premium Essentials for about $10 on the Navicat website (*http://www.navicat.com/en/download/download.html*). Both are available for Windows, Mac, and Ubuntu. If you just want to check it out for now, you can download Navicat as a free trial for 30 days.

For the purposes of this demonstration, we'll use Navicat Premium. The process in Navicat Premium Essentials should basically be the same.

Open Navicat and select Connection→New Connection→MySQL from the top menu.

Once you've created the connection, open the connection by double-clicking its name in the left column. Right-click on the connection name and select Create New Database from the menu (see Figure 11-5). Give the database a name that represents the project you're creating; I'm going to call this one *d7-demo*.

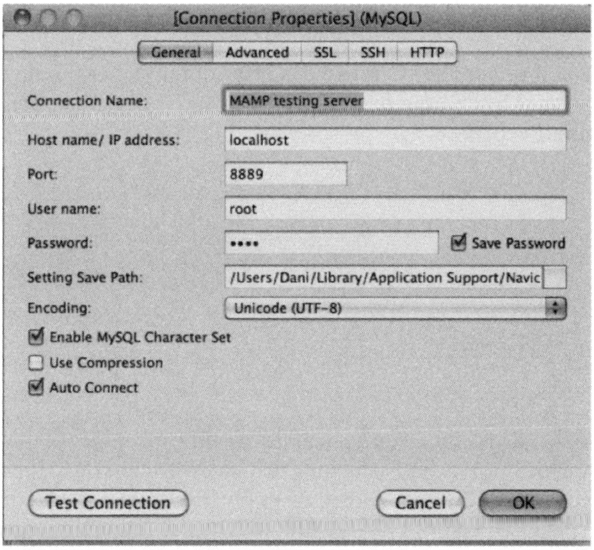

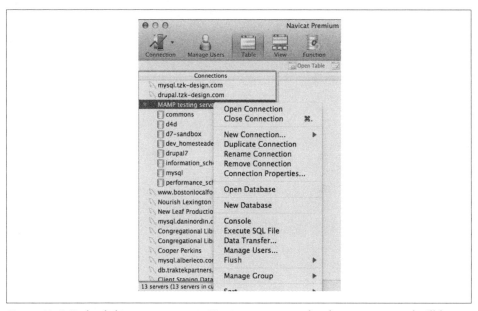

Figure 11-4. Connection settings in Navicat for our local MAMP server.

Figure 11-5. Right-clicking your server in Navicat gives you a handy context menu that'll let you perform key database operations.

That's it. Done. See how easy that was?

Using phpMyAdmin

If you decide you'd rather just stick with phpMyAdmin to create your database, you can start that journey by clicking the "Open start page" button on your MAMP home screen (see Figure 11-6).

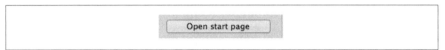

Open start page

Figure 11-6. The "Open start page" button will take you to your MAMP home page, where you can access phpMyAdmin.

Once you get to the MAMP home page, you'll see a tiny link under the MySQL heading that will take you to phpMyAdmin. Clicking that link will take you to the phpMyAdmin interface, where you can create a database simply by typing a name into the "Create new database" field (see Figure 11-7). Again, we'll call this one *d7-demo*.

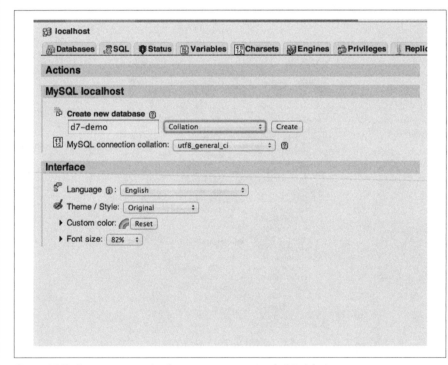

Figure 11-7. Creating a new database is pretty easy in phpMyAdmin.

The new database you create will come set up with all the privileges your *localhost* user needs to install Drupal. When it comes time to transfer the database from your local server to a staging or production server, you'll need a new database with different permissions—but that's for another time. For now, we press onward.

Step 5: Install Drupal

Now that you've created your database, go back into your favorite browser (I use Chrome: *http://www.google.com/chrome*) and go to *localhost:8888/d7-demo/install.php*. Choose the "standard" installation profile for now (see Figure 11-8); it will take care of some basic configurations for you. On the next page, select English as the installation language. If you need to install it in another language, there's a handy link on that screen that will show you how to do it.

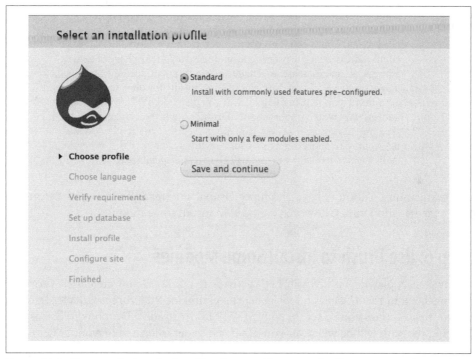

Figure 11-8. Choosing the Standard profile when installing Drupal will set you up with some basic functionality for your Drupal site.

Now it's time to add the values for the database you just created. On the screen that follows, enter the values you provided when you created the database. In my case, the database name is *d7-demo*, the host is *localhost*, and both the username and password are *root*.

You might be wondering why we're setting up our local Drupal database with a password that is obviously not secure. When you're developing locally, security is important, but not as important as when you're developing on a remote site. When you transfer this local version of the site to a remote server, for staging or production, you're actually going to create a new database (with a stronger username and password), and you'll sync the data from the local database to the new remote database.

Submit the form, and Drupal will install itself within a couple of minutes. When the installer finishes (see Figure 11-9) you'll be able to fill in some basic site details along with a username and email address for the administrative user account.

 The first user created in the installation process is given permission to do everything on the site, *always*. Therefore, it is strongly advised that you never use this user as your own personal account, but rather as an administrator account, and that you give it a strong password. The site might be just on your computer now, but when you move it online you'll need to make sure you preserve the user accounts. Drupal requires all email addresses for site users to be unique, so if you only have one email address, it makes sense to create a second email account, such as *admin.user@gmail.com*, that you use specifically for the administrator account. If you're using Gmail, you can also add a "+" to the email address to create a subaccount. Drupal 7 will recognize these as separate addresses; however, Gmail will send all the mail addressed to your subaddresses to your main account. For example, *dani+drupaladmin@gmail.com* will go to *dani@gmail.com*.

Congratulations! You now have an empty Drupal site, ready for content. Before we start playing with Drupal, however, we need to install some modules.

Step 6: Use Drush to Install Some Modules

Ready to start playing with Drush? Let's go back to our D7 Demo site. Open Terminal and navigate to the *d7-demo* folder using the command `cd ~/Dropbox/MAMP/d7-demo`. Again, this assumes you've set up your MAMP folder inside a Dropbox folder; if you haven't, the path will be wherever your *d7-demo* folder is located on your system.

Now we're going to start downloading some modules. For this project, we'll start with a few essential modules:

Pathauto and Token
    These modules help you automatically create sensible URLs for your site's content.

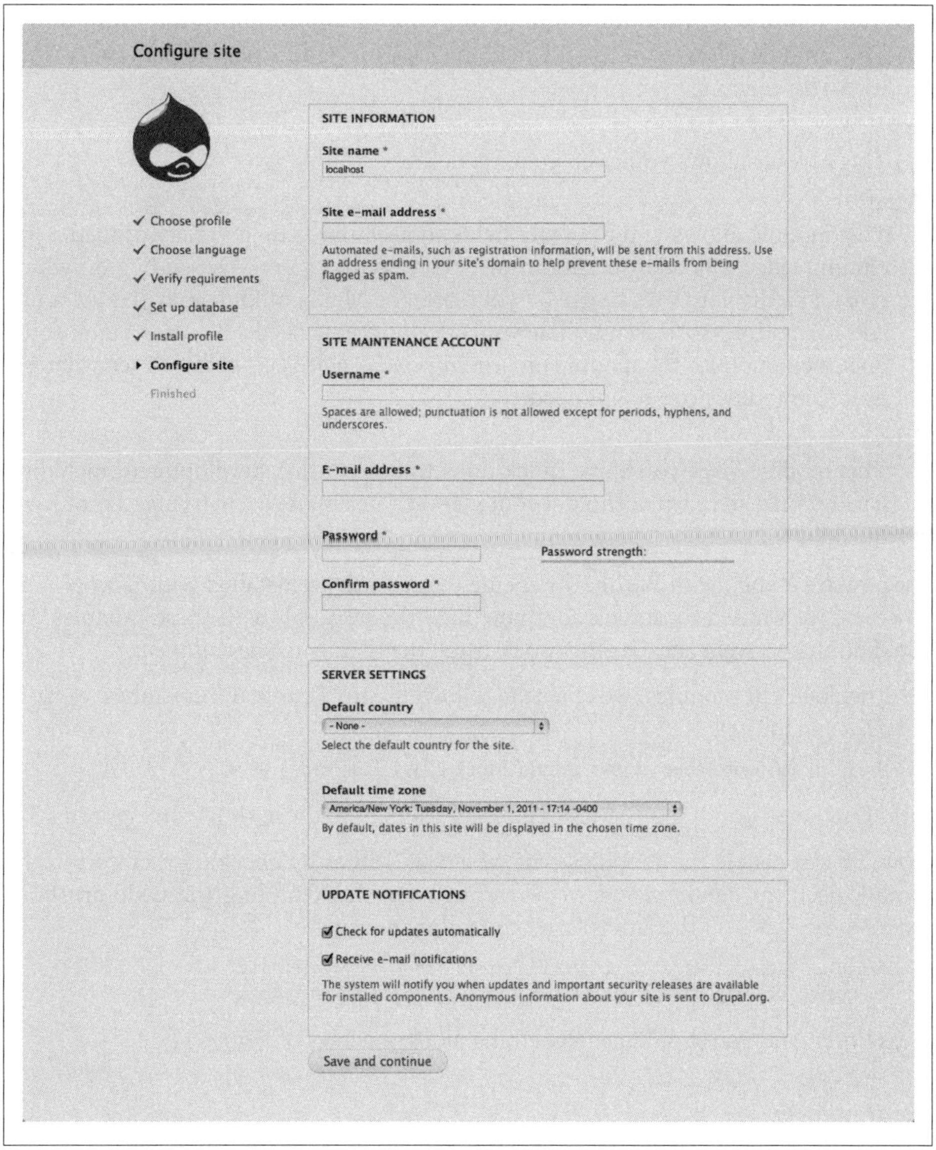

Figure 11-9. Once you've installed Drupal, you can set up some of the site's initial configuration.

Views and CTools

These modules help you create dynamic lists of content on your site. I've heard people say it's possible to have a Drupal site that doesn't require the Views module; however, I have yet to see one.

Block Class

This module allows you to add custom classes to individual blocks. This is very useful for theming.

Link

This module allows you to create Link fields.

Media

This module allows you to create fields to accommodate a variety of media, including video uploads, sharing from YouTube, and so on. Depending on which type of media you want to use on your site, the Media module may require a few add-on modules to accommodate your specific media needs. Be sure to look at the documentation for the module (at *http://drupal.org/project/media*) to see what additional modules you might need.

Devel

This module gives you some quick links to help during development, including letting you generate placeholder content—very useful if you're trying to prototype quickly.

For now we'll stick with Bartik, the theme that comes preinstalled with Drupal 7. If, however, we wanted to download a new base theme along with these modules, we could do that as well, and Drush would install the theme in */sites/all/themes*.

To download our modules, we enter the following into Terminal (remember, we're in our *d7-demo* folder):

```
drush dl pathauto token views ctools block_class link media devel
```

Press Enter, and you'll see a series of messages similar to those shown in Figure 11-10.

Now we can enable the modules that we need—either by checking them off in the Modules screen (*admin/modules*), or through Drush by adding the code drush en module_name. Let's try the latter. Enter the following code:

```
drush en views views_ui ctools media media_internet file_entity
    devel devel_generate link block_class pathauto token
```

Press Enter, and you should get something along the lines of Figure 11-11.

```
Danielles-MacBook-Air:~ Dani$ cd Dropbox/MAMP/d7-demo
Danielles-MacBook-Air:d7-demo Dani$ drush dl pathauto token views
 ctools block_class link media devel
Project pathauto (7.x-1.0) downloaded to
         [success]
/Users/Dani/Dropbox/MAMP/d7-demo/sites/all/modules/pathauto.
Project token (7.x-1.0-beta7) downloaded to
         [success]
/Users/Dani/Dropbox/MAMP/d7-demo/sites/all/modules/token.
Project views (7.x-3.0-rc3) downloaded to
         [success]
/Users/Dani/Dropbox/MAMP/d7-demo/sites/all/modules/views.
Project views contains 2 modules: views, views_ui.
Project ctools (7.x-1.0-rc1) downloaded to
         [success]
/Users/Dani/Dropbox/MAMP/d7-demo/sites/all/modules/ctools.
Project ctools contains 9 modules: views_content, stylizer, page_
manager, ctools_plugin_example, ctools_custom_content, ctools_aja
x_sample, ctools_access_ruleset, bulk_export, ctools.
Project block_class (7.x-1.0) downloaded to
         [success]
/Users/Dani/Dropbox/MAMP/d7-demo/sites/all/modules/block_class.
Project link (7.x-1.0) downloaded to
         [success]
/Users/Dani/Dropbox/MAMP/d7-demo/sites/all/modules/link.
Project media (7.x-1.0-rc2) downloaded to
         [success]
/Users/Dani/Dropbox/MAMP/d7-demo/sites/all/modules/media.
Project media contains 3 modules: media_internet, file_entity, me
dia.
Project devel (7.x-1.2) downloaded to
         [success]
/Users/Dani/Dropbox/MAMP/d7-demo/sites/all/modules/devel.
Project devel contains 3 modules: devel_generate, devel, devel_no
de_access.
Danielles-MacBook-Air:d7-demo Dani$ █
```

Figure 11-10. Drush downloads all the modules we ask it to into the sites/all/modules folder. Total time? About 30 seconds.

When doing certain things in Drush, you may end up with an error saying you've exceeded your memory limit. If this happens to me, I often fix it by going into *sites/default/settings.php* and adding the code `ini_set('memory_limit', '128M');` to the file. Search for the term `ini_set` in the text and put the code at the top of all those values.

You may have to change the permissions on *settings.php* in order to change the file; make sure you set it back to 444 (or 400, if you're very concerned about unauthorized shell access) when you're done. This ensures that, once you've made your changes, nobody else can change your file—particularly important when the site is live. The difference between 444 and 400 is who can read your file; 444 allows anyone to have read-only access to the file. This could potentially let users who manage to get into your server unauthorized read the file, which includes your site's database credentials; 400 makes sure that the only person and computer who can read the file is the web server running Drupal.

Drush also has its own settings file, *drushrc.php*, which you can adjust in order to give Drush more memory while keeping Drupal's memory at a reasonable limit.

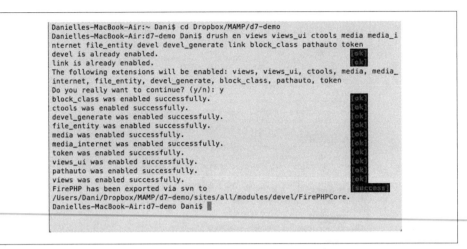

Figure 11-11. Enabling all our modules through Drush. Total time? About a minute.

So now, in about 10 minutes, we've done what it would have taken us well over an hour to do manually. This, dear reader, is why you should learn Drush.

In the next section, we'll go a bit deeper into actually prototyping a site with Drupal.

PART IV

Prototyping in Drupal

CHAPTER 12

Prototyping in Drupal

Some designers, such as independent designer and web strategist Jason Pamental,[1] whose interview appears in the upcoming sidebar, prefer to prototype sites directly in Drupal. Jason says that doing it this way lets him see things as they actually behave in the browser, rather than mocking things up in Photoshop or Fireworks, only to spend hours explaining to clients why the designs changed once they were implemented.

The trick to this approach, however, is not falling into the trap of simply decorating on top of what Drupal gives you, but rather, as Todd Nienkerk suggests in his DrupalCon session "Don't Design Websites, Design Web SYSTEMS!"[2]— letting Drupal's default behavior simply provide a guide for your design.

When a site doesn't require a ton of complex interaction (for which I do paper or interactive Axure prototypes), I'm a big fan of the "sketch, quickly wireframe or prototype, then start prototyping in Drupal" approach. Being able to see how the interactions I'm designing, and the content I'm designing around, can be implemented in Drupal can help me make smarter decisions about layout and functionality, because it helps me make sure that what I'm proposing can actually be done. In practice, my process often looks like this:

1. I'll create a bunch of sketches for possible page layouts, interactions, and so on, and choose one or two to start wireframing.

2. I'll create wireframes for the one or two best options and talk them over with the project team.

3. I'll work those wireframes into some kind of (non-Drupal) prototype, so the project team can see how the interactions should work.

4. We'll iterate those prototypes until we figure out the best solution for what we're dealing with.

---

1. *http://thinkinginpencil.com*

2. Check out the slide deck at *http://fourkitchens.com/presentations*.

5. I'll either start working on prototyping my assumptions in Drupal, or work with the team's developer to start prototyping right away while I work on the next area of functionality/content that needs fleshing out.

This is also one of the key reasons I break up work plans into specific functional areas of the site. It helps me focus the team's energy on getting one specific area working before we go too deep into the next area. This approach can be called many things; some think of it as Agile (from the software programming methodology) and others call it Lean (from the Lean Startup concept).[9] I tend to think of it as a Lean hybrid; the point is less about getting a Minimum Viable Product up and running within a couple of weeks, and more about being able to quickly get your head around the various complexities of a project, create a bunch of hypotheses to test based on your research, and start seeing how those hypotheses play out as quickly as you can.

From the Trenches: Jason Pamental, Web Strategist

Jason Pamental is an independent web strategist and designer who regularly writes and speaks on a variety of Drupal design topics, including web typography. He also serves as the Platform Architect at Schoolyard (*http://www.schoolyard.com/*), an open source system created especially for school websites, which is built using Drupal. You can learn more about Jason and his work at *http://thinkinginpencil.com*.

Dani: You've mentioned to me that you prefer to prototype in the browser, rather than in layout comps or sketches. Can you talk a bit more about that?

Jason: When you prototype in the browser, you can see what it really looks like. It doesn't matter what tricks you have in Photoshop, it's never going to translate exactly into how a web page will behave. So, over the years, I've started to see that if you have a good base theme or a handle on writing HTML, you get to a place much faster where you can actually explore behavior—especially when you're putting it right into a content management system. So you can explore more of the real life of a website quickly, rather than trying to mock up every different state of an interaction.

Dani: How do you come up with your ideas with a process like that? Do you go straight to code, or do you start with sketches and then move to code later?

Jason: In terms of the actual design process, there's always work that goes on in Photoshop or Illustrator. But oftentimes, that comes after a prototype's been built. We tend to have this "sandbox" version of a website that's been built out with all of the main pages and some of the default users there already. It's really quick to play with things and think about "How am I going to search?" and "How am I going to play with these things?" Once it's time to go into the look and feel, you have all the real stuff there to play with. Even as you're opening Photoshop or Illustrator, you know the real things that you have to be concerned with—the buttons, the navigation elements, and the real content on a page, and so on.

But even with that, there are pages and pages of sketches, notes, and things like that from early on in the process, especially for something complicated.

Dani: The flow that I've been moving toward lately is sketch, maybe wireframe a couple of pages, but then start prototyping in Drupal relatively quickly so that I can see how things are falling and how something's going to be implemented. The question I always ask myself is: how much of that workflow is based on the fact that I'm a team of one to three, as opposed to being one piece of a larger team? I notice, with larger teams, they often have more clearly defined roles, so there's not as much concern about whether you specifically can implement something, but more about whether it can be implemented by the team. Have you had experience with that?

Jason: I've worked on teams of varying sizes, from just me to managing a group of three to five people, to being a creative director at a company in Boston with 30 developers and a team of six designers. I've never been a big fan of having a person for every possible task and isolating the work they're doing. It's never seemed to work well.

Especially with a platform like Drupal at your disposal—even doing the site for CVS Caremark, which is a pretty significant project, it was still a team of five or six core people. There was a designer, there was a researcher and information architect, [and] there was me and a couple of developers who were helping me. That was pretty much it.

Dani: That's one of the benefits of Drupal. There's so much that's built for you that it's easier to make big websites with fewer people. I don't think it makes it any less complicated, but I do think it allows you to focus on more important parts of the experience than what the code is going to look like.

Jason: Exactly, and that's one of my favorite things about it. It lets you be a team that is iterative and reactive far more easily than when you have each person in their own separate role. I keep thinking of these companies that push development offshore, or to a partner company, where you have this enforced wall between design and architecture. Maybe there's some prototyping, but the real development happens somewhere else. In those cases, there's no way to just sit down with someone and discuss something, and then react to it right away.

Dani: While you're prototyping in the browser, do you find that there are any moments where you find yourself leaning on Drupal's defaults a bit too heavily?

Jason: That's an easy trap to fall into. Because you know something works, so you put your attention to something else, but what's already built doesn't always work in the best way. I think that's a constant challenge, and not one that's so difficult to overcome if you work smartly. One of the things that I have enjoyed about the process of working on the platform we've built for Schoolyard is that there's a common base point we're starting with. Every project, we get to smooth off more of those rough corners.

When you build up this set of defaults—this set of modules that you always use, this point from which you always start the process—it lets you build up these layers of sophistication. You can start building all these little things that add up to a much more refined experience. That's where taking the time to get to know the platform and just look for stuff and see what's out there—every time you do another project, it just gets better and better.

Working with Content and Content Types

In the Old Days, building a promotional website was a fairly straightforward affair. You'd go through a discovery process, create a couple of wireframes—generally for the home page and one or two interior pages—then mock up and iterate designs. When the client approved those designs you'd whip up a fancy template in HTML and start laying in the content and images.

Content, almost always, came later. You'd have a sense of the site map and how it might evolve—you needed that for navigation—but the actual content was rarely something you saw in the early phases of developing wireframes. Generally, this wasn't a problem; as you were coding the content by hand within the template, you could adjust the template relatively easily once you had content to work with.

With Drupal, as with many other content management systems, things aren't that easy. Some elements will be familiar, especially if you've gotten used to systems such as WordPress. At the most basic level, you're dealing with a series of page templates, and those templates put your content into specific areas of the page. You style those templates in your theme layer, and that makes the page look good.

What makes Drupal complex, but also terrific, is the amount of control you have over almost every aspect of the site's pages, including the specific way that content is formatted. The key to making sense of this complexity is to understand that *each page of a Drupal website is a collection of different pieces of content that are located within your site's database and files.* Because of Drupal's inherent flexibility, that content can be organized and formatted in any number of different ways—and it will need to be, in order to finish the project with a working site.

For this reason, I've found that two things are essential to getting started on any Drupal project:

- *Shifting the way you think about page layout for the Web.* You're not looking at it in terms of generic page grids anymore (although that's certainly a component of it). To actually succeed in creating a Drupal site, you need to think of a page layout in terms of how the information is organized on the page. What will the content be? What sections will you need, and how will they be organized on the page? How will the content be found or searched for—in top-level navigation, by browsing categories, or some other way? Visual design is an important component of that, but it should always come after this first issue has been dealt with.

- As a way of reinforcing the preceding bullet point, start *every Drupal project* with one to three samples of actual content that will appear on the actual site.

Over the years, I've seen some resistance to this concept—developers, for example, like to think in terms of building things quickly, and clients can have a hard time grasping the idea that they need to be able to provide content before they see page layouts. But there's a very specific reason for this need. As mentioned earlier, every page of your

Drupal site is constructed from different bits of content that are stored in different locations in the system and then are collected on the page. This means that to construct the actual pages, you need to start loading actual content into the system as soon as you can—and you need to know if there's anything in the final content that you'll need to accommodate in your design.

Drupal works by organizing content into different content types (see Chapter 1 for more information on content types). It also allows you to add and display as many custom fields within those content types as you can (which is very useful for making content look the way you want it to on the page). This flexibility is one of the key reasons it is imperative to work with actual content instead of placeholder text. Seeing the content allows you to visualize its fundamental components, and allows you to set some formatting parameters that will protect the client's content strategy after they take over management of the site.

The layout of a Drupal page can be constructed from any number of things:

- Actual node content (remember, Drupal calls content "nodes")
- Displays of views that organize several nodes together
- Blocks that can be created either with custom text/HTML or as views displays
- Menus that can be created in any number of ways
- Custom code built into the page template

For example, a standard Events page on a corporate website would likely consist of the following (see Figure 12-1):

- An Event content type, with a title, description, date, and link to an external website or registration page
- A view called "events" that lists all events in chronological order
- Displays based on the "events" view that would show as a block of titles and dates for the home page, an Events archive (showing events that have happened already), and an Upcoming Events page (showing events that haven't happened yet)

In addition to these, you might have categories for different types of events, links to external resources (such as a book to read or a packing list), and any other permutation of the Event content type your clients can come up with. Starting the process with dummy content only gets you so far; if the live content will be different from what you're assuming, you'll find yourself with a load of headaches before you know it.

Trial by Fire

My first major Drupal site was for a small-business owner. In our initial discussions we talked about doing a simple refresh of her existing site, which was only about a dozen pages, and I sold her on the idea of doing it in Drupal, which gave her more control

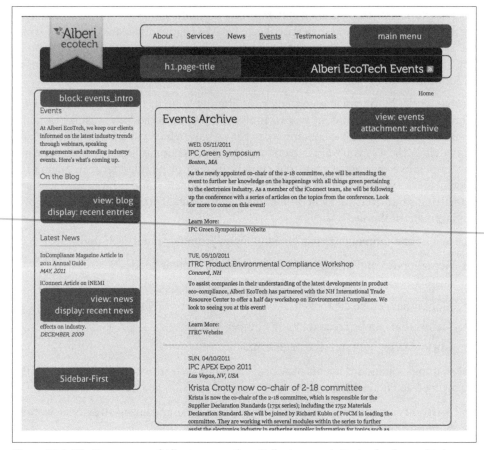

Figure 12-1. The Events page of Alberieco.com (http://alberieco.com). Design by the zen kitchen.

over content entry. We discussed the site map and the way that content was going to be organized, but she hadn't developed any of the new content yet. As was my process at the time, I worked up a proposed layout for the home page and an interior page, and she approved it with no problems. With the look and feel established, I started up an installation of Drupal and began creating the content types that would organize the site's content, working with generic placeholder text.

The site map we originally agreed on was fairly simple:

- A Services page that listed all the services her company offered
- An Events page that listed upcoming events (this would require an Event content type)
- A News page that listed current news (this would require a News content type)
- An About page that listed all the staff members and what they brought to the company

- A Resources page that listed resources for her clients
- A contact form that would allow users to get in touch with her for consultations

All of this seemed pretty straightforward. When the content started coming in it turned out that the Services page was actually several different services, each with 14 pages of descriptive content. The staff bios were two pages long. Events could be categorized, and would be navigated, in three separate ways. And the landing pages for each of these content sections should only show teaser content (i.e., a picture, a title that linked to the full content, and an intro paragraph). Most of her requests made perfect sense, but none of them had been discussed in our discovery sessions, nor were they reflected in the designs that had been comped and approved. Eventually, I had to redo all the work that had already been done, which threw the project into massive delays.

From that point on, I made it part of my discovery process to get samples of actual content from the client before I start working with Drupal on any project. While this policy isn't without its challenges, it has resulted in a much more efficient workflow over the years. This is especially true for large, complex sites—but as with the previous example, it can even be true of smaller sites.

Working with Content Types: A High-Level Overview

As mentioned previously, Drupal works by separating content into distinct content types. The best way to determine which content types your site will need is through the site map and wireframes that were done in the UX/discovery phase. Site maps and high-level navigation items will guide you in creating content types, while wireframes and site designs offer insight into the types of content you need to accommodate (text, images, video, etc.), what special fields you might have to create, and how those fields should be formatted.

If you (or someone on your team) developed a site map during the discovery or UX phase (see Figure 12-2), you can work directly with the site map to determine content types. Working with a printout, or in a program such as OmniGraffle, start marking up the site map with notes. These notes should include possible fields you might need, categories users might expect for the content, and other questions that arise from the site map. For example: do we want to have testimonials from clients? Should those appear as a block on several pages, or just as a page? How are we organizing news items? How many authors will be on the blog? This will help you get oriented, and you can better communicate to the client and the team what the content needs will be.

When you have sample content from the client, print out the content file (double-sided) and start writing on it. Note extra fields, taxonomy categories you'll have to create, and how to break up the content on the landing pages for that section. If wireframes (see Figure 12-3) or site designs have already been created, be sure to check them against the content you've received; you'd be surprised how often they differ.

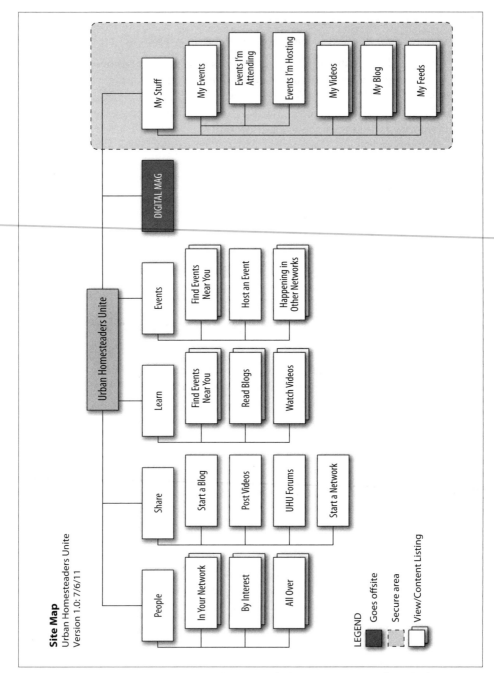

Figure 12-2. A site map can give you a head start on which content types you'll need. This site map notes with double boxes which content pages will be coming from Views; each of those types of content lists could be its own content type; for example, blog entries, videos, events, and so on.

The number of extra fields you include in a content type will vary; I've had projects where every content type was a title, description, and image, and I've had projects where every content type required anywhere from four to 30 extra fields, each of which had to be formatted and displayed in a certain way based on what situation the user was in at the time he was viewing it. This, if you haven't guessed yet, is why you need the content *first*—if you think you're doing the former and you find out you're doing the latter, your life will be very, very bad while you switch gears.

Once you've sketched out an overview of what you're really looking at and you've confirmed these assumptions with the client, it's time to start creating the content types themselves. Building out content types can be one of the most time-intensive pieces of creating a Drupal site if the content types you're working with are very complex.

First you start creating fields, then reorder them if you need to, change the way they're displayed (Do they need the field label? Should it be above the content or in line with it? Do you even need to show the field? Do we want to group them a certain way?), and create a single piece of content to test that it looks right on the page. For a very simple content type (e.g., most news content types, or basic page content types), this can take a few minutes. For more complex content types (e.g., a product description, or a content type that maps to several pieces of related content), this back and forth can take days.

In order to keep things moving along, we won't get into the basic process of how to create content types; if you have never done it before, check out the following video-based demos on creating content types in Drupal 7:

- *http://www.youtube.com/watch?v=iibPX5KBFu4*
- *http://yadadrop.com/drupal-video/drupal-7-creating-content-types*

Also, check out the next chapter for some modules that can help with managing the code that is output by content types and custom fields.

Organizing Your Content

Setting up content types is one piece of the content puzzle. Once you've gotten the content types somewhat organized and you have some sample content in the site, you want to start putting them into Views displays. I, like many of my Drupal brethren, have a love–hate relationship with Views. On the one hand, Views is an incredibly powerful tool for getting content to display in any possible combination you can think of. This makes it easier to build massively complex sites while keeping them relatively easy to maintain. On the other hand, Views can be so complex that even the most seasoned developers occasionally can't make heads or tails of it.

For the designer, or even the solo site builder, it's useful to have the basics down when it comes to Views. While the first few views you create will always leave you grinding your teeth, it's relatively easy to put them together once you get the system down. Additionally, Views allows you to clone views and individual displays, which makes it

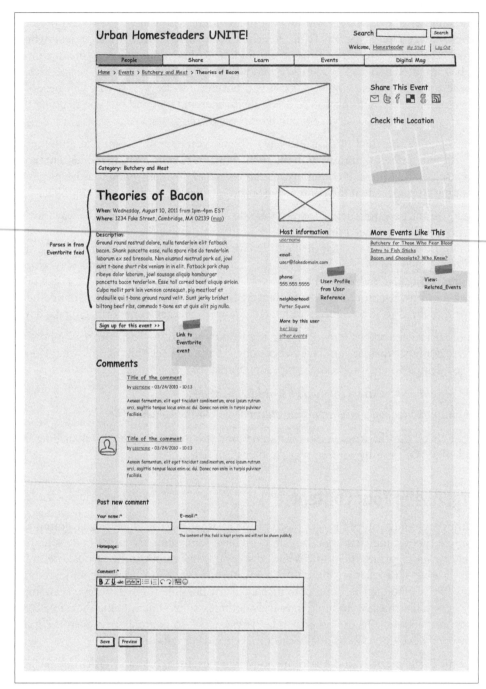

Figure 12-3. Annotating a wireframe can help you figure out where content is coming from in your Drupal site. In this mockup for a project in process, we're assuming most of the page information is coming in from an Eventbrite feed.

much easier to create additional views once you have the first one finished. For the purposes of this chapter, we're only going to discuss how to figure out which views you'll need, and how they should be displayed.

To figure out which views you need, start with your site map and any wireframes that have been created in the design process. Anything that looks like a list of content, titles, or links to content is most likely going to require a view. Sample views might include:

- A menu of recent blog entries for the sidebar of each page
- A menu of categories for a specific type of content
- A News page or Events calendar
- A staff directory or list of bios
- A list of blog posts related to the one a user is reading
- A jQuery slideshow of featured content on the home page
- A single entry from the blog that appears in the site's footer or in a promotional area on the home page

All of these things can be created with the Views module.

By default, Views allows you to create the following displays:

- Pages (i.e., a full page of content, which appears in the site's navigation)
- Blocks (i.e., a small block of content, which can appear anywhere on the site that you want it to)
- Attachments (i.e., a view with slightly different parameters that's attached to another view; this is useful, for example, if you want to display both Upcoming Events and Recent Events on the same page)
- RSS feeds

Each of these displays can be output in a variety of formats, including an HTML list (good for building sidebar menus or lists of related content), an unformatted list (the default display, good for displaying content on a page), tables, and multicolumn grids. Adding a few handy contributed modules can open up more possibilities for formatting your Views displays:

- JQuery slideshows. These are particularly helpful for creating featured content areas, or for highlighting specific projects or products. My favorite slideshow module is Views Slideshow (*http://drupal.org/project/views_slideshow*). While it has its limitations and dependencies, it's the most reliable of the slideshow modules I've seen.
- Calendars of events, or pages that have time-sensitive content. This is where the Date module (*http://drupal.org/project/date*) comes in handy.

The Date module comes with a submodule called Date Views. *You will need to enable this module in order to get Views to work correctly on anything that involves a date.*

- All manner of jQuery effects: accordions, sliders, and anything you can think of. While it is often advisable to build these things into your theme manually, many contributed modules are available that can create the formatting for you. Just be aware that many contrib models don't create the prettiest code.

We won't get into the basics of creating views in this book. However, there are quite a few excellent video tutorials that you can check out if you haven't played with the Views module yet:

http://lin-clark.com/blog/intro-drupal-7-intro-views-pt-1
> An introduction to Views, by Lin Clark (just ignore the Drush stuff).

http://www.metaltoad.com/Drupal-7-Tutorial-Creating-Edit-Content-Links-Views
> A very comprehensive tutorial from Dan Linn at Metal Toad Media on creating "edit content" links using Views. It also gives a quick overview of the new Views interface, which is a massive improvement over the last version.

http://nodeone.se/blogg/learn-views-screencast-series-summed-up
> An entire set of Drupal videos that walk through the Views process in a variety of contexts, by NodeOne in Stockholm, Sweden. I cannot recommend these videos highly enough.

Putting It All Together

In theory, each member of the team will be dealing with his or her own piece of this giant puzzle called building a website. In practice, especially on small or solo teams, you'll often find yourself switching back and forth among different phases of the content development cycle. A typical Drupal project, for example, might look like this:

1. Site map and wireframes are created and approved.
2. The designer (you) starts adding in visual elements.
3. The frontend developer (or you) starts creating content types and fields.
4. Site content comes in and looks different from the wireframes and designs that have been approved.
5. The frontend developer (or you) goes back and starts changing content types, fields, views, and so on, to mesh with the content files.
6. The client decides the content should be changed to match the designs.
7. The frontend developer (or you) goes back and starts changing content types, fields, views, and so on, *back* to where they were before.
8. And so on, and so on ... .

Somewhere in this whole mess, theming also has to happen. In larger teams, the designer will often work directly with a frontend developer to iterate designs and incorporate them into the site's theme. For smaller jobs or solo gigs, you're the one doing the lion's share of the design, theming, and content management. With time, you get used to it. A typical theming session for me usually involves tweaking the display of a field in my content type, then tweaking a display setting in one of the views I created, then going back into CSS and making adjustments—in infinite combinations.

This is the single most important reason why it's important to get actual content as soon as you possibly can. The more you can allow the content to inform your designs, the fewer headaches you'll have in the design and development process. Your team will cheer you, your client will love you, and your head will definitely thank you.

CHAPTER 13

Choosing Modules

Modules are one of the things that make Drupal terrific; however, they can also make Drupal frustrating to many people who are just starting to work with it. Knowing which module to choose, or which one you need for a specific project, can be a challenge. And sometimes a module that seems to be exactly what you need will end up causing more trouble than it fixes—either through refusing to play nice with other modules you've installed, or through messy code that causes major cross-browser issues.

That being said, many modules are incredibly useful when working with Drupal. Some, such as Block Class (*http://drupal.org/project/block_class*) and Pathauto/Token (*http://drupal.org/project/pathauto*; *http://drupal.org/project/token*), are so useful that I install them by default on any new installation. Others, such as View Reference (*http://drupal.org/project/view_reference*), I install only when I need that specific functionality.

So Many Modules; How Do I Choose?

There's no specific science to choosing the right Drupal module for a given project. However, the more sites you build, the more you'll begin to notice that specific modules become common for a given project. As you experiment, you'll also get better at weeding out the modules that aren't terribly good from the ones that are rock solid. Here are some things to keep in mind when choosing modules for your project:

When possible, fewer modules is generally better
> Bear in mind that every module you enable on a Drupal site adds code and other things the site needs to deal with in order to load the site. The more modules there are to deal with, the longer it takes for pages to load.

Look for modules that are actively maintained
> Each module's project page lists whether the module is actively maintained, how long ago the code was updated, and the date of the last release. In general, it's best to choose modules that are listed as "Actively Maintained" and have a recommended release date within the past six months. Figure 13-1 shows an example of an actively maintained Drupal module.

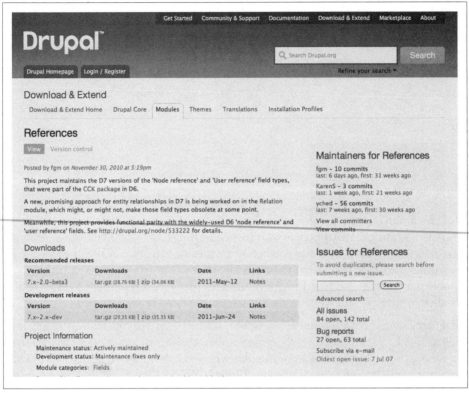

Figure 13-1. The Drupal project page for the References module. Notice the phrase "6 days ago" in the upper-right corner? That's a good thing.

If all else fails, reach out

Can't figure out what you're looking for? Can't find the right module for your specific functional needs? A good developer can often help you create custom functionality (and is worth every penny you spend—seriously). Often, though, you can find advice and support from the Drupal community just by asking at a community event or online. Searching on Drupal.org (*http://drupal.org*) for "[list functionality here]" can also help you find things you may not have thought to look for. Either way, don't worry; we've all been there.

What follows is an entirely incomplete and unscientific list of some of my favorite modules for Drupal 7.

Go-To Modules

The following modules have a home in almost every Drupal project I've done for the past three or four years. Some of them provide basic, commonsense functionality that's not available in Drupal core; others make theming or working with content easier.

Pathauto

(http://drupal.org/project/pathauto)

Pathauto helps you automatically create custom URLs for your site's pages. By default, Drupal will name every new piece of content "node/45" or something similar (the number represents the node's unique ID). This is bad not only for search engine optimization, but particularly for helping people find pages as your site grows in size. With Pathauto, Drupal will use the title of the node as a default URL, making things much cleaner. You can also configure the settings to give specific content types their own prefix; for example, blog pages can have the custom URL blog/[title] as their URL. Pathauto requires the Token module *(http://drupal.org/project/token)* to work properly.

Views

(http://drupal.org/project/views)

Views, in its simplest form, is a database query. It's one of the most powerful contributed Drupal modules, and presents some of the biggest learning curves, even to people who use it for years. Once you get used to it, however, you can use it to create almost anything on a Drupal site—from a simple list of blog entries to dynamic menus to (with some help from different modules) clickable calendars and funky jQuery widgets. Recent updates to Views with Drupal 7 have made it much easier to get started working with Views; while there's still a significant learning curve, it's much easier to cross. As mentioned earlier, Swedish Drupal shop NodeOne did a terrific series of videos on learning Views in Drupal 7. Check out *http://nodeone.se/blogg/learn-views-screencast -series-summed-up* for a whole lot of Views love.

 When you download Views, you also need to download Chaos Tools *(http://drupal.org/project/ctools)*, which Views depends on. CTools is also a dependency for a variety of very useful modules, including Context, discussed next.

Context

(http://drupal.org/project/context)

Context is a module that provides an interface for changing what's shown on a page (blocks, views, or other elements) depending on the user's location within the system, his or her role, or other contexts. This allows you to, for example:

- Display certain blocks only for a specific user role.
- Display the same block in two different regions on the page depending on what section of the site the user is in.

- Through Context Layouts (a submodule), create custom layouts that themes can switch to depending on where the user is in the menu structure.

While you can accomplish all of these things through different methods, using Context can greatly speed up the process once you get over the initial learning curve.

Webform

(http://drupal.org/project/webform)

Webform is a module that allows you to create custom forms (say, a contact form or a questionnaire) for your website. While Drupal comes with a contact form module directly in the core, its functionality is limited to sending fairly simple emails to individual users on the site. Webform gives you the opportunity to customize your contact form's content, as well as customize who receives the emails it generates. You can also use it to create custom surveys, which can be very useful for user research.

WYSIWYG

(http://drupal.org/project/wysiwyg)

Many Drupal developers (and even some designers) insist that they never use WYSIWYG editors. I'm not one of them. For one thing, clients expect them. We're accustomed to using them whenever we have to write something that's more than one sentence long—and the first time you leave one out of a site, you can guarantee your client will ask you where it is.

WYSIWYG depends on the Libraries module (*http://drupal.org/project/libraries*) in order to work; you'll also need to download an editor library from the Web. The configuration page for the module will give links to different libraries. The one that I find works best (or, at least, sucks least) is the TinyMCE library.

Mollom

(http://drupal.org/project/mollom)

Mollom is a service that helps block and trap spam on your site. To use the module, you have to set up a free account at *http://Mollom.com*, register the URL of your website for tracking, and copy your public and private API keys (given to you by the Mollom site when you register the URL) into the Mollom settings page (*http://<yoursite.com>/admin/config/content/mollom/settings*). The Mollom service is free for smaller personal and small-business/nonprofit sites; larger sites may require a paid subscription.

Media

(http://drupal.org/project/media)

Media helps you organize and store media (such as audio and video) on a Drupal site. You can use it both to upload files into the site directly, and to host audio and video from outside sources. One of the best features of the Media module is the ability to input a piece of media directly inside the content of a page, something that has been buggy in Drupal for quite some time. Be warned, however: the Media module may require additional modules, such as oEmbed (*http://drupal.org/project/oembed*), to accommodate media from third-party sources.

At DrupalCon in Denver, Dave Reid, one of the maintainers of the Media module, gave a great run-through on how to install and configure the Media module. My notes from that session are on my blog (*http://tzk-design.com/drupalcon-2012-session-notes-drupal -media*), or you can watch the session video at *http://denver2012.drupal.org/program/ sessions/drupal-media*.

Block Class

(http://drupal.org/project/block_class)

Block Class is a little module that does something very important: it allows you to give any block its own class, independent of what Drupal wants to call it. This is particularly useful, for example, when you want to create a block of featured content, or even a new class called "green" that you apply to random blocks in your theme.

For example, going back to our home page for Urban Homesteaders Unite, one of the things we're creating is an "about this site" block that describes what people can do here. If we look under the hood at what Drupal calls this block, we'll see something akin to Figure 13-2.

Now, we've already got some styling set in this block just from our typography defaults. But what if we wanted to add to this—say, make the headings a different color, or add a background color to it? Or, in the case of our mobile site, hide it completely? Drupal's default pattern is to give every element on the page a bunch of automatic classes based on what it is, where it is in the system, and a few other generic factors. Which class selector would we point to in order to make sure we don't accidentally end up styling other blocks as well?

Simply by installing the Block Class module, we can easily add a unique class to our block, directly in the Block configuration screen (see Figure 13-3).

This will allow us to customize the styles for that block using the `.welcome` selector, which will help us more quickly theme our site. It won't strip out the gobbledygook that Drupal outputs in the first place, but it at least gives us something we know to be unique to that block, and something that's named somewhat logically.

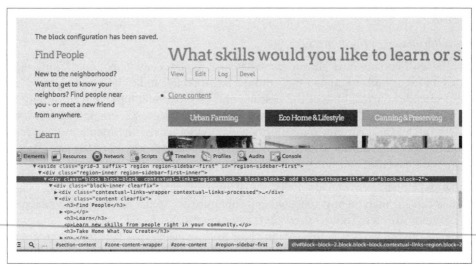

Figure 13-2. See that **long** list of class names that's highlighted? That's our block.

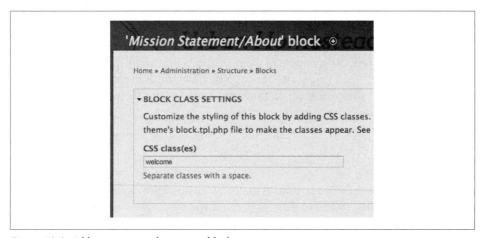

Figure 13-3. Adding a custom class to our block.

Not only is this useful for, say, establishing a common style for all sidebar menus on a given page, but if you're using a grid system such as 960.gs (see Chapter 7), you can assign grid values directly to blocks. This means that, rather than having to do a bunch of fancy tricks in your theme in order to accommodate a layout with blocks of multiple sizes, you can just give one block a class of `grid-4` and another a class of `grid-6`, and let the two float together in one region.

Semantic Fields

(http://drupal.org/project/semantic_fields)

Formerly called Semantic CCK, Semantic Fields (in Development Release as of this writing) helps you do exactly what it sounds like: turn your Drupal fields into clean, semantic code. The module lets you set up certain default field formats—that is, ways that certain fields are displayed in code—through a configuration interface, then apply those formats to a given field in your Drupal content type through the Manage Display interface. This means that you can, conceivably, turn code like this:

```
<div class="field field-type-filefield field-field-recipe-photo">
<div class="field-items">
<div class="field-item odd">
    <img width="200" height="200" title="" alt="" src="my-image.jpg" />
</div></div></div>
```

into this:

```
<img width="200" height="200" title="" alt="" src="my-image.jpg" />
```

without having to mess with template files or theme functions. As a fan of clean code, I can't begin to tell you how gleeful this makes me.

Fences

(http://drupal.org/project/fences)

Fences, a relatively new module, provides an alternative to Semantic Fields. While Semantic Fields requires you to go into a configuration screen to set up your field formats, Fences allows you to select the field's HTML wrapper (including various HTML5 elements, or no wrapper at all) while you're setting up the configuration for the field. Even nicer, it also makes sure that Views uses the field wrapper you've chosen for its field output, instead of the default field wrappers that Views imposes. The only drawback is that Fences does its magic through many custom *field.tpl.php* files, and if you want to alter the output of said files, you'll have to find and copy said *.tpl* file directly in your theme, or create a special function in *template.php* to change it.

Oh-So-Nice-to-Have Modules

While the aforementioned modules will prove useful on almost any site you build, the following modules should at least make it onto your "I might need this for something" list.

Field Group

(http://drupal.org/project/field_group)

Field Group gives you the ability to organize fields within a given content type into groups. For example, let's say you're creating an address book and you want to separate the mailing address from email/phone contact information. Using Field Group, you can display both sets of information in different groups, and theme them differently within your site. You can also display Field Groups as vertical tabs or horizontal tabs by configuring the Manage Display settings in your content type; this is very useful for dealing with complex content types that have a lot of fields.

Link

(http://drupal.org/project/link)

Link helps you create a Drupal field formatted as a link. Each link can have a title and a URL; when displayed, the title will show as a link to the URL you specify.

References

(http://drupal.org/project/references)

References gives you the ability to format Drupal fields as references to other content—such as nodes, user profiles, or taxonomy terms. This is useful if you want to show the author of a post, or related content for an article. It's also essential for implementations that involve multiple content types that relate to one another; for example, on a recent redesign of a large travel site, I used a combination of Views relationships and References to allow trips to share information about ships, locations, and other components that were related to the travel experience.

View Reference

(http://drupal.org/project/viewreference)

The References module, as you just read, makes it possible to reference a specific node or user within a field in your Drupal page—which is useful if you have related information to share after a blog post. But what if you want to show a bunch of related content, with some teaser information and an image? You could use a Node reference, and format the display of the field to show the content's Teaser display rather than just titles; however, doing this may cause Drupal to create a bunch of extra code that will slow down your site. Using View Reference, you can create a view that contains only the fields you want to display, formatted the way you want to show them, and reference that view directly in a custom field.

Block Reference

(http://drupal.org/project/block_reference)

Normally, to place a block on a page, you'd use the Block configuration screen to place it inside a region, and customize which pages or content types it belonged on. Block Reference, while it doesn't replace this process, gives you the ability to reference a Drupal block directly in a field. This is useful:

- When you want to place a block on only one page
- When you want to place a block within the Content region in a particular location (say, within a field group, or underneath a description)

Block Reference doesn't replace the Block configuration screen for all blocks; menus, for example, still work best when you use the Block configuration screen to place them. But for highly specific blocks that need to show up within a node's content, this is an incredibly useful module.

Submitagain

(http://drupal.org/project/submitagain)

Submitagain allows you to create an option when you're creating a content type—through a simple checkbox on the content type edit form—that will let you "Save and Add Another" when you create a piece of that type of content.

Why is this wonderful? Let's say you're doing an online directory of association members for your local trade group. You likely have a list of folks with name, address, and other contact information to enter into the site. Normally, you'd have to choose Add Content→Member (assuming you're working with a content type called "Member") from the administration menu each time you create a new member. With this module, you'd be able to add a member, click "Save and Add Another," enter another member, and so on. This is a major timesaver for clients who are using Drupal to manage a lot of online content.

I Don't *Need* This, but Ooh, It's Purty! Modules

The following modules are useful for adding a bit of whizbang to your sites.

Views Slideshow

(http://drupal.org/project/views_slideshow)

Views Slideshow allows you to create customized jQuery slideshows using Views data. This is useful when you want to create a banner of featured content on a site landing page, for example, or if you want to show a list of featured projects on your home page.

Colorbox

(*http://drupal.org/project/colorbox*)

Colorbox is a module that allows you to display images using jQuery overlays.

User Points

(*http://drupal.org/project/userpoints*)

User Points is a helper module that allows you to set up your site to give users "points" for doing things on your site. This is useful for community sites, where you want to encourage users to engage with the site in some way. The User Points project page lists a number of additional modules that the community has created with the help of the User Points module. If you're interested in building a community-oriented site, it's well worth a look.

HTML5 Tools and Elements

(*http://drupal.org/project/html5_tools*)

HTML5 Tools, which depends on the Elements module, helps you prepare your theme for HTML5 by giving you access to HTML5 form elements such as `<phone>`, `<email>`, and other lovelies. It also allows you to use these elements directly in your views.

@font-your-face

(*http://drupal.org/project/fontyourface*)

This module gives you an administrative interface for importing and browsing web fonts from a variety of sources, including TypeKit, FontSquirrel, and more, and implementing them in your site's theme using the `@font-face` property. This promises to make working with web fonts significantly easier; while with certain font services you can download the font files, import their stylesheets into your theme's CSS, and work with them that way, the @font-your-face module is especially good for implementing hosted web fonts, such as TypeKit and Fontdeck, that don't necessarily have downloadable fonts you can load into your theme.

A Completely Incomplete Listing

As mentioned before, the modules discussed in this chapter are hardly a complete listing of everything you might need in a Drupal installation. But remember the point: once you know what you need the site to do, it's that much easier to find a module that can help you do it. Have fun creating!

CHAPTER 14

Making Views Sing—Using Views to Enhance a Layout

Thus far we've had a chance to look at sketching and wireframing designs, creating style tiles and layouts to explore design directions, and different options for prototyping and iterating on those designs. So what happens when you're dealing with a design that's already been created and you're getting ready to put it into Drupal? Understanding how Drupal stitches pages together can help you find the holes in implementation, and even help you improve the original layout. As an example, let's take the single event page shown in Figure 14-1, created by Tricia Okin of Papercut (*http://papercutny .com*) for the Brooklyn Urban Homesteaders Unite site.

The original layout for this page, created before the project was going to be built in Drupal, was inspired by the way that Eventbrite.com (*http://eventbrite.com*) displays events. At first glance this page would be pretty easy to build in Drupal.

But what if we could make it even better?

To do that, we need to consider a couple of things based on the overall vision for the site (a way to get urban homesteaders together for different events), and the way that Drupal will be organizing the site's content:

- Each event is created by a user of the site who is serving as the host of the event.
- Each user will have a profile, with contact information, a brief bio, and a link to things the user has done on the site.

Given these two things, what if, rather than having users repeat their contact information as part of each event, you could pull it directly from the host's user profile? This would allow potential attendees to put a face to the event, and learn more about the person who is about to teach them this stuff.

This is the type of situation where getting things into Drupal early makes the most sense. While it's still important to think about what this might look like—consider, for example, the greybox comp in Figure 14-2—by starting to prototype this directly in

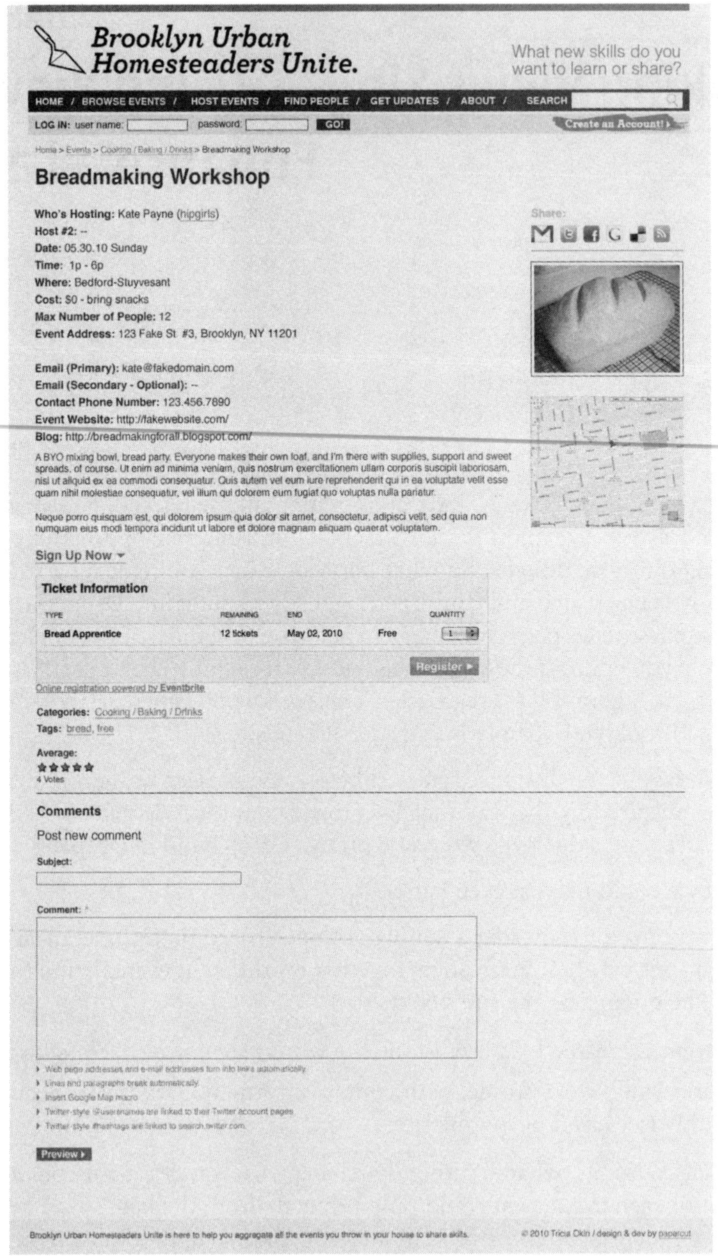

Figure 14-1. Original design comp for an individual event page on Urban Homesteaders Unite.

Drupal we can start working out the kinks in our design early, before they cause problems later on.

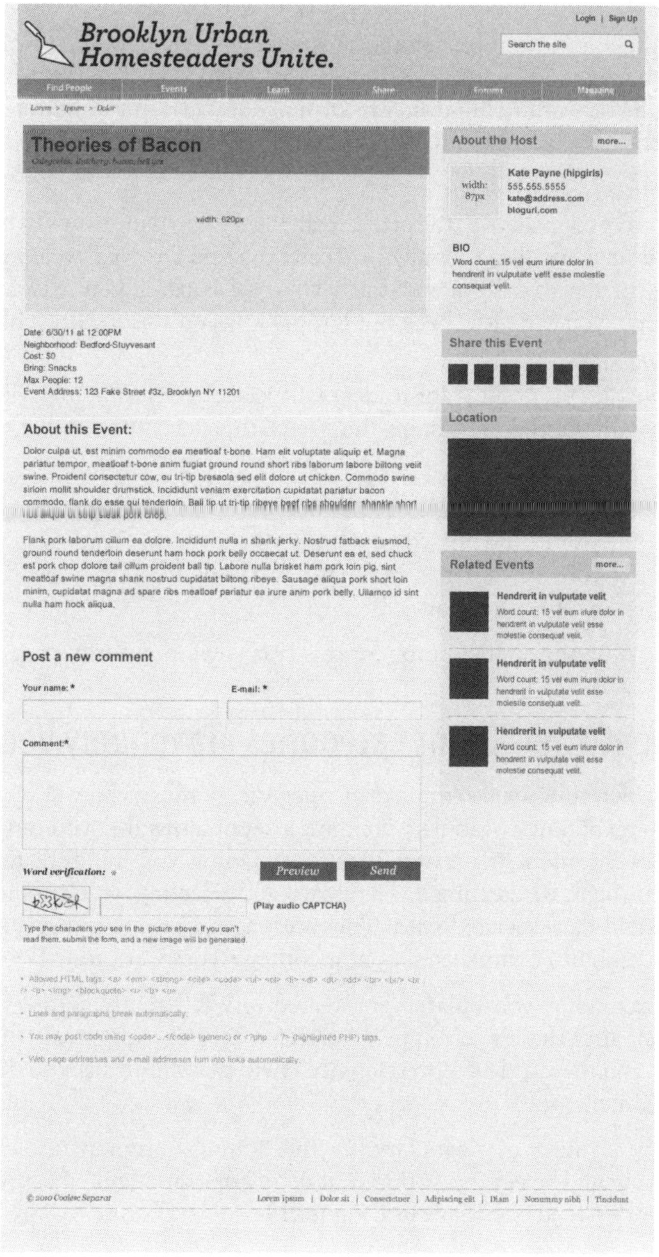

Figure 14-2. A new mockup for the Events page, taking into account the ability to automatically feed in the host's bio information.

But I'm Not a Developer—What If I Don't Want to Code?

Admittedly, much of this approach requires a certain willingness to work directly in Drupal, which may (and usually does) mean touching code. The bad news in this situation is that if you want to build sites in Drupal but you don't want to figure out how to deal with the code, you essentially have two options:

Partner up with a good developer
> You can meet them all over the place, from local Drupal meet-ups to online at *http://groups.drupal.org*. Occasionally, you can even find Drupal developers on Twitter simply by asking a question with the hashtag #Drupal. If you're feeling brave and super-nerdy, you can also check out Drupal folks on various IRC channels.[1]

Don't create the site
> I'm serious. If you don't want to deal with code and you aren't willing to pay a developer, you shouldn't be doing things in Drupal. Many folks don't want to hear this, but it's the truth.

That being said, if you're willing to learn and you don't mind spending a bit of time messing around, you'll find that prototyping directly into Drupal isn't without its headaches, but it's often easier than you may have thought. In rare cases it doesn't even require you to step into code at all.

Here's how I set up the configuration for this crazy-awesome event page in Drupal 7.

Step 1: Create the "Event Categories" Taxonomy Vocabulary

Taxonomy, which you can also think of as *categories* or *tags*, is how Drupal categorizes content. Each taxonomy vocabulary contains a set of terms that you can apply to one or several types of content. In previous versions of Drupal you could create vocabularies as you needed them, by creating a vocabulary and selecting which content types the vocabulary could be associated with. This was easier in some respects than the new system, but could turn complicated as new content types were added.

In Drupal 7, taxonomy vocabularies are treated very differently. Rather than creating the vocabulary after the content type, you create it *before* you create the fields for a content type, and then add a "term reference" field that points back to the vocabulary within your content type.

We'll start by creating a vocabulary. In the administration panel, choose Structure→Taxonomy and select the "Add vocabulary" option. Name the new vocabulary "Event Categories" and click Save (see Figure 14-3).

---

1. IRC: Internet Relay Chat. Used heavily by Drupal developers to have conversations and help one another in real time. I have no idea how it works or how to get set up on it, but if you meet a nice developer, he or she will often be more than happy to show you.

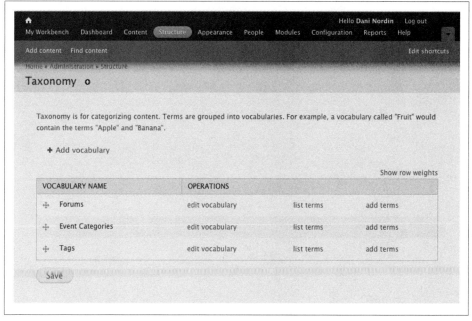

Figure 14-3. See that little + next to "Add vocabulary"? You'll see that a lot on Drupal admin screens. Wherever you see it, it allows you to add something to whatever section you're in.

Now that you've created your vocabulary, you can add terms by clicking the "add terms" link. When you're done adding terms, choose "list terms" to see the terms you've created. Figure 14-4 shows the terms I included in my Event Categories vocabulary.

Now that you've created your taxonomy vocabulary and added some terms to it, it's time to create the Event content type.

Step 2: Create the Event Content Type

Creating a content type starts the same as creating a taxonomy vocabulary. This time you select Structure→Content Types from the admin menu and click the "Add content type" link.

When creating a content type in Drupal 7, it's important to remember each step involved:

1. Set up the field's default settings, then click the Save and Add Fields button to add fields.
2. Add any fields you need in your content type, then click the Manage Fields tab to manage how fields are displayed.
3. Use the Manage Display area to set up how fields are displayed in different contexts (e.g., "teaser" content versus a single page entry).

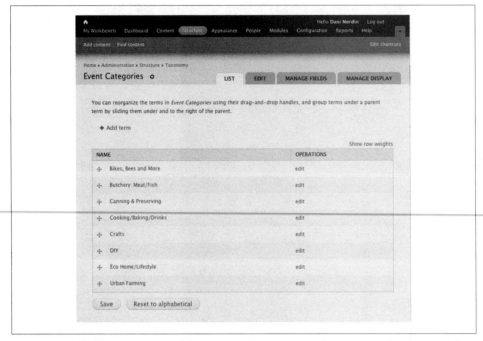

Figure 14-4. All of the terms I created for my Event Categories vocabulary. Note that they come from the home page mockup listed at the beginning of the chapter.

This last bit, involving the Manage Display area, can trip you up if you aren't careful. Because Drupal depends on content, and content can change during site implementation—more fields are added or removed, new categories are decided on, and so forth—you may find yourself periodically going back and forth adjusting the content types you've created on your site. This is especially true of complex implementations, but it can happen just as easily on a small corporate site. A helpful way to remember it is this: *Manage Fields* controls where fields show up on the form you use to create new content; *Manage Display* controls how and where they show up when that content is displayed.

Figure 14-5 shows what my Manage Fields screen looks like after setting up the Event content type.

I won't get into a tutorial on creating fields here; if you've never created a content type or added fields before, Sweden's NodeOne has an excellent series of screen-casts (*http://dev.nodeone.se/en/learn-drupal-7-with-nodeone*) that covers the basics of creating basic sites in Drupal 7. I will point out a couple of things, however:

Figure 14-5. My Manage Fields configuration screen, with all the fields from my Event content type.

- The Cost field is set up as an Integer field with a prefix of "$" and a suffix of "USD," so when rendered, it will show as "$10 USD."
- The Audience Capacity field is also an Integer field, with a suffix of " guests," so when rendered, it will show as "12 guests."
- The "Groups audience" field is a byproduct of the Organic Groups module.[2] As we currently have two primary locations for this site's events—Cambridge/Somerville and Brooklyn—each location is set up as its own group. Thus, an event can belong to either the Cambridge/Somerville group or the Brooklyn group; it'll show up on the home page of whatever group you're in.

2. *http://drupal.org/project/og*

Now that we have our fields put into the content type, we need to manage how they're being displayed. For this, we'll need to visit the Manage Display tab. Before we do that, however, let's add a test event and check it out to see where we're starting from. Figure 14-6 shows my starting point.

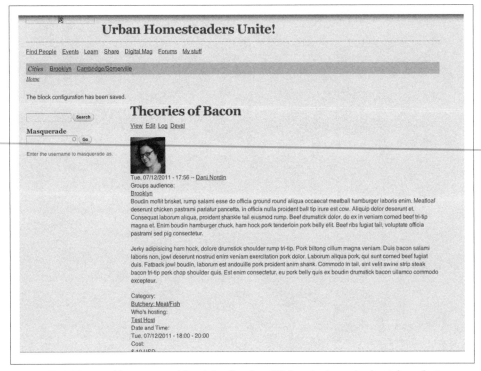

Figure 14-6. The new Event page, with minimal styling. Wait—that's not in the right order!

As you can see, there's a whole lot that's out of order right now:

- The additional fields are all out of order.
- A bunch of stuff is showing that I don't really need, such as the "Groups audience" and author information underneath the title.

Let's go back to the content type and make some adjustments to the way things display. I'm starting with something similar to what appears in Figure 14-7.

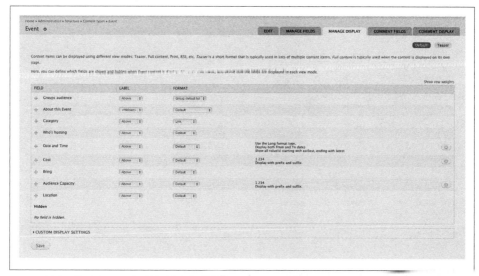

Figure 14-7. The Manage Display tab in the Event content type.

First I'll hide some of the things I don't need to see, by setting the Format of the "Groups audience" and "Who's hosting" fields to Hidden. From there, I'll set the Labels of all the fields except for "About this Event" to be Inline instead of Above. Then I'll rearrange the fields in the correct order:

1. Date and Time
2. Location
3. Cost
4. Bring
5. Audience Capacity
6. About this Event

Now the Manage Display settings look as shown in Figure 14-8.

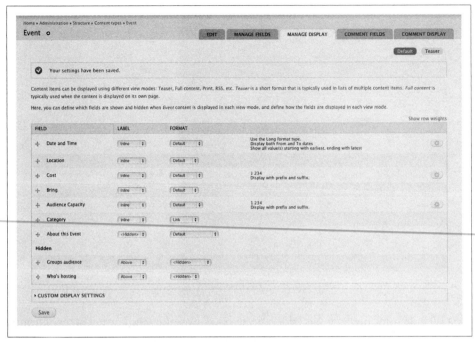

Figure 14-8. Organizing the fields in the content type to better fit the mockup.

Easy, right? Now let's see what it looks like in the sample event (see Figure 14-9).

Now, there are a few things that are still missing here. First of all, I don't want to show the author information in the content, and I haven't included an image with the content, which I'll need for my Views displays (and to make the page more visually interesting). This will require a couple of steps. First, in the Event content type, I'll go back to the Edit tab and uncheck "Display author and date information" under Display Settings (see Figure 14-10).

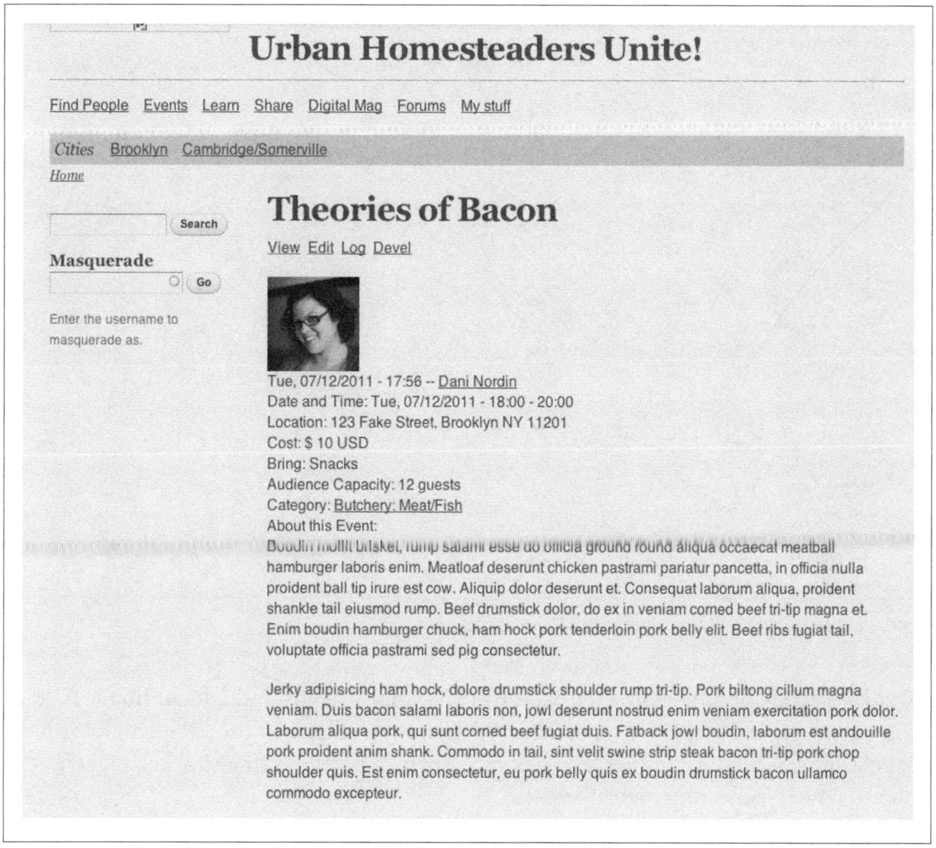

Figure 14-9. Getting closer. But it still needs work.

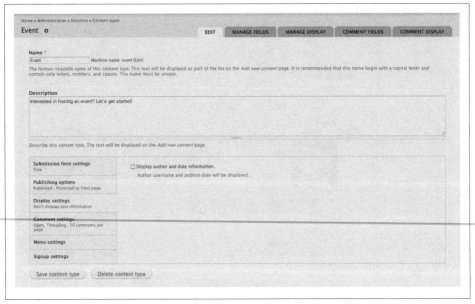

Figure 14-10. There's always something you forget.

After I save the content type, I'll go back into Manage Fields and add an Image field to the content type. Next I'll go into Manage Display and set up the Image field to have a label that's hidden. I can then go back into my published event and add a placeholder image. Now it looks like Figure 14-11.

Now I realize another problem: I have to set up image styles.

Step 3: Create an Image Style

Image styles are the Drupal 7 method of handling, resizing, and displaying images. You can have as many image styles as you like, and the system will automatically handle cropping, resizing, and maintaining the files for you. For our events, we had an event image size of 620 pixels wide by 280 pixels tall. To create an image style, select Configuration→Image Styles from the Admin screen and click the "Add style" link to add a new image style. I'm going to call my new style "grid-8" (as I'm using a 12-column grid, and 620 pixels is eight columns wide; more on grid systems in Chapter 6), and I'm going to set up the style to Scale and Crop to 620 × 280 pixels (see Figure 14-12).

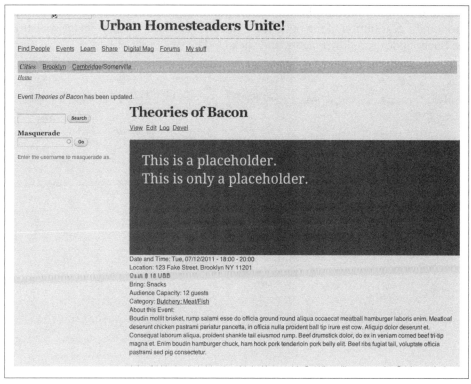

Figure 14-11. Well, now, that's an awfully big image.

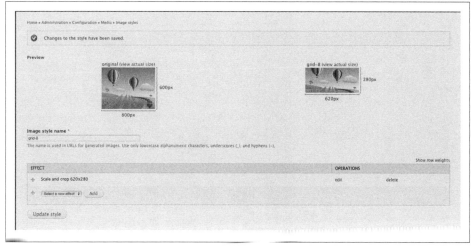

Figure 14-12. Configuration settings for my Events banner. Calling it something generic, such as the column width, allows you to use it universally wherever you need an image that size. Thus, if you create a new content type and want to style it the same way, you'll be covered.

From there, I'll go back into the Manage Display screen for the Event content type and click on the gear button to the right of the Image field, select the new image style from the Image Style drop-down menu, and click Update (see Figure 14-13).

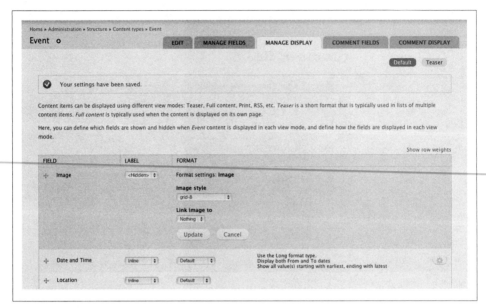

Figure 14-13. Selecting the new image style.

Now, if I refresh the page, I can see the results of these steps (see Figure 14-14).

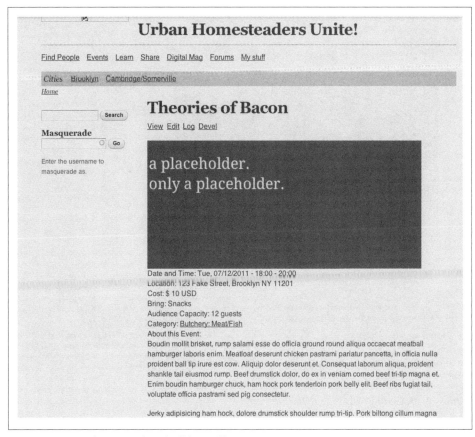

Figure 14-14. Look, Ma! It shrunk all by itself!

Now it's time to start styling this puppy. After updating the styles for field labels, moving stuff around with page titles, and removing those blocks from the right sidebar, I have what appears in Figure 14-15.

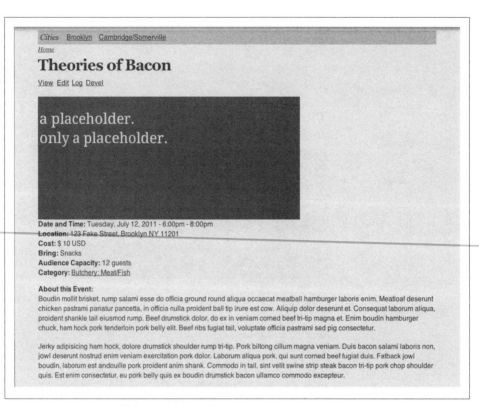

Figure 14-15. Getting still closer to the mockup.

At this point I'm getting much closer to what I mocked up (see Figure 14-16).

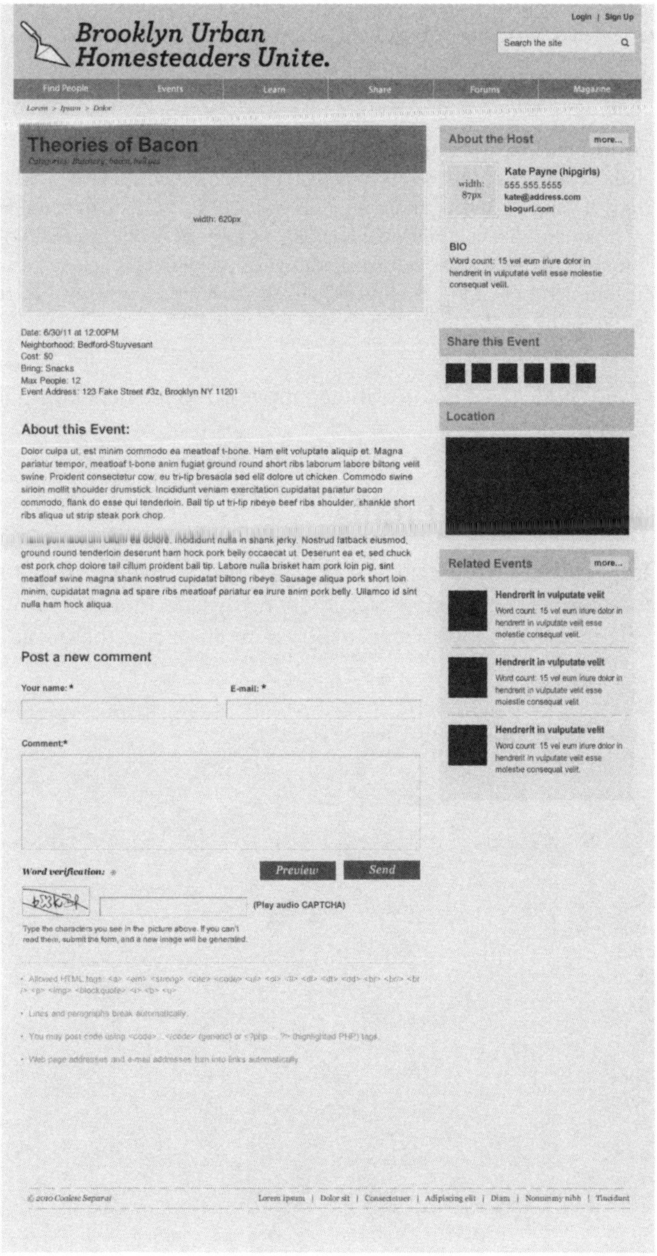

Brooklyn Urban
Homesteaders Unite.

Login | Sign Up

Search the site

Find People   Events   Learn   Share   Forums   Magazine

Lorem > Ipsum > Dolor

Theories of Bacon
Categories: Blahblory, bacon, balfyou

width: 620px

Date: 6/30/11 at 12:00PM
Neighborhood: Bedford-Stuyvesant
Cost: 50
Bring: Snacks
Max People: 12
Event Address: 123 Fake Street #3z, Brooklyn NY 11201

About this Event:

Dolor culpa ut, est minim commodo ea meatloaf t-bone. Ham elit voluptate aliquip et. Magna pariatur tempor, meatloaf t-bone anim fugiat ground round short ribs laborum labore biltong velit swine. Proident consectetur cow, eu tri-tip bresaola sed elit dolore ut chicken. Commodo swine sirloin mollit shoulder drumstick. Incididunt veniam exercitation cupidatat pariatur bacon commodo, flank do esse qui tenderloin. Ball tip ut tri-tip ribeye beef ribs shoulder, shankle short ribs aliqua ut strip steak pork chop.

Ham pork laborum culum ea dolore, incididunt nulla in shank jerky. Nostrud fatback eiusmod, ground round tenderloin deserunt ham hock pork belly occaecat ut. Deserunt ea et, sed chuck est pork chop dolore tail cillum proident ball tip. Labore nulla brisket ham pork loin pig, sint meatloaf swine magna shank nostrud cupidatat biltong ribeye. Sausage aliqua pork short loin minim, cupidatat magna ad spare ribs meatloaf pariatur ea irure anim pork belly. Ullamco id sint nulla ham hock aliqua.

Post a new comment

Your name: *   E-mail: *

Comment:*

Word verification: *

b386Y

(Play audio CAPTCHA)

Type the characters you see in the picture above. If you can't read them, submit the form, and a new image will be generated.

· Allowed HTML tags: <a> <em> <strong> <cite> <code> <ul> <ol> <li> <dl> <dt> <dd>
 <b>
 <p> <img> <blockquote> <i> <b> <u>

· Lines and paragraphs break automatically.

· You may post code using <code>...</code> (generic) or <?php ... ?> (highlighted PHP) tags.

· Web page addresses and e-mail addresses turn into links automatically.

About the Host   more...

width:
87px

Kate Payne (hipgirls)
555.555.5555
kate@address.com
blogurl.com

BIO
Word count: 15 vel eum irure dolor in hendrerit in vulputate velit esse molestie consequat velit.

Share this Event

Location

Related Events   more...

Hendrerit in vulputate velit
Word count: 15 vel eum irure dolor in hendrerit in vulputate velit esse molestie consequat velit.

Hendrerit in vulputate velit
Word count: 15 vel eum irure dolor in hendrerit in vulputate velit esse molestie consequat velit.

Hendrerit in vulputate velit
Word count: 15 vel eum irure dolor in hendrerit in vulputate velit esse molestie consequat velit.

Preview   Send

© 2010 Cosine Separat   Lorem Ipsum | Dolor sit | Consectetuer | Adipiscing elit | Diam | Nonummy nibh | Tincidunt

Figure 11-16: A quick reminder of where I am headed.

And the only code I've added so far is a bit of CSS in the theme to set some text defaults. Now it's time to start working on getting the rest of this stuff into Drupal. The first step: getting the user data to show up on the page.

 If it seems like we're jumping around a bit here, that's because we are. Believe it or not, this is pretty typical in building Drupal sites, particularly if you're building them on your own or in a very small team. Each component of a site plan will have its own set of needs, and will often require going back and adjusting things as you go. This is why I always recommend breaking down site plans by specific sections of functionality; for more about this, check out Chapter 1.

Now that the event node is set up, it's time to move on to the next component: the user profile connected to the event.

Step 4: Create the User Profile

By default, Drupal gives each user his or her own profile, which you can see by going to *site.url/user* in your browser. However, there really isn't much to show on this page. For example, Figure 14-17 shows a screenshot of my /user page before adding anything to it.

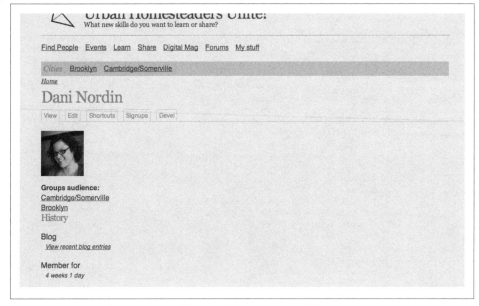

Figure 14-17. Drupal's core user profile—cute but not very useful.

In order to include the contact information and other interesting bits that I'll need to include with the Event page, I need to install a module. The Profile2 module (*http://drupal.org/project/profile2*) is Drupal 7's answer to Drupal 6's Content Profile (*http://drupal.org/project/content_profile*), as well as an interesting replacement for Drupal 7's core Profile module. With Profile2, you can create different "types" of profiles and associate them with different roles, add fields, and do other useful stuff. For right now, I just need the basics: contact information, website, and so on. To include this information, choose Structure→Profile Types from the admin menu. The Profile Type screen will show you a "Main profile" type; that's what I'm going to start with. The Profile2 module essentially treats profiles as though they were content types, which means you can add fields just as you would with a content type (see Figure 14-18).

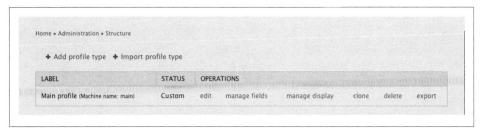

Figure 14-18. The Profile Type screen from Profile2. You can see how it looks like the content type editing screen.

For my purposes, I'll add the following fields, using the same basic procedure used for creating the Event content type:

- Phone number
- Website or blog URL
- Bio
- Interests, which will be a Term Reference field that links to the Tags taxonomy vocabulary
- Types of Events, which will be a Term Reference field that links to the Event Category vocabulary

Figure 14-19 shows what it looks like when I'm done.

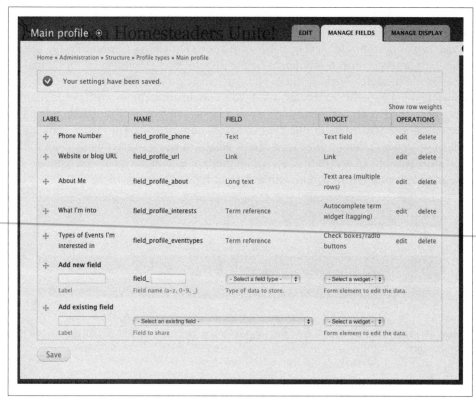

Figure 14-19. The finished profile fields.

When creating fields, it's generally a good idea to use the name of the content type in the field's machine name (e.g., "profile_about"). This helps you find the fields you're looking for in other areas, such as views. The exception to this is fields that are used among many content types, such as an Image or File field, or taxonomy fields that belong to more than one content type.

Now that I have the fields created, it's time to populate the test users with some profile content. Figure 14-20 shows what my profile looks like now that I've filled it out a bit.

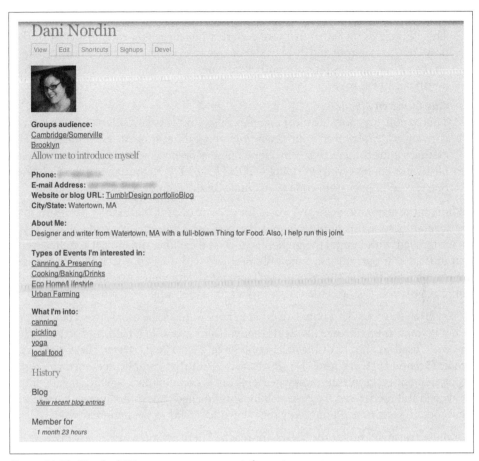

Figure 14-20. Hey, look! You can see my contact information now!

Step 5: Get Profile Content into the Event Page

Now that I have an Event content type and additional information in my user profile, I have to figure out how to stitch all of this together so that all this information is actually showing up on my sample Event page. There are a few options for doing this:

The User Reference module

This module allows you to turn a User Reference field into a content type, and populate it with content. While we have this already in the Event content type, the only option for displaying this field is the user's username as a link to the user's profile. This isn't what we're looking for.

A Related User view

This option, using Views, is more complex but gives you the most control over how content is output and displayed. For example, we have some extra information on the profile, such as Interests and Event types; we really don't need those to show up on our Event page.

Creating a custom .tpl file

This option, arguably the most complex, also isn't very sustainable. You'd start by copying *node.tpl.php* in your theme file and calling it *node--event.tpl.php*. (This assumes your content type's machine name is *event*; you can create a custom *.tpl* file for any content type by adding *--CONTENTTYPE* to the name of the file.) From there, you'd use custom code to manually insert each field into the *.tpl* file.

Although the last option can give you a lot of control over the code you output, there are several reasons this approach isn't the best one. For one, it's code-heavy; if you aren't familiar with Drupal theme hooks, it can take a long time to get it right. Even if you did figure it out, this isn't the only problem with this approach. If you choose a different theme for the site, or you accidentally delete your custom *.tpl.php* file, the entire page will break, and the user information will disappear again.

You also have to consider a bunch of other factors. What if the user leaves a field empty? What if you want to change the fields that you show, or add a field, and so on? While the code used to simply display the content of a field (e.g., `<?php <h2><?php print render($content['field_NAME']); ?></h2> ?>`) isn't that complicated once you figure it out, it doesn't take into account whether the field contains data—which means empty fields will still render and the page will look unfinished. Additionally, you have to add new code to your *page.tpl* file every time you add a field to your content type.

For these reasons, I prefer the Views approach. There are a few reasons for this:

* It's as close as you can get to putting code in a *.tpl.php* file without having to put code in a *.tpl.php* file.

* It's reusable in other areas of the site. Since much of this implementation involves relating data to other data (user information on events, events related by category, etc.), setting up the logic once gives you something you can easily clone and relate to other content types, pages, and so forth.

Here's how I set it up.

Setting Up the View

It took me several tries, and a few frantic Twitter posts, before I figured out the best way to create this view. The key, apparently, is to use Views relationships, which are a complex and mystical art that seems to elude even some of the best developers I know. The important thing to remember for this example is this: you want to set up a view of content/nodes of the Event content type, *not* a view of users or profiles. This is where I got stuck; intuitively, you would think that users and profiles would be basically the same thing, that both would be available to a view, and that you could somehow use the User Reference field as a way to pull that data into your view. As it turns out, that's sort of what happens, but you have to go about it in an odd way.

So, we start by setting up a view, showing Content of type Event, and a block with an unformatted list of fields. Figure 14-21 shows the starting screen for my view.

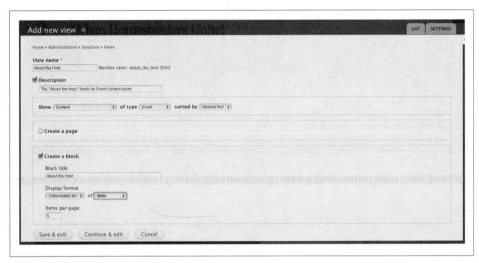

Figure 14-21. Starting off my view for the host information.

Once we have our initial setup done, it's time to start adding settings. Here comes the interesting part: if you were, right now, to start adding fields to this view, you would only see fields that belong to the Event content type. This, however, isn't what we want. We want the user information that relates to the user we've identified in the "Who's hosting" field. For this, we need to set up a couple of relationships.

Setting up a Views relationship is fairly simple once you're used to it, but the logic is complicated at first glance. The way to think about it is that when you create a Reference field, whether it's to a node, a user, or anything else, you're essentially creating a relationship between the node that contains the field and whatever you're referencing. This means that, when I created my Theories of Bacon event and referenced my Test Host user in the "Who's hosting" field, I created a relationship between the Theories of Bacon event and the Test Host user. Now, in my view, I can use that relationship to make Views let me use the content and fields of that related thing (in this case, my Test Host) inside my view (see Figure 14-22).

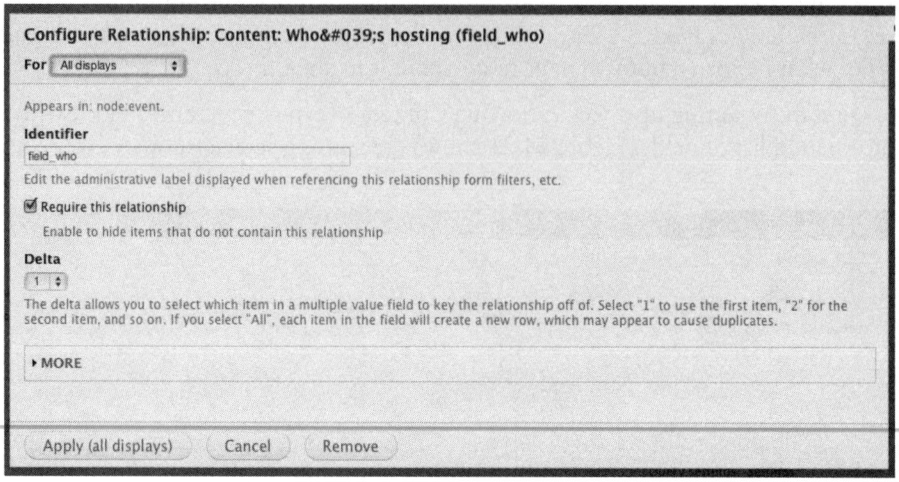

Figure 14-22. Setting up my "Who's hosting" relationship.

Here's another trick: users and profiles, in Drupal, are treated as different things if you're using the Profile2 module. This means that if I set up my view with only the "Who's hosting" relationship in it, all it will let me include in my view is the default user information. In other words, all I can include is the user's name and picture. What about all the fields I added to the user profile? How do I include those?

The answer is—you guessed it—create another relationship. This time, the relationship is to the profile connected to the user in the "Who's hosting" field (see Figure 14-23).

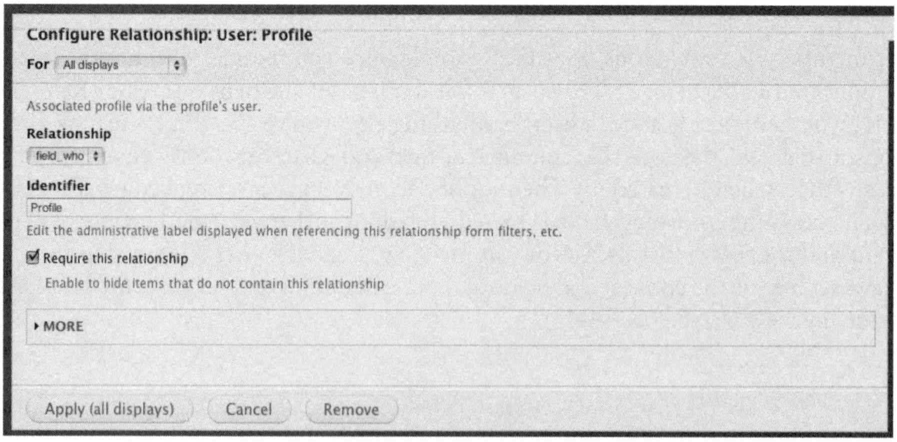

Figure 14-23. Adding the Profile field to my relationships.

At this point, I can now add all the fields that I need for my block (see Figure 14-24).

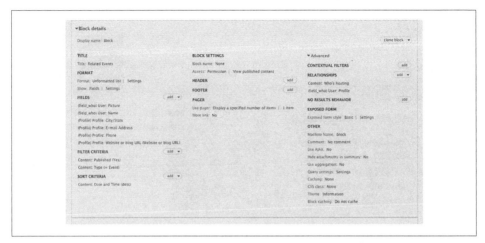

Figure 14-24. Adding the fields to the view. Now I can place this block and have at it.

Now that I've got the view all saved and ready, if I go to Structure→Blocks in my Admin menu, I should see my new block all set to put into my Event node. I'm going to start by configuring it to show up in the Sidebar Second region (the righthand sidebar) and only on Event content types (see Figure 14-25).

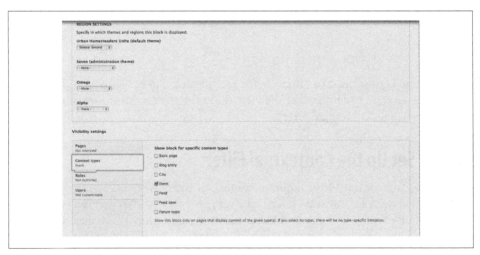

Figure 14-25. Configuring my "Who's hosting" block in the Blocks configuration screen (Structure→Blocks).

Now, if I go back to my event (see Figure 14-26), I should see my "About the Host" block, with Test Host's user information right underneath the user's picture ...

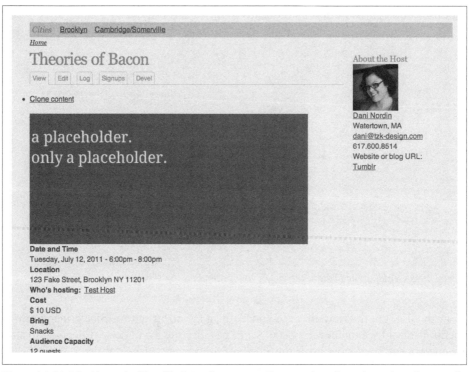

Figure 14-26. My About the Host block is all set on my Event node ... but why isn't it showing the right user?

... or not.

This is where I got tripped up. Because the relationship can only give you the fields to put in your view, in order to make the view select the *right* user information, you also have to work with contextual filters.

Step 6: Set Up the Contextual Filter

In prior versions of the Views module, contextual filters were called *arguments*. The difference between a contextual filter and your garden variety Views filter is in its specificity; while you can use standard Views filters to select global variables, such as the type of content or whether it's published, contextual filters use something on the page—usually in the form of some kind of numeric ID, which Drupal attaches to nodes, groups, and taxonomy terms—to determine how it filters the content.

Here's the basic idea:

1. Figure out which component (field, node ID, group ID, etc.) contains the "context" you want to filter on.

2. Set that up, in a "default" argument.

3. Publish and prosper.

Since I'm basing this view on the "Who's hosting" field, my first instinct was to create the contextual filter based on that field. However, the argument needs a default value to work, and the option that made the most sense, User ID from URL, turns up either the node's author or nothing at all, depending on which settings you choose (see Figure 14-27).

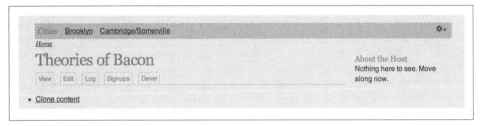

Figure 14-27. Yeah ... OK, no.

After an hour or two of trying different things and banging my head against the keyboard, I finally gave up and set up my contextual filter with a default value of the node's author. This, at least, had a value that showed up, and I could work on other pieces of the project while I stewed over my failure.

It was a couple of days later, when I ran into my friend Jacine Luisi, that I was finally able to figure out the issue. Jacine is a frontend developer who runs Themery in NYC,[3] and she's one of many friends I've been lucky to find in the Drupal community over the years. In what was meant to be a quick chat over Skype, I ended up mentioning this Views issue to her and she was kind enough to spend an hour or so working out the issue I was having. Here's her explanation of how it works:

> I was off on what the argument should be, stupidly... because the block is totally disconnected from the page content and needs to be manually fed the context, which in this case is the node ID.

> It needs to grab that from the URL, so I set the argument to "Provide default value: Content ID from URL" on the Content: Nid field.

> So, now it has its context. Then the relationships kick in. There are 2 relationships:

> The first is on the "Who's hosting" field. It will use the contextual filter (argument) and require that the field for the NID of the content we are viewing matches the user specified.

> The second is the "User: Profile" which allows the use of the other fields you wanted, but wouldn't be required if all you wanted was the user picture and name.

Figure 14-28 shows what that configuration looks like.

---

3. *http://themery.com*

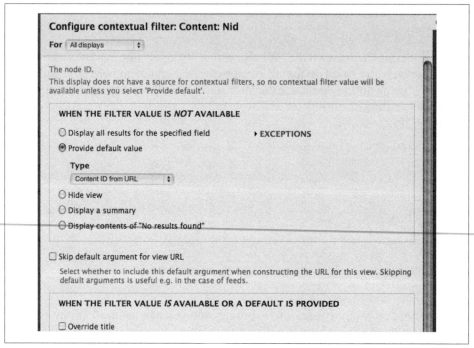

*Figure 14-28. My new contextual filter, with the **right** default value.*

And now, if I save the filter, I can go back to my page and see the result (see Figure 14-29).

Step 7: Set Up the Related Events Block

Now that I have the host information block set up and I've taken a moment to refresh my coffee, it's easy enough to create a "related events" view and place the block it creates into my sidebar. The process was remarkably similar to what I did with the host information, with the following exceptions:

- Instead of configuring our contextual filters by the node ID, we're using the taxonomy term from the Event Categories vocabulary.
- Since this is just pulling fields from the Event content type, we don't need to worry about relationships.

Figure 14-30 shows how that contextual filter was set up.

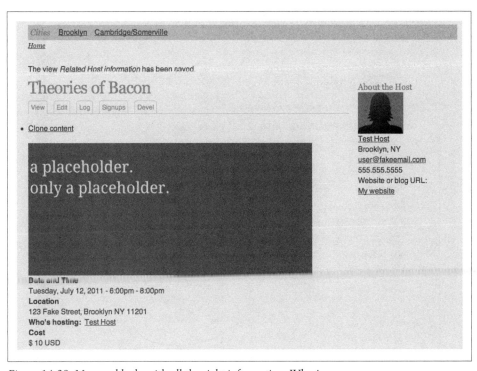

Cities   Brooklyn   Cambridge/Somerville
Home

The view *Related Host information* has been saved.

Theories of Bacon

| View | Edit | Log | Signups | Devel |

- Clone content

a placeholder.
only a placeholder.

About the Host

Test Host
Brooklyn, NY
user@fakeemail.com
555.555.5555
Website or blog URL:
My website

Date and Time
Tuesday, July 12, 2011 - 6:00pm - 8:00pm
Location
123 Fake Street, Brooklyn NY 11201
Who's hosting: Test Host
Cost
$ 10 USD

Figure 14-29. My new block, with all the right information. Whee!

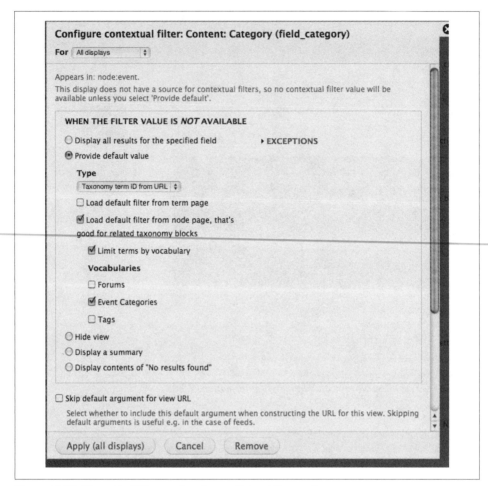

Figure 14-30. Contextual Filter settings for my Related Events view.

Now, if I go back to my Blocks administration screen (Structure→Blocks) and enable the Related Events block using the same configuration I used with the About the Host block, I should see a selection of related workshops available for theming (see Figure 14-31).

From here, it's easy to start theming this whole thing so that it looks a bit closer to my design. After some CSS love and a little Drupal tweaking, my updated page looks like Figure 14-32.

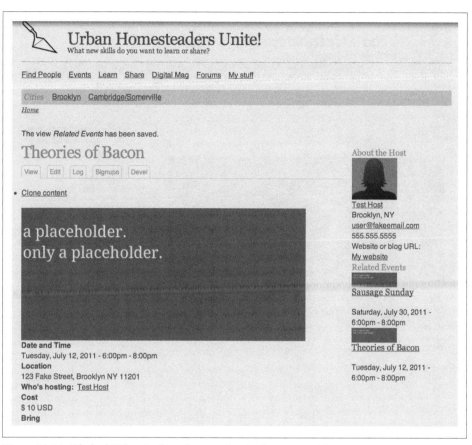

Urban Homesteaders Unite!
What new skills do you want to learn or share?

Find People   Events   Learn   Share   Digital Mag   Forums   My stuff

Cities   Brooklyn   Cambridge/Somerville
Home

The view *Related Events* has been saved.

Theories of Bacon

View   Edit   Log   Signups   Devel

- Clone content

a placeholder.
only a placeholder.

Date and Time
Tuesday, July 12, 2011 - 6:00pm - 8:00pm
Location
123 Fake Street, Brooklyn NY 11201
Who's hosting: Test Host
Cost
$ 10 USD
Bring

About the Host

Test Host
Brooklyn, NY
user@fakeemail.com
555.555.5555
Website or blog URL:
My website
Related Events

Sausage Sunday

Saturday, July 30, 2011 -
6:00pm - 8:00pm

Theories of Bacon

Tuesday, July 12, 2011 -
6:00pm - 8:00pm

Figure 14-31. Oh, look! There's also a Sausage Sunday happening. Neat!

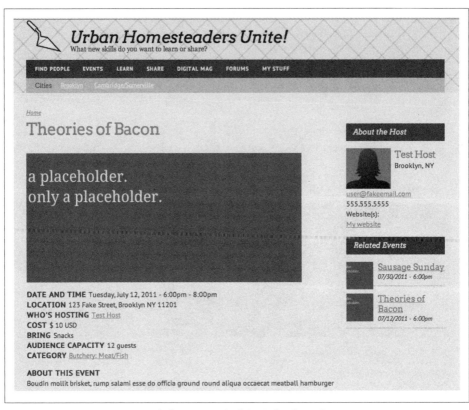

Figure 14-32. My Event page with theming applied. Isn't that better?

So, What Did We Just Do Here?

At this point you might be wondering why on earth I dragged you through all that. The reason is simple: in my experience, unless you're working on a large team where every person has a distinct Thing to Do, this is how the process goes. While it's tempting to put together a stack of wireframes, layouts, and so forth, and hand them off to developers to implement, the reality of working with any web-based framework is that certain things just work better if you go *with* the system rather than *against* it. Understanding the system, by actually creating stuff within Drupal, is one of the best ways to figure out how to work with it.

This doesn't mean you can't innovate, or create designs that are truly beautiful. But the point of good design isn't reinventing the wheel; it's partially about incorporating design patterns that have been shown to work well, and partially about finding areas where you can improve an experience that isn't optimal. Taking advantage of some of the defaults that Drupal gives you isn't copping out; it's smart design.

CHAPTER 15

Making Views Sing—Controlling Views Markup

As we discussed previously, much of the code that Drupal will output on any given page may come from Views—whether it's a page full of blog entries, or a block of taxonomy terms in your sidebar. The beauty of this is that it gives you a tremendous amount of flexibility in terms of what information you display on the page, and how it gets displayed. The challenge, however, is in getting your Views output to display in a way that:

- Allows you to theme it easily—in other words, it isn't impossible to find out what things are called so that you can style them.
- Doesn't make you cringe when you look at the code.

In previous versions of Views, the only way to manage the code that Views created was to override everything that Views spit out—from creating custom *tpl.php* files to actually rewriting the results of Views queries. In Drupal 6, you could use the Semantic Views module (*http://drupal.org/project/semanticviews*) to specifically manage the output of a Views field. While you still may have to do a little bit of rewriting to create truly semantic Views code, the latest versions of Views give you a number of ways to control the code that it creates—if you know how to use them.

As an example, let's take our Event Categories block for the home page of Urban Homesteaders Unite. Figure 15-1 shows the layout for the home page.

The first thing we have to figure out is this top box with all the pictures in it; technically, it's a list of Event categories, which is a list of taxonomy terms in the Event Categories vocabulary. But how do we associate the terms with a specific image? And how do we make each term a different color?

The process (which, by the way, is much easier in Drupal 7 than it was in Drupal 6) goes like this:

1. Add an image to the taxonomy term by adding some fields to the vocabulary itself.

Figure 15-1. Our mockup for the home page.

2. Add a representative image to each term in the Event Categories list.

---

3. Set up the view to output specific code for the list of terms, and give each instance of the term name its own class, which we can then theme.

Step 1: Associate an Image with a Taxonomy Term

In order for each term in the Event Categories vocabulary to have its own image, I first needed to add an image field to the vocabulary. To do this, I went into Structure→Taxonomy and chose "edit vocabulary" next to the Event Categories vocabulary. From there, I selected Manage Fields to add my Image field (see Figure 15-2).

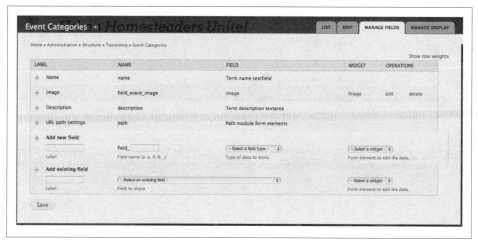

Figure 15-2. Adding the Image field to the vocabulary.

Once I added the field, I went into the Manage Display tab for the vocabulary to make sure the label for the image would stay hidden in the default view for the term. I may decide later to change how it's displayed (or hide it altogether), but for now, I'll leave it set to the `grid-8` image style, which we specified in the event page we put together in Chapter 14 (see Figure 15-3).

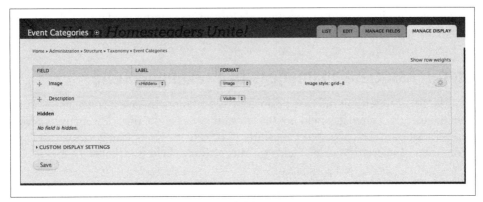

Figure 15-3. Changing the display of the Image field.

Now it's just a matter of adding an image to the individual terms. If I go back to the vocabulary page and click on "list terms" (see Figure 15-4), I can edit each category to be associated with the image I've chosen for it.

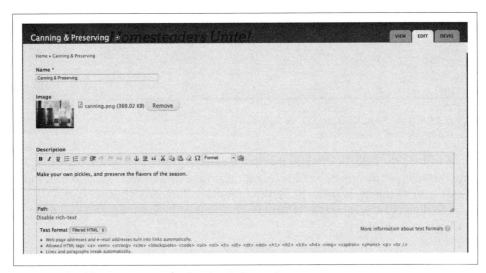

Figure 15-4. Adding an image to the Canning & Preserving category.

Once I had an image associated with each term in my Event Categories vocabulary, it was time to create my view.

Step 2: Create the Event Categories View

The initial Event Categories view was pretty simple. As the goal was simply to give a visual list of taxonomy terms, all I needed was a list of taxonomy terms that showed the name of the term, linked to the term page itself, followed by the image I'd added to each term. Figure 15-5 shows what my initial settings looked like.

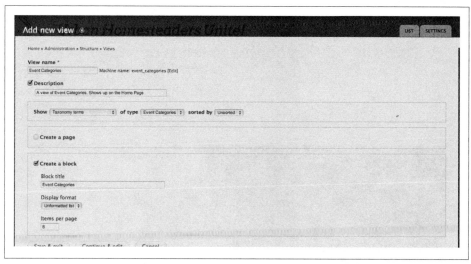

Figure 15-5. My initial view settings. Note that I'm looking to show "Taxonomy Terms," not "Content."

Once I had the view set up, it was time to select the fields I needed, and set up my filters. To begin, I just wanted to add the Image field; "Taxonomy term: Name" is added by default. I also wanted to limit the terms I showed to just the Event Categories vocabulary. Figure 15-6 shows what the settings looked like once I was done.

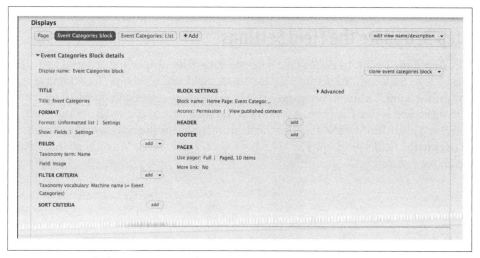

Figure 15-6. My Block Settings page in the view. Now the fun begins.

Now that I had all my settings put together, I was ready to enable the block via the Blocks administration (Structure→Blocks) and see my new view on the home page (see Figure 15-7).

Figure 15-7. Well, that's ... something.

In order to get this looking correct, I have to start tweaking some of my view settings.

Step 3: Update the Field Settings

The first thing I want to do is make sure the images are displaying at a good size. For that, I'll go back into the settings for my Image field and set the preferred image style to "grid-3_long," which is an image style I created that scales and crops all images to 205 × 180 pixels (see Chapter 14 for how to set up a new image style). While I'm at it, I'm going to go into Style Settings for the field and uncheck the box that adds the default classes to the field's markup. This'll help me get rid of some code overhead that I don't need (see Figure 15-8).

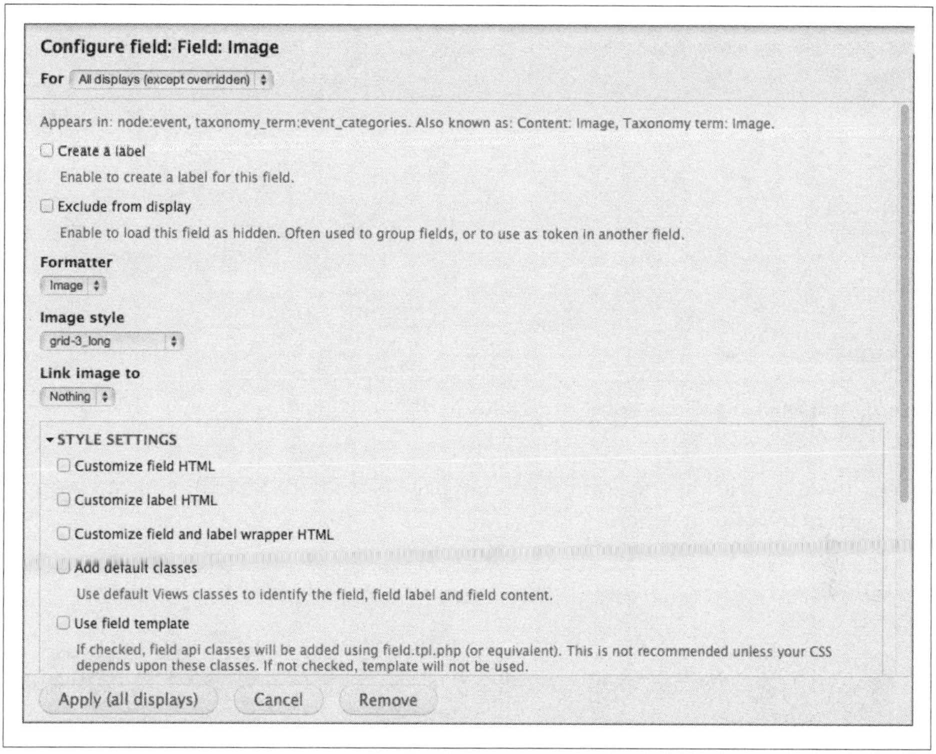

Configure field: Field: Image

For All displays (except overridden) ⇕

Appears in: node:event, taxonomy_term:event_categories. Also known as: Content: Image, Taxonomy term: Image.

☐ Create a label

    Enable to create a label for this field.

☐ Exclude from display

    Enable to load this field as hidden. Often used to group fields, or to use as token in another field.

Formatter

Image ⇕

Image style

grid-3_long ⇕

Link image to

Nothing ⇕

▼ STYLE SETTINGS

    ☐ Customize field HTML

    ☐ Customize label HTML

    ☐ Customize field and label wrapper HTML

    ☐ Add default classes

        Use default Views classes to identify the field, field label and field content.

    ☐ Use field template

        If checked, field api classes will be added using field.tpl.php (or equivalent). This is not recommended unless your CSS depends upon these classes. If not checked, template will not be used.

(Apply (all displays))   (Cancel)   (Remove)

Figure 15-8. Customizing the Image field.

 Style Settings are a relatively new and incredibly useful addition to Views. Although it's not without its bugs (e.g., the Views template still wraps every field in its own `<div>` tag unless you go into the Field settings for the view and tell it not to include any default markup), it allows you to control the markup your view creates with much more granularity than previous versions of Views. In Drupal 6, this level of control over markup can also be achieved using the Semantic Views module (*http://drupal.org/project/semanticviews*).

Now that I've done that, I also want to make sure my view's rows float next to one another, as shown in my design comp. Since I'm using a version of the 960 Grid System in my theme (see Chapter 6), all I have to do is add a class to my Format settings for each row of the view. I'm going to give each row a class of `grid-3`, which makes each row three columns wide, and `alpha`, which removes the left margin and helps things float more easily in the container (see Figure 15-9).

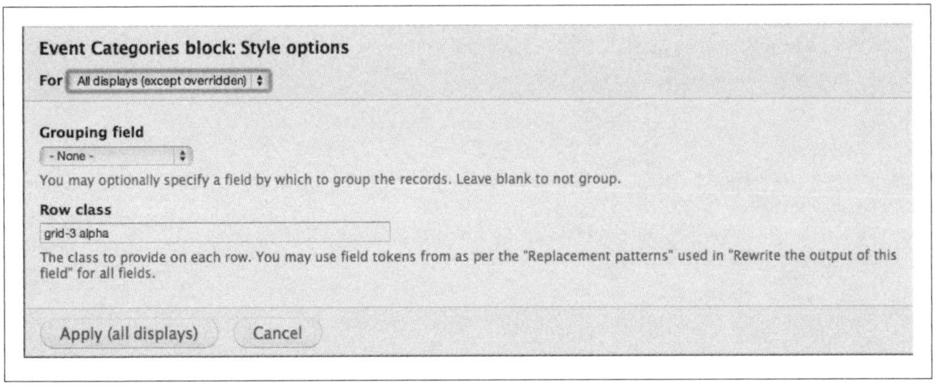

Event Categories block: Style options
For
All displays (except overridden)
Grouping field
- None -
You may optionally specify a field by which to group the records. Leave blank to not group.
Row class
grid-3 alpha
The class to provide on each row. You may use field tokens from as per the "Replacement patterns" used in "Rewrite the output of this field" for all fields.
Apply (all displays)
Cancel

Figure 15-9. Setting up some sensible grid settings for the row format.

Now, if you look at the block on the home page (see Figure 15-10), you can see that I'm starting to get somewhere.

Event Categories
Urban Farming
Eco Home & Lifestyle
Canning & Preserving
Butchery: Meat & Fish
Cooking, Baking & Drinks
Crafts
DIY
Bikes, Bees and More

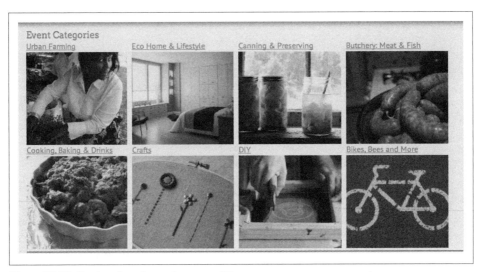

Figure 15-10. Getting close. I can almost smell it.

But I still have to deal with the term names. The goal is to style each term name with a different background color; this will require a unique class for each term name. How do I do that?

Step 4: Add a Custom Class to Each Taxonomy Term: Name Field

The answer is to use tokens, which Views calls *replacement patterns*. Tokens are little bits of text, usually surrounded by brackets (e.g., `[link]`), which you can use to replace other text. So, for example, I can create a custom class for each instance of the Taxonomy Term Name field, by inserting a token for the name into the CSS class for that field.

The first step in adding a class to my field is to find the actual token; to do this, I had to pretend I was rewriting the field.

If you click on the name of any field in your Views settings, you'll see a few drop-down areas that let you set up different parameters for the field. With the Image field, you already saw the Style Settings variable. If you check out the options under Rewrite Results (see Figure 15-11), you'll notice the option "Rewrite the output of this field." This is highly useful, especially if you want to create very specific code from Views. The rewrite options are what I'll use to create my custom class.

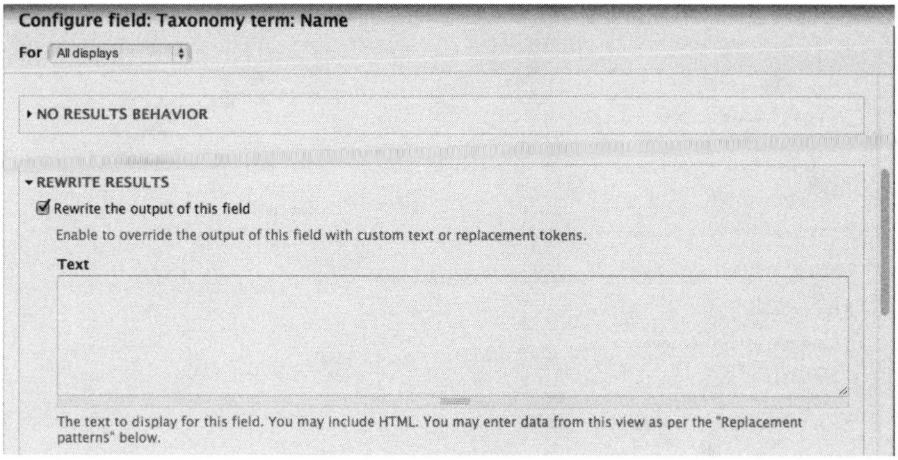

Configure field: Taxonomy term: Name

For `All displays ⬥`

▸ NO RESULTS BEHAVIOR

▾ REWRITE RESULTS
☑ Rewrite the output of this field
  Enable to override the output of this field with custom text or replacement tokens.

  Text

  The text to display for this field. You may include HTML. You may enter data from this view as per the "Replacement patterns" below.

Figure 15-11. Choosing the option to rewrite the field's output allows you to do many things.

In order to find the token I needed for my new Views class, I had to check the option to rewrite the field output. Underneath the checkbox, you'll see a new drop down called Replacement Patterns (see Figure 15-12). This will give you a list of the replacement patterns you have available.

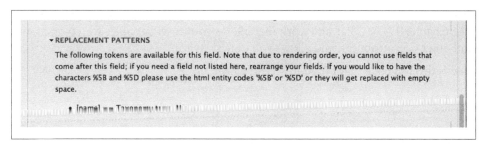

▾ REPLACEMENT PATTERNS
  The following tokens are available for this field. Note that due to rendering order, you cannot use fields that come after this field; if you need a field not listed here, rearrange your fields. If you would like to have the characters %5B and %5D please use the html entity codes '%5B' or '%5D' or they will get replaced with empty space.

    • [name] == Taxonomy term: N...

Figure 15-12. My list of replacement patterns.

Looking at the options (there's only one, since I'm just loading in the term name), I see that [name] is the replacement pattern that I want. Now I can uncheck the option to rewrite the field's output, and set up my Style Settings for the field (see Figure 15-13).

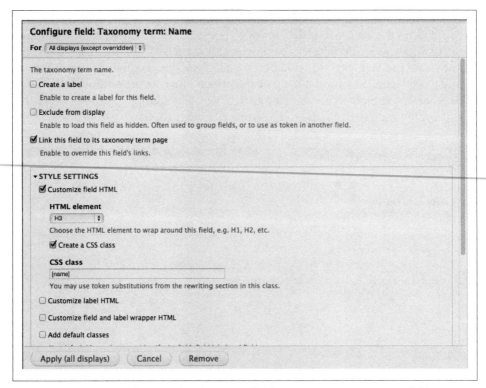

Figure 15-13. My new and improved Style Settings for the "Taxonomy term: Name" field.

Step 5: Style Away

Now, if I go back to my home page and inspect the code that Views just created, I'll see what's highlighted in Figure 15-14.

From there, it's a simple matter to start putting this together in CSS. I work with LESS (see Chapter 17), a CSS framework that allows you to set variables for colors, fonts, and other CSS attributes, and allows you to nest styles.

Here's the *.less* code that I used to style the headings:[1]

---

1. If you haven't heard of *.less* yet, you're missing out. Check out Chapter 17 for an overview, or go to *http://incident57.com/less* to download Less.app for Mac for *free*.

Figure 15-14. Hey, now—I have a new class name to use in my Name header!

```
/* 1.0 Colors & Fonts

    1.1 Colors */

@gray: #8D8D7D;
@dkgray: #4D4545;
@mdgray: #666;
@ltgray: #999;
@palegray: #ccc;

@red: #D32F00;
@orange: #D17103;
@cyan: #47A7BF;
@dkcyan: #183b44;
@green: #89A155;
@gold: #eeb200;

/* 2.0 Homepage Event Categories block */
#zone-content .homepage-events {
    .views-row {
        margin-bottom: 2em;
        text-align: center; /* center the image in the container */
        overflow: hidden; /* hide the excess when it resizes */
    }

    h3 a {
        font-size: .75em;
        display: block;
        padding: .5em 0;
        color: white;
        text-decoration: none;
        text-align: center;
    }

    .Bikes-Bees-and-More {
```

```
        background: @green;
    }

    .Butchery-Meat-amp-Fish {
        background: @red;
    }

    .Canning-amp-Preserving {
        background: @gold;
    }

    .Cooking-Baking-amp-Drinks {
        background: @dkcyan;
    }

    .Crafts {
        background: @cyan;
    }

    .DIY {
        background: @ltgray;
    }

    .Eco-Home-amp-Lifestyle {
        background: @dkgray;
    }

    .Urban-Farming {
        background: @orange;
    }
}
```

When I go back into my browser and refresh the page, I see Figure 15-15.

So, What Did We Just Do Here?

As you can tell from the process I just illustrated (and the example in Chapter 14), there's a lot you can do with Views. But part of working with Views is understanding the code it creates and how to manipulate that code to get the results you want. Knowing how it works—even if you're not the one implementing a particular site—can make it easier to envision how a given project might look in the end, and make it easier to create beautiful layouts that will be easier for your team to implement.

For example, I worked on a massive site overhaul with my friend Claudio Luis Vera (@modulist on Drupal.org (*http://drupal.org*)). Claudio was working on wireframes and design layout, while I focused on prototyping the site in Drupal 7. During the design process, Claudio kept getting stuck on a particular piece of the design puzzle and was unable to come up with what a given page should look like—until he started thinking in terms of how Views might output the content. Simply by understanding what Views

Figure 15-15. My finished block. How pretty!

would do with the content, he was able to rapidly create and iterate designs, and we were able to more easily implement them in the prototype—and the final product.

This is the value in having an understanding of Views. It can be challenging to master, but once you get the basics down, it's that much easier to get your job done.

CHAPTER 16

Getting Started with Drupal Theming: Base and Child Themes

And now it's time for the Fun Stuff: turning your design into a theme. In this chapter you'll learn how to break down a layout for theming, choose a base theme, and create a child theme to hold your customizations. In the next chapter you'll learn how to work with LESS to make coding CSS easier.

Breaking Down a Layout for a Drupal Implementation

The most important part of working in Drupal, particularly in terms of creating and implementing layouts for a given page, is figuring out where the content in a layout is coming from and how to manage the code that Drupal is creating. This is, arguably, the biggest difference between building sites in Drupal and building them with straight HTML. Whereas it's fairly straightforward to mock up a page in HTML once you have an idea of what it should look like, everything that goes into your Drupal site comes from somewhere in the site's database; your code simply tells Drupal how to render the content it pulls from that database.

Content in a Drupal layout can come from any number of places.

Nodes

Any individual piece of content, in Drupal terms, is called a *node*, and it's displayed using a file called *node.tpl.php*. If you're dealing with the layout of a single page and are only concerned with how the actual page content is displayed, you're likely dealing with *node.tpl.php*.

While *node.tpl.php* can help you control certain aspects of how Drupal displays individual nodes—for example, if you want to move the page title, or change the markup that controls the node's container—if your content type has custom fields, as many content types do, you'll want to manage those in the Manage Display tab, available by going into the admin area for your content type. From there, you can manage how fields are organized on the page, how and if their labels are displayed alongside the field, and even the format of the field display.

Blocks

Blocks are, essentially, little bits of content that you can put anywhere in your Drupal page. Not only can you create your own blocks through the Blocks administration screen (Structure→Blocks), but many modules, such as Views and Drupal's Menu system, create blocks for you that you can then place somewhere on your site. A good rule of thumb is this: if something's going into a sidebar or footer, or it's not part of the main content, it's likely coming from a block.

Views

Views helps you create lists of content to put in various places on your site. As you saw in the practical examples in Chapters14 and 15, I used Views to create a custom "Who's Hosting" block for my Event page, with user profile information based on a User reference field; I also used it to create a block of related events for the sidebar, and a list of categories for events with associated images. Views works by setting up your defaults (what Views is pulling out of the database) and parsing it into different displays depending on your needs. Anywhere you have a list of content, you likely have a view.

For example, Figure 16-1 is an annotated layout of the Urban Homesteaders Unite home page.

If I break this down according to the numbers I annotated on my layout, I'll see:

- Numbers 1, 2, 4, 5, 6, 7, and 8 are all blocks.
- Numbers 2, 7, and 8 are blocks built with Views.
- There's no actual node content on the home page.
- Number 3 is a menu, and comes from the Menu core system.

There's no hard-and-fast way to know exactly where a bit of content is coming from on the page (e.g., depending on the regions in your theme, block 6 could actually be coming in as content from the home page; I'm creating it as a block because it's easier to theme that way), but there are a few things that are safe to assume:

- Anything that is in the menu bar comes from the menu system.
- Anything that looks like a list of content, users, or taxonomy terms comes from Views displays.
- Anything that is contained within its own little box on the page, and doesn't look like it came from Views, is likely a block.

Figure 16-1. A rough home page mockup for UHU, with annotations.

Once you have an idea of where content is coming from, it's easier to figure out how you're going to put things into Drupal. Even if you're just creating a layout for someone else to implement, knowing how things are going to be implemented and learning the design patterns that Drupal gives you will make your job infinitely easier.

Remember: an important part of good design is understanding the constraints you're dealing with, and how much you can stretch against those constraints. You'll hear this from me several times before this book is done, but trust me: going *with* Drupal, rather than *against* it, will take you far. And you can still do gorgeous design. Really.

Choosing a Base Theme

Back when I was using WordPress to build most of my sites, the process of theming (i.e., applying the look and feel to a website) was relatively simple. I'd mock up the design that I was thinking about, head over to *http://wordpress.org*, and find a theme that had the same structure as the site I was designing. Then I'd hack apart the files, customizing them with my own CSS and images. Changing the HTML output was pretty simple as well; as long as I could pick out the few bits of PHP code that were making the site render content, and not mess with them too much, it wasn't a big deal to customize container names or change the format of a given page.

When I did my first Drupal site, back when Drupal 6 was still relatively new, I thought the process would be about the same. I mocked up my template, went to *http://drupal .org*, and started searching for a contributed theme that looked sort of like what I was going for. Then I started trying to customize it according to what I'd mocked up.

I cried my way through that first site. And drank more coffee than I care to talk about.

As I started to chat with other designers about this problem, I realized I wasn't alone. Drupal's theme layer is impressive, flexible, and powerful; it's also confusing as hell until you get used to it. The biggest layer of confusion is this: while in WordPress it's generally fine to download a theme package and start hacking it up to customize it, you don't want to do that in Drupal. Why? Because Drupal keeps tabs on that theme file and includes it in any updates you make to your site's code. This means any customizations you make will be *gone* as soon as you update the code. All of them. Really.[1]

The other problem with hacking themes directly is making sense of the code. While some themes allow you to make any customizations you need directly in the template files (files that end with *.tpl.php*), many advanced themes put most of their theme overrides directly into *template.php*, a set of PHP functions that controls various aspects of the way Drupal renders the page. In fact, I've seen themes where everything—including how various grid classes are rendered—is thrown into *template.php*. This means that, unless you're really cozy with PHP and don't mind spending your time writing theme functions, you'll be lost the moment you try to customize a theme.

---

1. All. Of. Them.

This is where choosing a good base theme comes in handy. A *base theme*, in Drupal terms, is a theme that contains minimal styling, contains a good number of templates (*.tpl.php* files) that you can duplicate into your child theme and customize, and renders code in a way that you can customize via CSS. The base theme, ideally, handles most of the heavy lifting in terms of rendering the page layout, and setting reasonable defaults for font sizes, form elements, and the like. By creating a *child theme* derived from this base, you create all your customizations in a separate set of files within the */sites/all/ themes* folder, which keeps your custom code safe—and helps you debug issues without having to worry about the base theme getting wrecked. It also lets someone else (the theme maintainer) worry about updates to the theme's underlying structure; since your customizations will mostly involve CSS and the occasional *.tpl.php* file or theme function, they often won't be borked by security updates.

How to Choose a Base Theme

Choosing a base theme is a matter of personal preference. Drupal.org (*http://drupal .org*) offers quite a few to choose from, and every site builder has his or her favorite. Whichever you choose, make sure your base theme has the following:

A way to deal with code and CSS files that makes sense to you
> If you've never worked with Drupal themes before, it might seem like none of them are organized in ways that make sense; however, some themes are more confusing than others. I prefer to avoid themes that throw all the page rendering information into functions in *template.php*; while I don't mind dealing with some PHP, trying to sort through another developer's theme functions in order to make a relatively small change gets overwhelming quickly. An exception to this rule is themes whose *template.php* code is very well commented; Square Grid, which clearly labels the places where a themer would make changes in order to edit grid classes and other variables, is a great example of such a theme. I also avoid themes that separate each aspect of the page into separate CSS files that you have to sort through.

The ability to spit out relatively clean code
> You won't always be able to find the ultimate, beautiful semantic markup you might want from a base theme, but you can at least get close. If you can't get exactly the code you want out of your base theme, there are a couple of modules that can help. Check out Chapter 13 for examples.

Enough tpl.php files so that you can customize the code easily if you need to
> At the very least, a good base theme should have its own version of *page.tpl.php*, *block.tpl.php*, and *node.tpl.php* available for you to customize. You may not need to customize it in your child theme, but having it there is useful in case you will need to.

Whichever base theme you select, you'll want to save it into */sites/all/themes* and enable it in your Appearance settings (see Figure 16-2).

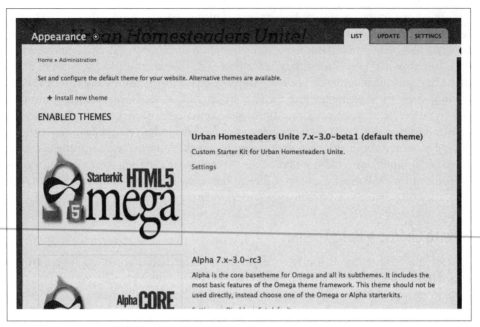

Figure 16-2. The Appearance settings page lets you enable themes in your Drupal site, and set the default theme for your particular site.

It's very likely that you'll end up trying out a few base themes before you settle on one you like. On the recommendation of a few friends in the Drupal community, I tried Zen (*http://drupal.org/project/zen*) a few times before realizing I couldn't make sense of it. After giving up on Zen, I switched to the NineSixty base theme (*http://drupal.org/project/ninesixty*), which is based on the 960 Grid System (960.gs). NineSixty was, and still is, one of my favorites to work with; the grid system enables me to quickly make adjustments to the layout, and the code is cleaner than many base themes I've worked with, particularly once I started creating my own starter kit with some of the more onerous extra `div`s deleted.

In the past year or so, as HTML5 and responsive design has become more of a priority, I've started trying out Omega (*http://drupal.org/project/omega*). Omega is an HTML5-based theme with three versions of the 960.gs grid at the ready and a completely responsive layout (which resizes according to your browser window). While it's not without its share of stuff to figure out (including a whole lotta *template.php*), one of my favorite things about Omega is the ability to customize the grid for each section of the site. For example, on Urban Homesteaders Unite, I use a 12-column grid on the header, but a 16-column grid in the Content region, which gives me a bit more flexibility in the layout.

Another interesting aspect of the Omega theme is the ability to update my page defaults through a GUI in the theme settings page (see Figure 16-3). This frees me to experiment with different layouts as I need to, without having to search through code and tweak

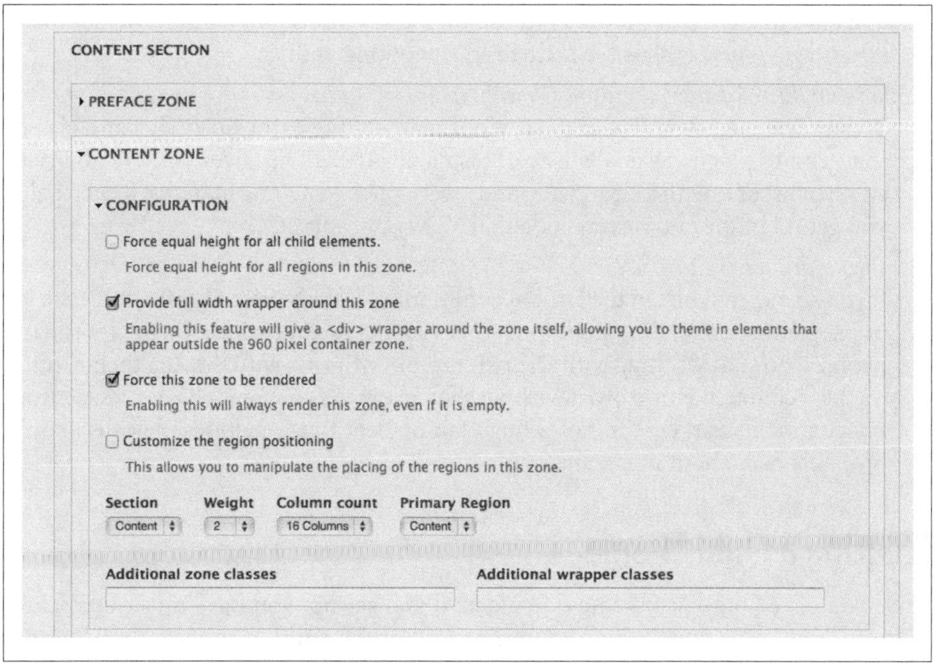

Figure 16-3. Updating the Content region defaults in Omega's snazzy region settings GUI.

grid numbers here and there. I don't know if it's faster than tweaking code directly, but it's certainly a bit more idiot-proof.

For my most recent projects, including the Drupal for Designers website (*http://drupal fordesignersbook.com*) and my own website (which we did the layout for in Chapter 7), I've started working with the Square Grid theme (*http://drupal.org/project/squar egrid*). This theme, created by Laura Scott of PingV Creative, has the advantage of being relatively lightweight, has a grid framework similar to (but more flexible than) 960, and like Omega, incorporates responsive design principles, including content-first layout. The only minor drawback is that, in order to set up your initial grid outside of the default options, you have to go into *template.php*; however, the theme has terrific documentation, and a well-commented *template.php* that makes it very easy to make updates once you know the math.

Other Base Themes to Try

Now that I've given you my favorites, here are some other base themes to try, based on recommendations from friends in the Drupal community:

Tao (*http://drupal.org/project/tao*)
Tao is a base theme that simply resets a lot of Drupal's default page rendering behavior. Its goal is to sit back and let your subtheme do its job. It does assume a focus on preprocessors (i.e., setting up things in *template.php*), which might mean

you have to deal with a lot of PHP and theme functions, but it also provides many advantages, such as sensible code to start working with.

Mothership (http://drupal.org/project/mothership)
> This theme does what it can to strip out many of the extra `<div>` tags and classes that tend to plague Drupal's way of displaying data. This gives you the ability to start your theme with a clean slate, and creates nice, semantic markup. It even helps you get rid of the crazy extra code that Views can spit out.

Zen (http://drupal.org/project/zen)
> If you spend any time in the Drupal community, frankly, you're going to hear a lot of people recommending Zen. In fact, it's such a common base theme that many people who start working with Drupal start out working with the Zen theme, often on the recommendation of a developer they know. As you might have guessed from my comments earlier, I'm not a huge fan of Zen, but I include it because you'll probably hear about it at some point.

Creating a Child Theme

Once you have your base theme downloaded and set up, you have to set up a child theme into which to put all your customizations. Some themes, such as Zen and Omega, come with a set of starter kits that you can simply copy into your */sites/all/themes* folder and rename; with other themes, you may have to manually copy the files you need into a new folder. To start with, all child themes should contain three files:

- A *blank template.php* file, which will hold any theme functions you decide to put into it. Note that this file should be *blank* initially; copying the *template.php* file from your base theme will cause errors when you try to access your site.
- A *<THEMENAME>.info* file, which you can copy from the base theme.
- A *styles.css* (or something similar) file, which will be referenced in your theme's *.info* file and contain all of the CSS customizations for your child theme.

If you plan to override any of the base theme's *tpl.php* files, you can also copy those into your child theme. However, generally, I avoid doing that unless I need to create a new template region, or change the base theme's grid layout.

To create your child theme, you'll start by modifying the theme's *.info* file. The *.info* file defines the page regions, CSS, and JavaScript files that your theme will use. For example, here's part of the content of the *.info* file that comes with Omega's HTML5 starter kit:[2]

```
name = Omega
description = <a href="http://drupal.org/project/omega">Omega</a> extends the Omega
```

---

2. If you're interested in trying out Omega, it's recommended that you work with one of the starter kits that come with the theme *instead* of trying to copy the one that comes with Omega itself. Omega's *.info* file is copious and full of interesting settings that don't need to be copied into your child theme.

```
theme framework with some additional features and makes them available to its
subthemes. This theme should not be used directly, instead choose one of the Omega
or Alpha starterkits.
core = 7.x
engine = phptemplate
screenshot = screenshot.png
version = 3.x
base theme = alpha

; REGIONS
; REQUIRED CORE REGIONS
regions[page_top] = Page Top
regions[page_bottom] = Page Bottom
regions[content] = Content

; END REQUIRED CORE REGIONS
regions[user_first] = User Bar First
regions[user_second] = User Bar Second
regions[branding] = Branding
regions[menu] = Menu
```

If you've copied your base theme's .info file into your child theme's folder, you can
generally delete everything in the "stylesheets" and "scripts" sections. The information
on whatever regions your base theme has identified, however, must stay where it is.
Regions are specific areas on the page where you can place content—usually through
the Blocks administration screen (Structure→Blocks). You need to remember a couple
of things when modifying your .info file:

- As mentioned before, any regions your base theme has defined should *stay in the file*. Any regions that are set up in your child theme's template files, but aren't listed in its .info file, could break your theme.

- Themes have two names: the Machine Name and the Human-Friendly Name. Machine Names are always written in lowercase, with underscores instead of spaces (e.g., my_awesome_theme), while Human-Friendly Names can have uppercase letters, spaces, and so on (e.g., My Awesome Theme).

- The top bit of information (name, description, core version, engine, etc.) should stay at the top of the page. Drupal requires this information to make the theme work. Most of it should stay the same as what's in your base theme, with the exception of the name and description.[3]

- Additionally, you want to include base theme = *MACHINE_NAME* underneath the top set of descriptive information. In the Omega example shown earlier, you can see that Omega uses Alpha as its base theme; if you were creating a child theme from Omega, you would change that text to base theme = omega. Likewise, if you were creating a child theme based on NineSixty, which doesn't have its own base theme, you'd add base theme = ninesixty to your child theme's .info file.

---

3. If you want to learn more about what goes into a theme's .info file, check out *http://drupal.org/node/171205*, which has a complete list of the types of information you can put in there.

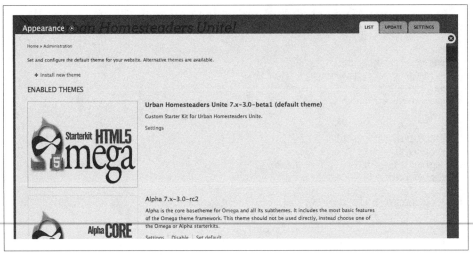

Figure 16-4. Setting our theme defaults.

Once you've updated the descriptive information and identified the base theme you're working with, you want to include any stylesheets or JavaScript files that you want to include in your theme.

For example, here's the updated *.info* file for my Urban Homesteaders Unite theme (which is based on the HTML5 starter kit that comes with Omega):

```
name = Urban Homesteaders Unite
description = Custom Starter Kit for Urban Homesteaders Unite.
core = 7.x
engine = phptemplate
screenshot = screenshot.png
base theme = omega

; REQUIRED CORE REGIONS
regions[page_top] = Page Top
regions[page_bottom] = Page Bottom
regions[content] = Content

; OPTIONAL STYLESHEETS
css[mobile.css][name] = Mobile Styles
css[mobile.css][description] = Your custom CSS
    for the mobile version of your website (mobile first).
css[mobile.css][options][weight] = -89

css[styles.css][name] = Main Styles
css[styles.css][description] = Your main custom CSS file.
css[styles.css][options][weight] = 10
```

From there, you should be able to enable your theme through the Appearance menu, set it as the default (see Figure 16-4), and plug away at your *styles.css* file.

Other Things You Should Know About Base Themes

Now that you've gotten the hang of editing your theme's *.info* file and making a child theme, there are a couple of other things that you should bear in mind when working.

Clear the Theme Registry!

Anytime you add a new element to your *.info* file—whether it's to add a new region to your page, or add a new stylesheet (e.g., I sometimes like to add a separate stylesheet for the navigation on sites with complex navigation styles), you must clear your theme registry. Sometimes, for really sticky issues, you can also try clearing all the caches. You can clear all caches by going into Configuration→Performance and clicking the Clear all Caches button. If you're feeling super-nerdy, you can also use the command `drush cc all` to clear the caches from within Drush, the command-line tool for Drupal.

 You don't have to clear the cache every time you do something simple, such as changing the CSS in your theme; but if you make a change and nothing happens, clearing the cache will often help.

Working with Regions

Regions are Drupal's way of laying out containers for content in a given theme. Many themes, such as Bartik and Omega, come with a copious volume of regions—all with odd names such as "Triptych," "Postscript," and "Preface"—for your block organization pleasure. This is, in fact, one of the things you want in a base theme—the more regions you have, even if you use none of them, the more flexibility you have in your layout. The trick is to understand what the regions mean, and to use your layout to guide where you put things.

In Drupal 6, your theme's regions would be overlaid directly in the Blocks administration screen. In Drupal 7, things are different. If you look at your Blocks administration screen (Structure→Blocks), you'll see this link: "Demonstrate block regions <theme name>" (see Figure 16-5).

If you click that link, you'll see a page that shows all the regions you have available in your theme (see Figure 16-6).

As you can see, there's a lot to work with here; however, it's not always easy to re-member which region is where, or how things are going to show up. For that reason, I tend to keep either a print or a sketch of my theme's regions in my project file as I'm working. If I lose track of something, I just refer to my printout and I'm good to go.

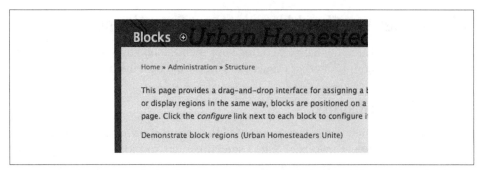

Figure 16-5. If you go into Blocks administration, you'll see a link that will let you show the theme's associated regions.

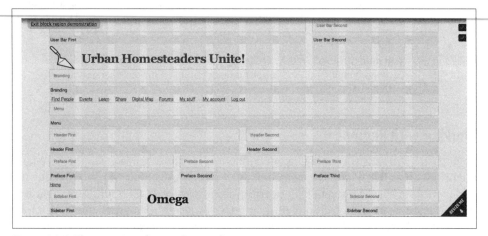

Figure 16-6. Theme regions for our Omega theme.

Please, Tell Me More!

We've really just scratched the surface of working with base themes in Drupal 7. If you're itching to learn more (and I just know you are), check out *http://drupal.org/node/ 225125*, where the lovely folks in the Drupal community have running documentation on how to create a subtheme, with commentary. You can also add comments and questions to the documentation page, simply by logging in with your Drupal.org (*http: //drupal.org*) account.

CHAPTER 17

Making CSS Easier with LESS

LESS[1] is a dynamic stylesheet language that allows you to code CSS more efficiently. Not only does it allow you to create variables with sensible names that you can reuse anywhere in your stylesheet, but it also allows you to *nest CSS styles*, which is a huge timesaver—especially when working in Drupal, when you might find yourself styling several different selectors within one page or block of the site.

In LESS, you'll create your code in a file with the extension *.less*. Once you've created your code, you compile it into a *.css* file either using a JavaScript call in the browser (there's even a Drupal module for it—see *http://drupal.org/project/less*), or using Less.app (available for the Mac at *http://incident57.com/less*) to compile it and upload the *.css* file to your server.

Creating Variables

Variables are little bits of code that you can call at will in your stylesheet. My favorite use for variables is in picking out colors. For example, let's assume your site uses a specific shade of brown (#572700) in a variety of places throughout the layout. In regular CSS, you'd have to input each instance manually, and you'll more than likely have the color written down—with a bunch of other colors used in your layout—on a pad somewhere near your desk.

Using LESS, you'd define the color once using `@brown: #572700;` and then call the color wherever it appears using `color: @brown;` or `background-color: @brown;`.

This allows you to not only code more quickly overall (no need to keep referring to that page of scribbles on your desk every time you need to call the color), but also *change* colors quickly if you realize down the line that a particular color just wasn't working out. Instead of having to do a find and replace for the color's hex value, you can just change the settings on the @brown variable and save your .less file.

---

1. *http://lesscss.org/*

The Mighty Mixin

Mixins are similar to variables, in that you call them in much the same way. However, they are different from variables in the following three ways:

- They start with a dot (.) instead of an @ symbol.
- Instead of a general variable that you can call anywhere in your syntax, a mixin can only show up as its own line of CSS.
- Unlike variables, a mixin can combine many lines of code into one neat little property that you can plug into your CSS whenever you need it.

The syntax for a mixin is exactly like standard CSS, for example:

```
.brown-link {
    a {
        padding: 1em;
        background-color: @brown;
        color: white;
    }

    a, a:hover {
        background-color: @orange;
        color: @brown;
    }
}
```

The difference is that, instead of having to retype all this code whenever you need a brown link in your document, you simply call that mixin in your code for the area you're working on, for example:

```
#Menu ul>li {
    float: left;
    margin-right: 1em;
    .brown-link;
}
```

Mixins work best for bits of unwieldy code you use all the time, such as font designations, CSS3 variables that require multiple lines of code, and anything else you find yourself typing over and over again. They're also good for properties that may change as you work. I often set up font conventions as mixins in the top of my *.less* file using a generic font stack, and change the font stack when I've decided which fonts I'm going to use.

Nested Selectors and Styles

The other, and perhaps most important, feature of LESS is the ability to nest your CSS selectors inside their parent selectors. This not only makes your stylesheet shorter and more organized, but it also helps you understand how different selectors relate to one another. You'll see an example of this awesomeness a bit later; first, we'll discuss how LESS actually gets turned into usable CSS.

Compiling the Code

In order for LESS to work on your site, it needs to be compiled into regular CSS. If you're on Mac OS X, you can download Less.app,[2] a free application that will compile your *.less* file into CSS every time you save the file. Simply keep the app (see Figure 17-1) open while you work, drag your theme's folder into it, and every time you save the file, it will compile your work into a *.css* file in the theme folder.

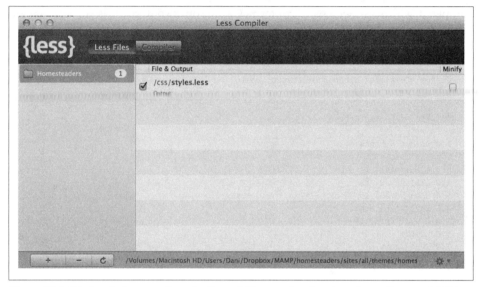

Figure 17-1. The handy Less.app "watches" any folder you drag into it and compiles your LESS into CSS as you work.

If you aren't on a Mac, or you're working in OS X 10.5 or earlier (Less.app only works in 10.6 and later), there are other options for compiling your *.less* files:

The LESS CSS Preprocessor module (http://drupal.org/project/less)
This module claims to process any *.less* file you add to your theme's *.info* file. I've never used it, so I can't vouch for how well it works. If you have the ability to use Less.app, I'd use it before installing a new module.

The Less.js JavaScript (downloadable from http://lesscss.org/)
This JavaScript file will process your *.less* files directly on the server if you include it in your theme's *.info* file.

2. *http://incident57.com/less*

Although both of these are perfectly fine options, I prefer using Less.app for one major reason: *I hate worrying about my JavaScript not running.* Additionally, in an average Drupal installation, you're going to have quite a few *.js* files running on your site just because you installed Drupal core and a couple of modules. Adding *Less.js* to the mix just adds another thing for the server to do when it serves up a page, and that adds weight to your site that you won't want to worry about. So I highly recommend that you use Less.app if you can.

Working with LESS: Organizing Your Stylesheets

Confession: I'm hyper-organized when it comes to my CSS. Everything is ordered and numbered, with a distinct table of contents. Call me obsessive-compulsive, but it works. Whether I'm working in straight CSS or LESS, every file starts about the same. Here, for example, is the table of contents for my Urban Homesteaders Unite theme:

```
/*
Custom styles for Urban Homesteaders Unite
Authors: Dani Nordin, tzk-design.com and Tricia Okin, papercutny.com

**Table of Contents**

1.0 Colors & Fonts
     1.1 Colors
     1.2 fonts
2.0 CSS3 Behaviors
3.0 Page Defaults
4.0 Navigation Menus
5.0 Drupal Defaults
6.0 Custom
7.0 Typography

*/
```

This way of organizing my CSS allows me to set up my page defaults near the top of the file, and put all my custom stuff at the bottom. This helps me create a more natural flow while I'm theming; I'll start by theming the Big Stuff (fonts, color standards, etc.), then move into page-level or template-level variables. Note that I do include the global typography at the bottom of the file; this ensures that any of my custom typography shows up before my global typography, instead of being overridden.

Setting Up Color Variables

Before I switched to using LESS, I would incorporate color values into my table of contents, for example:

```
**Table of Contents**

Color Values:
gray: #8D8D7D;
```

```
dkgray: #4D4545;
mdgray: #666;
ltgray: #999;
palegray: #ccc;

red: #D32F00;
orange: #D17103;
cyan: #47A7BF;
green: #89A155;
gold: #eeb200;
```

That way, if I was in the middle of a big theming push, I could just do a quick "find" on the color I needed by name, and copy/paste it into what I was theming without having to remember the hex value. Now, with LESS, I'm able to do the same thing, but instead of writing `color: #D32F00;` in my code, I can write `color: @red;` and Less.app will compile it into the CSS I need to make my object's text red. This means that in my *styles.less* file, I'll start off by defining those color variables:

```
/* 1.0 Colors & Fonts
      1.1 Colors */
@gray: #8D8D7D;
@dkgray: #4D4545;
@mdgray: #666;
@ltgray: #999;
@palegray: #ccc;

@red: #D32F00;
@orange: #D17103;
@cyan: #47A7BF;
@green: #89A155;
@gold: #eeb200;
```

After defining colors, I'll define the font mixins. As noted earlier, LESS allows you to use entire bits of code as variables (mixins). This is especially handy when working with CSS3 properties such as rounded corners and drop shadows (which usually require multiple lines of CSS). For my font mixins, I'm going to define some general defaults, using fonts that my partner Tricia and I have decided on:

```
/* 1.2 Fonts */

.serif-italic {
    font-family: 'ArvoItalic', Georgia, Times New Roman, serif;
}

.headings {
    font-family: 'ArvoRegular', Georgia, Times New Roman, serif;
    font-weight: normal;
}

.serif {
    font-family: Georgia, Times New Roman, serif;
}

.sans {
```

```
        font-family: 'PTSansRegular', Helvetica, Arial, san-serif;
    }

    .sans-italic {
        font-family: 'PTSansItalic', Helvetica, Arial, san-serif;
    }

    .caption-bold {
        font-family: 'PTSansBold', Helvetica, Arial, san-serif;
    }

    .caption-regular {
        font-family: 'PTSansCaptionRegular', Helvetica, Arial, san-serif;
    }

    .narrow-regular {
        font-family: 'PTSansNarrowRegular', Helvetica, Arial, san-serif;
    }
```

The use of the descriptors `.serif-italic`, `.serif`, and `.sans` is intentional; as the fonts may end up changing during the design phase, using generic descriptors such as these allows me to change fonts sitewide simply by changing the font stack in a few lines of code. Less.app then compiles the code into what I need. Using a generic name for the mixin also allows me to change the font without being tied to the name of the original font I chose. Now, let's say I wanted to change the headings in my site. I'd use the `.headings` variable as a line in my CSS:

```
h1, h2, h3, h4 {
    .headings;
    color: @orange;
}
```

When Less.app outputs the CSS file, the preceding code will translate to:

```
h1,
h2,
h3,
h4 {
    font-family: 'ArvoRegular', Georgia, Times New Roman, serif;
    font-weight: normal;
    color: #d17103;
}
```

Brilliant, right? This is why I love using LESS. The next step is to define any CSS3 mixins I need. For this site, we're keeping things pretty low-key; the only things we're really using are rounded corners for a few boxes here and there. For this, we'd put this in our code:

```
/* 2.0 CSS3 Variables */

.round-sm {
    /* all corners */
    -webkit-border-radius: 5px;
    -moz-border-radius: 5px;
    border-radius: 5px;
```

```
}

.round-lg {
    /* all corners */
    -webkit-border-radius: 10px;
    -moz border-radius: 10px;
    border-radius: 10px;
}
```

Now, if we wanted to style everything with the class selector button to be green with rounded corners, we could add the following to our code:

```
/* Form elements */
.button {
    .serif-italic;

    a {
        color: white!important;
        .round-sm;
        background-color: @green;
        padding: 1em;
    }

    a:hover {
        background-color: @cyan;
    }
}
```

When it's compiled into CSS, we'll have something that looks like Figure 17-2.

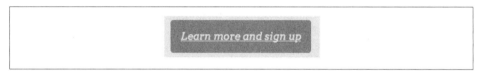

Figure 17-2. Our lovely button

Why LESS Is Awesome (Besides the Obvious)

Aside from the sheer volume of code you can prevent yourself from having to write (your carpal tunnel will thank you), one of the things that makes LESS especially awesome when you're working in Drupal is the way it helps you organize your CSS according to parent-child relationships, which is essential to theming in Drupal.

In most cases, when theming Drupal elements you'll be theming specific containers—say, all views of a certain type, or a Featured Content block—and everything within those containers. In standard CSS, it's very easy to find yourself losing track of where you are in the hierarchy when you start getting into more complex relationships; this is especially true with navigation menus, where you have a multitude of selectors, and their immediate descendants, to deal with. But with LESS's nested styles, you can start from the top down and keep everything in one place. For example, here's the sample LESS from the Event page that we walked through in Chapter 14:

```less
/* 6.2 Event Node */

.field-name-field-event-image {
    margin-bottom: 1em;
}

.about-host {
    .user-picture {
        float: left;
        margin-right: .5em;
    }

    h3 {
        margin: 0; padding: 0;
    }
    .username {
        font-size: 1em; line-height: 1.3em;
    }
}

.related-events {
    .views-row {
        margin: 1em 0;
        padding-bottom: .5em;
        border-bottom: 1px dotted @gray;
    }

    h4 {
        margin: 0; padding: 0;
    }

    .date {
        .sans-italic;
        font-size: .85em;
    }

}
```

Note that each block—`.about-host` and `.related-events`—starts off as its own thing, and all the elements that lie within those blocks are styled within the block. This not only helps you organize your code (you will no longer end up with that handful of random styles thrown at the bottom of your stylesheet at the last minute), but it also helps you actually understand the parent-child relationships. Over time, I've been able to more easily figure out where my best top-level selector is—should I deal with the body of a page? the content area? a single block?—and create CSS that gives me the look I want for a specific section of a theme without accidentally overriding CSS in other areas of the site.

Working with LESS on a Team

While there is much that is terrific about working with LESS, there is one minor sticking point. If you are working in LESS on a project that other people are contributing to, each person on the team who is touching the CSS of the project must also be working in LESS.

Since LESS depends on being able to compile your *.less* files into *.css* files, anyone who wants to add to the styles of a given site needs to update the *.less* file, *not* the *.css* file, and compile that *.less* file into standard CSS code. If, for example, one of your colleagues decides to change or add CSS to the site, and he adds it into *styles.css* (like many of us instinctively would), the moment that you go back into *styles.less* and make updates, everything your colleague just wrote in *styles.css* will be overwritten when you compile *styles.less*.

If you're working on a project with a team—say you and another designer are working on a startup, and both of you will be theming the site—it's important to discuss this early in the project. If possible, train your colleague on how to use LESS syntax (it's really easy, once you get used to it) and point him or her to Less.app; if your colleague can't use Less.app for whatever reason, consider downloading *Less.js* from *http://lesscss .org/* and adding it to your theme's *.info* file (make sure you download the *Less.js* file to a folder called *js* in your theme folder as well), and let the server compile it for you.

PART V

Making It Easier to Start Projects

CHAPTER 18

Using Features

Along the way, you (like me) might find that many of the sites you work on tend to have the same general sections. You'll have an events section, some testimonials, a blog, or some other type of functionality that always turns out pretty much the same way. Or, let's say you're a member of a team of folks working on a specific project. You're plugging away at a local copy of the site, updating a view so that you can correctly theme it, when you realize that none of the changes you just made to the view will translate to the site that everyone else is working on.

Enter Features. Features is a Drupal module that allows you to pack up specific chunks of functionality—content types, views, and so on—and export it as a custom module that you can then install on any site you want.

Let's look at the first example: commonly built functionality. Many sites I've created over the years include some sort of events page. Each event has a date and time, a location, title, and description, as well as a link to register for the event or learn more at an external website. Once the content type was created and content was entered, you'd create a view that would populate the Event page, and maybe include a block display for the sidebar.

In order to create this section, you'd do each task separately, with each one taking anywhere from half an hour to several hours, depending on the complexity of the Event content type. With Features, you can create the task once, export it as a feature, and install that feature on any number of sites.

To start working with Features, download and install the Features module (*http://drupal.org/project/features*). You should also install Strongarm (*http://drupal.org/project/strongarm*), which will help you maintain the configurations of your feature (particularly important for including content types).

For our Events feature, we'd create:

- An Event content type, with several custom fields
- An Events view, with upcoming events as one (page) display, an events archive as an (attachment) display, and a block display that features a list of events for a sidebar listing

Once you have everything set up the way you want it, go to the Features panel by clicking Structure, and then Features. You will arrive at a screen similar to that shown in Figure 18-1.

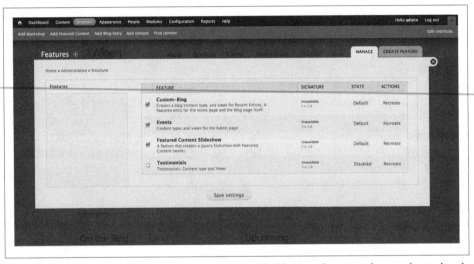

Figure 18-1. The Features window on a Drupal 7 site build. Note that some features have already been created and installed.

To create your feature, click on the Create Feature tab. This will give you a screen like the one in Figure 18-2.

In the first set of fields, you set up your feature defaults. We'll call this one Events and give it a description of "Creates an event content type, and views for an events listing." In the Version field, enter "7.x-1.0" (meaning it's a Drupal 7 feature and this is the first iteration of it). It's important not to leave those first three fields empty; they help create the *.info* file for your new custom module.

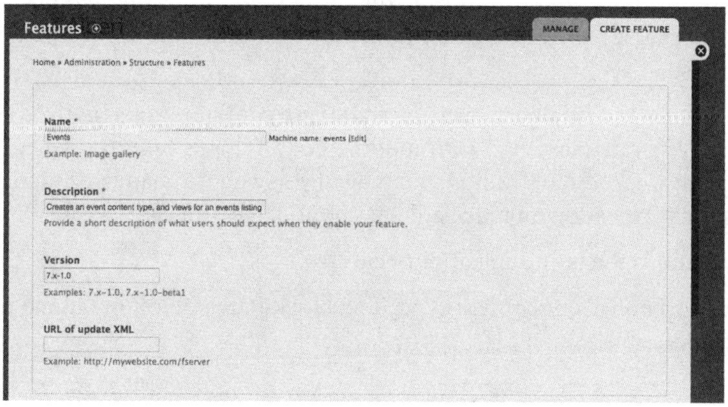

Figure 18-2. Setting up our Feature description.

Finally, choose Views from the Components list and then choose the view you created for your Events section. If your work depends on a specific contributed module, such as Semantic Fields, Fences, or Display Suite, and that module didn't show up in the Dependencies section, add it under Dependencies in the Components list.

By the end of all this work, you should have something that looks like Figure 18-3.

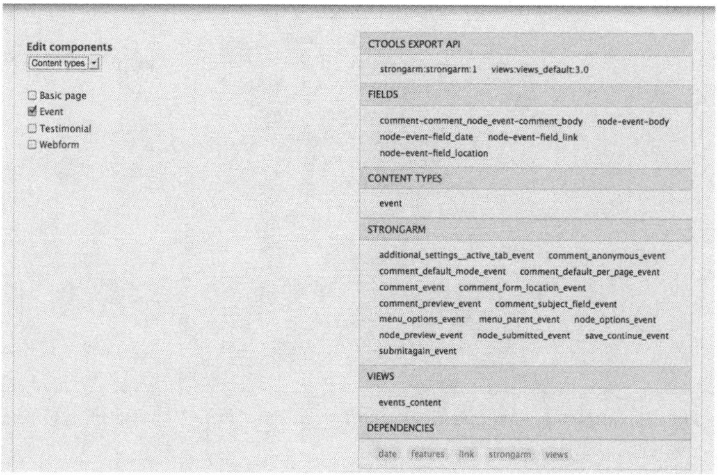

Figure 18-3. Your finished Components list. In addition to what's here, you can also include specific modules required by your content types, such as Fieldgroup.

Once all your components are assembled, you can download your feature by clicking the Download Feature button. Your feature will download as a *.tar.gz* file, which you can unpack and install into a "custom" directory under your *sites/all/modules* folder. Then you can enable the feature either under the Modules list or by returning to Structure→Features.

What features do, essentially, is turn your database configurations (in the form of content type, views, variables, etc.) into module code. This is fantastic when you want something that works out of the box. But what if you want to change your new feature's default settings? How do you make edits without destroying the feature?

That, my friend, is the best thing about Features.

Let's go back to our Event content type. The block I created on my home page looks like Figure 18-4.

Upcoming Workshops

Tue, 05/10/2011
ITRC Product Environmental Compliance Workshop
Concord, NH
To assist companies in their understanding of the latest developments in product eco-compliance, Alberi EcoTech has partnered with the NH International Trade Resource Center to offer a half day workshop on Environmental Compliance. We look to seeing you at this event!

Link To Page:
ITRC Website

Figure 18-4. The Upcoming Workshops block, built from one of the Views displays in the feature.

It looks beautiful, but I want "Link To Page" to say "Learn More" instead. Since the "Link To Page" label is part of my Events view, I can go into that display, change the label of the Link to Page field to "Learn More," and save the view. Now my display looks like Figure 18-5.

Workshops

TUE, 05/10/2011
ITRC Product
Environmental
Compliance Workshop
Concord, NH

To assist companies in their understanding of the latest developments in product eco-compliance, Alberi EcoTech has partnered with the NH International Trade Resource Center to offer a half day workshop on Environmental Compliance. We look to seeing you at this event!

Learn More:
ITRC Website

Figure 18-5. The Views display, fixed up a bit.

But when I return to the Features tab (see Figure 18-6), I notice that the database has overridden the Events feature I just created.

When you override a feature, it's important to make sure you update the code. The reason for this is twofold. First, if you're using the feature as part of a development workflow (e.g., you're developing the site locally, but you have to push changes to the server), updating the feature's code and pushing it to your remote server gives you the opportunity to transfer the changes from your local site to the remote site with relative ease. Second, updating the code keeps you safe from potential problems with your database down the road.

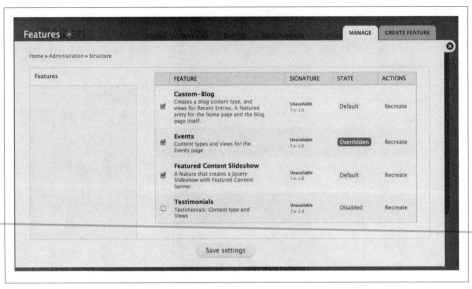

Figure 18-6. When you change an aspect of a feature, the feature shows as Overridden in the listing.

There are two ways to update your features. One way is to re-create the feature using the Recreate link on the Features page. Download the feature again, and replace the code in your *sites/all/modules/custom* folder. Refresh the page, and everything's all set.

The other way to do it, which is much quicker, is on the command line. The Features module comes with a set of Drush commands specific to managing features:

- `drush features` gives you a list of all the features installed on your site.
- `drush features-update` *FEATURE_NAME* updates code for a feature that the database has overridden.
- `drush features-revert` *FEATURE_NAME* reverts to the original code a feature that the database has overridden.

Remember, you should use all of these commands from inside your Drupal installation. In Figure 18-7, you'll notice that I used `drush features-update events` to update my Events feature.

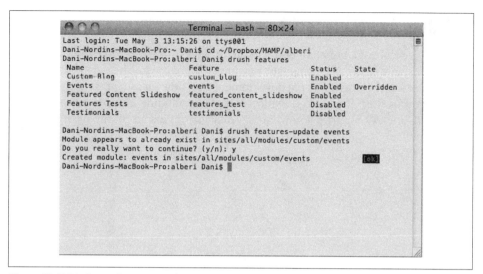

```
●●●              Terminal — bash — 80×24
Last login: Tue May  3 13:15:26 on ttys001
Dani-Nordins-MacBook-Pro:~ Dani$ cd ~/Dropbox/MAMP/alberi
Dani-Nordins-MacBook-Pro:alberi Dani$ drush features
Name                        Feature                       Status    State
Custom Blog                 custom_blog                   Enabled
Events                      events                        Enabled   Overridden
Featured Content Slideshow  featured_content_slideshow    Enabled
Features Tests              features_test                 Disabled
Testimonials                testimonials                  Disabled

Dani-Nordins-MacBook-Pro:alberi Dani$ drush features-update events
Module appears to already exist in sites/all/modules/custom/events
Do you really want to continue? (y/n): y
Created module: events in sites/all/modules/custom/events         [ok]
Dani-Nordins-MacBook-Pro:alberi Dani$
```

Figure 18-7. Updating features on the command line—three commands and you're done.

In the short amount of time I have been working with the Features module on my sites, I've seen both benefits and challenges to this workflow. The biggest benefit to this workflow is its portability and speed. Developing locally saves time; you don't have to worry about waiting for an FTP server to accept your file, or about accidentally up-loading the wrong file and wondering how to get it back. Additionally, since working in Drupal is so often a dance between configuration in the database and tinkering with code, Features allows you to get this same speed on your local machine without having to worry (too much) about syncing a database between your local and remote machines.

Speaking of syncing a database, it's important to note that Features won't export the *content* in your work to code. As such, if you're using Features to prototype something that involves a number of content types or complex node relationships, you'll still have to re-create any content you added on your local machine when you install or update the feature. This, in fact, is the one case where it might make more sense to sync data-bases back and forth instead of using Features; during one project, I ended up having to re-create about 30 pieces of content on the staging site after updating my feature, which was officially Not Fun.

Still More Awesomeness Awaits

So far, you've learned a bunch of new ways to protect your work and make your life as a Drupal designer easier. Now that we're inching toward the finish line, it's time to talk about my absolute favorite Drupal development trick: the Drush *.make* file. With this one file, you can use Drush to download Drupal, including any contrib or custom modules, themes, or libraries you want—even a custom install profile—within about five minutes.

CHAPTER 19

Working with Drush Make and Installation Profiles

As you continue working in Drupal, you'll likely notice that you use certain modules again and again. Normally, you'd start a project by downloading and enabling each module manually; you may even end up compiling, as I did for a while, a checklist of modules that belong on every project. While a checklist is a convenient way to remember all the modules you typically use, it still takes time to download and install the modules. Even using Drush to do it can get monotonous at times—and if you're using a lot of modules, it's easy to make a mistake and type the wrong filename. Although you could also create a local installation that serves as a "base install" with all your configurations and just copy the database over and over, it takes time and effort to keep the code and modules updated in the base installation, and creating a new site requires not only copying those files into a new folder, but copying the database as well. It's not the worst workflow, but it's not the most efficient either.

What if there was a way for you to run a script that would download Drupal for you, download and unpack all your modules and base themes, and basically create your file structure for you so that you can get to work on designing something awesome? That's what Drush Make is for. Drush Make is an extension for Drush that will allow you to specify:

- Which core version you want to download (e.g., 6.x or 7.x)
- Which modules you want
- Which base theme you'd like
- Any external libraries or other bits of code you want

It also allows you to *download/unpack it all into whatever folder you're in*. Combine this with an installation profile that enables the modules you want, sets your base theme as the new default, and establishes other key settings, and you can have a new site up and running within about fifteen to thirty minutes—with many of your most commonly used defaults already set up.

Step 1: Install Drush Make

To start using Drush Make, you first need to install the extension, unless you are using Drush version 5 (see the upcoming note). It's best to do this in a hidden directory in your home folder, rather than in the *drush* directory. The reason for this is simple: at some point you may end up upgrading Drush, and if you do, and Drush Make is in the main */drush* directory, you've just deleted Drush Make.

 As of Drush version 5 and later, Drush Make is part of the main Drush package. This means two things: 1) if you already have Drush version 5, you don't need to follow the steps to install Drush Make—you already have it; and 2) if you're upgrading your version of Drush to version 5 and you have installed Drush Make using the steps that follow, you must delete your copy of Drush Make from the *.drush* directory.

Follow these steps to install Drush Make:

1. Download the project from *http://drupal.org/project/drush_make*.

2. Unpack the *tar.gz* file into your working folder (again, this is your home folder).

3. Move the folder into a hidden directory called *.drush*. Start by navigating to your home directory:

   ```
   cd ~
   ```

4. Then make a hidden *.drush* directory:

   ```
   mkdir .drush
   ```

5. Finally, move the *drush_make* folder into your new hidden directory:

   ```
   mv drush_make ~/.drush
   ```

Now you need to create a *.make* file for it to run. If you go back to the project page for Drush Make, you'll find a sample *.make* file under the "Documentation and Resources" heading, called *EXAMPLE.make*; copy the text from that file and paste it into a new file in your favorite text editor (I'm using Coda, but you can also use TextWrangler for Mac or a similar free text editor). Now you can start customizing it any way you want.

Each *.make* file starts with specifying the version of Drupal core that you're working with and the Drush Make API version. To help keep things organized I like to include comments in my files that are preceded by a semicolon:

```
; Specify Drupal core and Drush API version
core = 7.x
api = 2
```

Specify the actual Core project (a.k.a. Drupal core):

```
; Core project
projects[] = drupal
```

Now you want to specify the modules you want to download. Note that Drush Make will only download versions of modules that are compatible with the version of Drupal you're specifying, and those that have current recommended releases. This means that, while I'd normally include `semantic_fields` in my "Theming Helpers" section, I can't because it's not in recommended release yet. You can still use Drush to download the module, however, once the *.make* file finishes running.

I like to group modules based on what they're used for, or based on a specific dependency, with comments. For example, I'll just start with Views, CTools, Pathauto, and Token, which are common to most Drupal installations:

```
; Standard modules
projects[] = views
projects[] = ctools
projects[] = pathauto
projects[] = token
```

Then I'll add some of my favorite theming helper modules, and the WYSIWYG module, with its dependency, Libraries:

```
; Theming helpers
projects[] = block_class

; WYSIWYG
projects[] = wysiwyg
projects[] = libraries
```

Then I'll add a base theme (in this case, Omega):

```
; Base theme
projects[] = omega
```

Now, I'll save the file as *make_basic.make*, in a *makefiles* directory in my home folder.

Here's where the magic happens. Let's say that now I want to create a new Drupal installation for a client project. I'll start in *Terminal.app* by navigating to my *MAMP* folder and creating a new directory for the project. I'll call it *make-test* for now.

```
cd ~/Dropbox/MAMP
mkdir make-test
```

Now I navigate into my new folder and call my *make_basic.make* file using Drush:

```
cd make-test
drush make ~/makefiles/make_basic.make
y
y
```

When I'm done, I'll see something approximating Figure 19-1 in Terminal.

If I go back into the Finder and navigate to my new *make-test* directory, I'll see something similar to Figure 19-2.

```
Danielles-MacBook-Air:.drush Dani$ cd ~
Danielles-MacBook-Air:~ Dani$ cd Dropbox/MAMP
Danielles-MacBook-Air:MAMP Dani$ mkdir make-test
Danielles-MacBook-Air:MAMP Dani$ cd make-test
Danielles-MacBook-Air:make-test Dani$ drush make ~/makefiles/make_basic.make
Make new site in the current directory? (y/n): y
Project information for drupal retrieved.                    [ok]
Project information for views retrieved.                     [ok]
Project information for ctools retrieved.                    [ok]
drupal downloaded from                                       [ok]
http://ftp.drupal.org/files/projects/drupal-7.7.tar.gz.
views downloaded from                                        [ok]
http://ftp.drupal.org/files/projects/views-7.x-3.0-rc1.tar.gz.
ctools downloaded from                                       [ok]
http://ftp.drupal.org/files/projects/ctools-7.x-1.0-beta1.tar.gz.
Make new site in the current directory? (y/n): y
Danielles-MacBook-Air:make-test Dani$ █
```

Figure 19-1. Drush Make downloading everything I need for my Drupal installation.

Why This Is Lovely

If you've done Drupal sites for any length of time, you've likely noticed that there are certain modules—or a specific base theme—that you return to over and over again. Using *.make* files, you can set up a file to download everything you need for a specific use case—say, a standard promotional corporate site, or a web community—and running that one file will download everything you need to get started in *about five minutes.*

Getting Started with Install Profiles

Once you have a *.make* file ready, with all the modules and other things you typically use for a project, you may want to make your life even easier by creating an install profile that enables all your modules for you, and sets up a few of the configurations you have to reset over and over again. Although install profiles can be tricky to set up, they can be huge timesavers. While the *.make* file does the hard work of downloading and unpacking most of your modules for you, you can set up the install profile to actually enable all those modules, along with a host of other things, such as the following:

- Setting up default user roles and permissions (such as editor, administrator, and other commonly needed user roles)
- Setting up appropriate input formats (such as adding <h1>–<h4> tags and the like)
- Populating the database with some sample content
- And much more!

In Drupal 7, profiles are set up like modules and need the following to work:

- A *<profilename>.info* file that sets up your dependencies (the modules that are enabled when the profile is used to install Drupal)
- A *<profilename>.install* file that actually installs Drupal for you
- A *<profilename>.profile* file that sets up your configurations for you

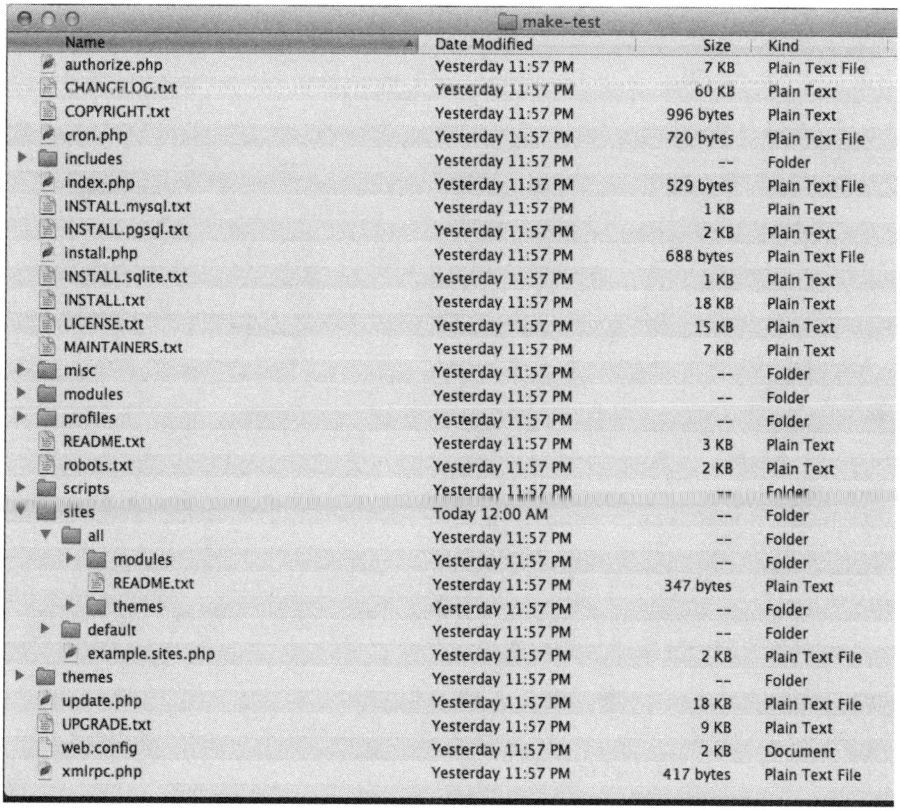

Figure 19-2. In about a minute, I downloaded my entire Drupal installation, a base theme, and the modules I need to get started, in the right locations. Sweet!

The documentation for install profiles at *http://drupal.org/node/1022020* provides a great starting point for making your own install profile. I like to start my new profile by copying and modifying the Standard profile that comes with the Drupal 7 core (located in the *profiles* folder). It should also be noted that, for certain things, such as a specific configuration of content types and views (such as an Events section, or a News section), you're better off packing it up into the Features module, which we talked about in the preceding chapter.

PART VI

Working with Clients

CHAPTER 20

Proposing and Estimating Projects

Over the years, I've learned to break the discovery process into two distinct phases. The first, outlined here, happens prior to estimating the project, and gives me the background I need to create a proposal and estimate for the project. The second, more comprehensive phase happens during and after the project kickoff. This phase, described in Part I, is where we start framing the design challenge that we're facing, fleshing out the user experience, and making sure the client is on board with our approach.

Preproposal Discovery: What You Need to Know

The initial discovery phase should give you enough information about the client, the project's goals, and the level of complexity for you to put together an accurate proposal. During this phase, you want to learn:

- Who is the client?
- How well do they know the business and themselves?
- Who are they trying to reach?
- What's the real goal here? What are they hoping their site will accomplish for them? Are they satisfied with their customers, or are they looking to branch into new markets?
- What kind of functionality will they need? Can you handle it on your own, or will you need to bring in external resources?
- What's the decision-making process within the organization? Are you dealing one-on-one with the main decision maker, or does everything have to go through one or more layers of red tape before it can be approved?
- What kind of content are you working with? Does the client have examples to show? How many pages, sections, and so on? How do they expect people to access or organize the content?
- How big is their budget?
- How open are they to your ideas and approach? What "vibe" do you get from them?

All of these questions should help you get a sense of what it will be like to work with the client, and whether you'll be able to create a productive working relationship. During initial conversations with potential clients, I often start putting answers to these questions in a standard project brief (available in Section 8) that will get fleshed out in the project kickoff meeting at the beginning of the discovery phase. I also include it as a download from my website for potential clients to fill out before we estimate projects. While it doesn't replace an initial phone call to flesh things out, it's very good at helping to weed out clients who may be more interested in price shopping than in hiring a serious design team.

From the Trenches: Richard Banfield, Fresh Tilled Soil

Fresh Tilled Soil, based in Waltham, Massachusetts, designs dynamic interfaces for web startups. I sat down with founder and president, Richard Banfield, to discuss how the company chooses and works with clients.

Dani: You guys definitely seem to have longer-term relationships, where you are working with clients through multiple iterations of their business. Was that intentional?

Richard: Absolutely. We had an awakening a few years ago where we realized that we couldn't roll through this roller coaster day by day—where you've got a project and then nothing, and then a project and then nothing. We wanted clients who wanted to work with us as partners, we wanted long-term contracts, we wanted to provide something that couldn't be outsourced to a foreign country—and that means we had to become high-end consultants providing high-end product development, essentially. We also decided to spin off the smaller projects to Super Web-O-Matic [a subsidiary business that specializes in affordable WordPress sites for small businesses], which takes care of the smaller projects, so we don't get distracted. [Super Web-O-Matic] is a different process, a different business model.

It was a very deliberate thing. If you're a UI/UX designer, you're essentially a partner to the executive team of the company you're working with. So you can't be anything but the absolute best thought leadership consultant. You're not just a hired gun. If you're a hired gun, certainly you'll be outsourced.

Dani: It's interesting that there are people who will think of UX designers as hired guns. And they're trying to hire a UX designer because they've heard they need one—and not because they have an investment in the user experience of their product and making something that people actually want to use. Do you find you run into clients like that?

Richard: We established something that we called "the lens," and it's sort of a way of [identifying] ideal versus nonideal clients. This lens includes things like, does this person have the money to do the thing they want to do? Also, is this a challenging and exciting project that we'd feel passionate about? Is this a client that respects the role of a business like ours as a partner to theirs, or are they just going to treat us like a vendor? Is there good chemistry there—will we have good communication, or is it always going to be that every single conversation we have has to go through legal counsel, or it's going to be a fight or something?

For entrepreneurial clients it's something that goes even deeper. For example, is this a client who's worked on a successful project before? First-time entrepreneurs tend to be exhausting, because they think they can do more than they can. They're not really open and coachable. If they haven't gotten a couple of wins or failures under their belt, they're unrealistic about what they can do and can't do.

Dani: I also tend to find that they can be, not cheap, but scared about money.

Richard: They don't understand the value of what you're doing, so they'll nickel and dime you on something and you'll say, "Why are we talking about a thousand dollars here when we're building a million-dollar business?" There's no way that I can do a good job if I'm thinking, "S***, I shouldn't spend that extra hour making this perfect." I'm going to start cutting corners, because I'm worried that you're going to beat me up on the invoice? How am I supposed to do a good job? It's taken us six years to get to that point where we can say, "This is what we know it's going to cost, because we've done 200 of these projects. No amount of cajoling or arguing is going to change that, because we know what it's going to take to create a successful project, and we're telling you that, and you should listen to it because we've done 200 projects like yours." If they can't work with that, there are other people who they can go to, but this is what we can do to bring value and create something successful.

I think the good clients recognize this immediately—they know what that means, they know what the value is—and they put the checks down. The ones that nickel and dime you over every little detail in the contract? Those are red flags. Those are people you don't want to work with.

Pricing a Project: Fixed-Bid Versus Hourly

The question of how to charge for Drupal is a sticky one. On the one hand, most significant web projects will carry with them a level of uncertainty that makes an hourly rate attractive. What happens when the client needs extra changes? What happens when a certain functional problem is trickier to solve than you had accounted for, and you end up spending twice as many hours as you had intended? These are very valid reasons to charge hourly for your work, and many developers I know have no problem getting clients to agree to hourly billing.

That being said, many clients (and designers) prefer a fixed-bid approach. Clients can equate the hourly approach with a ticking clock that must be shut off before things get too expensive, and that often means quality gets sacrificed in the name of doing things quickly. I've especially seen this in consulting work. For example, working with a client to reposition their brand can require anywhere from 20 to 100 hours of time to really see results; however, many clients working with an hourly rate will cut the process off as early as six hours in, afraid of getting a huge bill at the end of our work together. As a result, the client doesn't get the results they were hoping for, and they end up feeling they wasted their money.

Using a fixed-bid approach attaches a very real and specific value to your work that clients have an easier time dealing with. It also helps with creating consistent income and cash flow; if, during the process of learning Drupal, you find yourself building websites much more quickly than you used to, a fixed bid allows you to charge the same (or more) than you used to when you were still learning the ropes.

I have found the following tricks to working with fixed-bid pricing:

Keep very detailed time records
> Over time, you'll start to realize how long things actually take to build.

Have a contract that specifically states what clients will get from you
> In estimates, I always account for up to three iterations of a site's look and feel, with one opportunity to completely redesign it. Anything above and beyond that becomes a change order, and results in hourly charges.

Work with clients to establish payment schedules
> With smaller clients, I tend to take an initial deposit and then break the rest of the balance into monthly installments, regardless of when the project is finished. This helps me plan cash flow, while giving the client a chance to budget for the work. Other designers prefer a milestone-based approach, with one installment due upon approval of the designs and another due at the end of the project. Both approaches carry certain risks. With the monthly billing approach, you get paid sooner and more regularly, but it can be harder to define where, exactly, a project ends. With the milestone-based billing approach you risk running into a negative cash-flow situation at any point where the project runs into delays. And believe me, it will run into delays.

Ultimately, whether you bill on an hourly or fixed-bid basis, you still have to be able to give the client an approximate idea of what their job will cost and how long it will take to complete. The best process I've seen for estimating Drupal projects comes from CivicActions in San Francisco; its Estimating Spreadsheet[1] is a brilliant way to break up the individual pieces of a Drupal project by hours needed for specific team members. For working with distributed teams, I find translating the spreadsheet into a Google Doc offers a great way to collaboratively come up with numbers for a proposal.

Writing the Proposal

Once you've collected the initial discovery, and estimated what resources you'll need and how much the project will take to build, it's time to craft a proposal. At a minimum, a good proposal should include:

---

1. Available as an OpenOffice download at *http://civicactions.com/estimating-worksheet*. It should also open in Mac's Numbers application or Microsoft Excel. I've also imported it as a Google Doc with some success.

- Your initial assessment of the project's goals, audience, and objectives, based on your discovery sessions with the client.
- A statement of work that describes what you'll deliver to the client. This should include a number of original concepts you'll deliver, as well as how many rounds of revisions are included in the budget. It should also include a list of deliverables you'll need from the client in order to proceed, and a note about what happens if they're late on their deliverables.
- Estimated prices for the project you're discussing. Many teams like to give a low and a high bid, with the note that pricing is based on the information you have on hand and that new information, such as additional stakeholders or new content that wasn't discussed up front, may push the project into the upper price range.
- Any terms and conditions that apply to the project. This should include things such as a pricing schedule, what happens if you or the client decides to cancel the project, and how you'll deal with issues such as delays or new information.

In addition to these things, some teams find it helpful to include:

- An overview of the design and development process, which gives the client an idea of what to expect.
- Case studies or images of previous design work done for other clients.
- A more detailed scope of work, which would include Drupal-level deliverables, such as custom page templates or content types included in the estimated cost. Include this information with caution; not all clients understand "DrupalSpeak," and it could cause confusion.
- Bios of team members, and other information about the company.

In my work with clients, I use two proposal formats. For larger projects, especially ones where I have to put together a team for the project, I use a proposal format adapted from Chicago design firm Rogue Element's proposals.[2] The format has the benefit of being both concise and comprehensive, and it's easily adaptable to any studio's needs.

For shorter projects, I use an amended proposal, or work agreement, that includes just the set of information in the first of the two preceding lists. I use this format for smaller projects (e.g., budgets around $5,000 or less), or for repeat clients. For new clients, I may also include a bit of information about the studio and a list of previous design work.

A sample of both the proposal and the work agreement is available in Part VII. The content is unique to my studio and the project involved, but the format is free for you to adapt as you need to.

---

2. Which you can find in this article: *http://www.howdesign.com/article/proposal/*.

CHAPTER 21

Getting Clients to Love You, Even When You Have to Tell Them "No"

There comes a time in every Drupal project where you are going to have to say "no" to something your client wants. This could happen for a number of reasons. Your client could have seen an amazing widget on somebody else's site and feel they *must* have it on theirs. Or they suddenly decide that what they really need to "engage their community" is a full set of social media tools that customers can use directly through their site. Regardless of the reason, you've already set the scope for the project, you're probably already worried about meeting your deadlines, and you need to find a way to diffuse this situation without losing your patience or the client.

There are a few things to remember when this happens to you:

- Most of the time, the client will actually have a very good reason for making this suggestion.

- Just because something can't be part of the site now doesn't mean it can never be; in fact, these types of conversations often lead to future enhancements.

- The client needs to know they've been heard, and to know what you're going to do about it.

This is why it's so essential to have up-front documentation that clearly describes the technical and design scope of the project, user objectives, and business goals. The documentation won't prevent these ideas from cropping up; but it will give you a foundation for the conversation you need to have with the client when they do.

For example, let's say you contracted with the client to build a simple, mostly promotional site with an events listing, news page, blog, and contact form. You've gotten through the discovery phase and have already started theming and approving designs, when the client realizes she'd really love to add some interaction to the mix. She has seen other companies that have forums where users hang out, converse, and help one another. She has heard that Drupal "makes it easy" to add forums to a website, and she wants to implement it straightaway.

First, does Drupal actually "make it easy" to add a forum to your site? Technically, yes. Forums are part of Drupal's core functionality, and you can enable the forum simply by clicking a button on the Modules page. However, enabling the forum is just a tiny piece of what's actually involved in creating a forum. You have to figure out where it belongs in the site's architecture, decide who has access and who doesn't, set up the appropriate permissions, and style it to mesh with the rest of the site's look and feel. Also, the client will have to promote the forums, create categories for forum topics, get people actually using them, and monitor them consistently for trolls and spammers. What we think of as "easy" at first glance rarely is easy once we're in the process of making it happen.

There are several ways to approach the challenge of pushing back, most of which will at some point involve referring the client back to the documentation you created at the beginning of your project. My approach is to say, "Great idea! Let me ask just a few questions to figure out how this can work ... ." This assures the client that you're listening to them, but also helps them talk through the business logic behind the request, and understand everything that actually goes into fulfilling their request. Often, this approach will either talk them out of the idea completely or put it in the works for the next iteration of the site. Either response is a good resolution.

To elaborate on this example, any of the following questions could work with most reasonable clients, depending on where you are in the project plan:

- "A discussion forum could be great! How were you planning to promote it? Do you have resources to monitor it for spammers and trolls?"
- "I like that idea, but one of our business objectives was to focus on the organization's human-friendly approach to customer service. A user forum might give the impression that you prefer your customers to handle issues among themselves. What do you expect the user will gain from the forum?"
- "That sounds like a great idea, but right now, our push is to get the basic functionality into the site before launch on Tuesday. Do you want to have a discussion about adding it to the next iteration of the site? I'll work up some estimates on what it would cost."

There are a few things to note about this approach. First, clients really love it when you tell them they've had a great idea. Second, you're making it clear that although the idea is good, they have to be prepared to do some work to make it happen.

Third, and this is the really important part: you're not pointing to a specific document and saying, "If you remember the piece of paper you signed ... ."

In my early days of working with clients, I used the "that's not in the contract" line frequently, and it never ever worked. Something about referring people back to legal agreements sets up the conversation to be combative; the client ends up perceiving that you're trying to pick a fight with them. Referring to themes that you'd agreed on in the course of discovery shows the client that you're interested in seeing how this new idea might work with what was already agreed upon, and you want to find a solution that works for everybody.

This process of dealing with client requests that push a project beyond the original scope has caused some teams to adopt a hybrid Agile approach to Drupal projects. While the process still involves defining the scope of work and planning things out up front, design and development happen together, iteratively and collaboratively. This helps teams keep everyone on track while accounting for the inevitable bumps in the road that come with designing for Drupal. Says Four Kitchens' Todd Nienkerk of his company's Agile process:

> We rarely say "no" to a client with regards to adding functionality, but we do explain that:
>
> - Adding something before launch means something else needs to be pushed back.
> - Their current budget doesn't really allow for this extra work, so let's reprioritize or find more money, etc.
>
> Scrum provides a very handy framework for this discussion because all ideas, regardless of how enormous or superfluous or whim-driven they may be, go into the project backlog for future discussion. Usually having it in the backlog—i.e., captured somewhere for the client to see every so often—is enough to make them happy and never actually push for that feature to be implemented.

That's Easy for You to Say ...

Of course, this approach doesn't always work. Occasionally, you run into the type of client that I like to call "the Dictator." They grab ideas completely out of left field and present you with them, and you're expected to take the ideas and run with them. If you try to spin the conversation back to the scope that was agreed upon, they get hostile and say things like, "This is what I hired you to do," or "Just make it happen."

Or, worse, you could also run into the type of client that loves everything you do, gives you complete creative freedom, and gives you absolutely no direction, feedback, or restraints—but will come up with an idea once a week that absolutely won't fit into the budget, and can't understand why when you explain it to him or her.

When you run into either of these types of clients, you have to make a choice. Is it more important to preserve the client relationship, or to stand your ground and risk walking away from the project?

I'm fortunate in my career to have grown skilled at managing "difficult" clients. But the most important part of this skill is to know myself well enough to know the types of clients I just can't work with. In my career, the handful of times a project has gone sour can be directly attributed to deciding to take on a project despite the obvious conflicts between myself and the client. If you're on a team, it can be easier; you have other team members you can lean on when things get too difficult for you to handle. If you're working solo, or as part of a small, distributed team, it can make you wonder why you got into this field in the first place.

Either way, part of managing your career is learning how to navigate difficult situations with grace. If you find yourself faced with a client who refuses to hear the word *no*, it's on you to evaluate whether their request can be accommodated within the current budget and to make any adjustments that need to be made, including possibly letting the client go.

The "Professional Relationship" Clause

Recently, I gave a brief talk on the state of designers and UXers in the typical Drupal team. During discussions after the talk, I mentioned the "Professional Relationship" clause I include in all of my work agreements that establishes the working relationship I expect with clients, and states that I (or the client) can terminate the agreement if one of us isn't living up to the terms of this relationship. This statement—in which I basically told clients how I expected them to treat me, and what they could expect of me in return—resulted in expressions of shock and curiosity by all the people in the room, most of them developers.

The reason I put the clause into my contracts was simple. As a self-employed designer, I'm selling my time and energy. If that time and energy is being sapped by abusive or disrespectful clients, I need to be able to address the situation proactively in a way that protects my business and my sanity. The "Professional Relationship" clause, which encompasses a few bullet points on the front page of the contract, helps clients understand that I'm here to help them—and if they won't respect that, they should find someone else to work with.

I put the clause into my contracts with the help of Jessica Manganello, a client, friend, and cofounder of New Leaf Legal,[1] a terrific team of entrepreneurial lawyers in the Boston area. She and I got together to look at my contracts after a particularly nasty situation with a client who turned abusive after ignoring his project for more than a year. Although he had clearly breached his end of the contract, I had also set up my initial contract, which I cobbled together from sample contracts I got from a copy of *Legal Forms for Graphic Designers*[2] and the AIGA's website,[3] with no way for me to get out of a project that wasn't working out. Establishing the clause helped me make it extra clear to clients that I meant business, and I have yet to meet a client who refused to sign as a result of the clause.

If you want to consider adding the clause to your contracts, you can find it in my sample work agreement in Part VII. If you want a contract that fully covers all the bases, give Jess at New Leaf a call.

1. *http://newleaflegal.com*

2. *http://www.amazon.com/Business-Legal-Forms-Graphic-Designers/dp/1581152744*

3. The AIGA is the international association of graphic designers, based in the United States (*http://aiga.org*).

CHAPTER 22

After the Handoff—
The Project Retrospective

Unfortunately, this critical step [of reflecting on a project after its completion] is nearly always ignored by professional designers. Assessment implies internal criticism, something many companies prefer to leave up to public relations or external product reviews. The assessment [of the project's success] must be at a user and project level, rather than a quality assurance level, and benchmarks for success have generally not been developed or acknowledged within corporate America. In many high-pressure design consultancies, to reflect is to waste time. Reflection is not productive and is frequently viewed as a poor use of money and resources.[1]

The case study: some designers swear by them as a valuable marketing tool; others refuse to do them, insisting that there's just "too much work to do" or that images of their work will speak for themselves. I've even heard designers say that clients don't like reading case studies. I've never seen this, but then, I've never quite subscribed to the idea of being "too busy to read."

Let me state one thing emphatically: *reflecting on your work—whether you share it in the form of case studies or not—is vitally important to your career as a designer.* Whether you are part of a team, are an independent designer, or are working in corporate America, taking time to think about a project—how it went, what went right, how you can make things better next time—is one of the most important things you can do. Every time I've reflected on a project, no matter how well or how horribly it went, I've learned something valuable I can use in the future. Reflecting on "nightmare" projects has proven particularly valuable; not only does it give me a way to move on from them productively, but it also gives me a wellspring of lessons for those inevitable "have you ever had a project that just went *horribly?*" questions that clients or job interviewers sometimes like to spring on you.

The time you take to reflect at the end of a project depends on the project, and often on your role in the project. When I'm leading a project I've done before and all goes

---

1. Kolko, Jonathan. 2011. *Thoughts on Interaction Design* (Morgan Kaufmann), p. 34.

well, a simple retrospective can take as little as a half hour with a coffee and my journal; if I'm part of a larger team, or if the project hits some bumps in the road I wasn't anticipating, it can take much longer. The process you use is up to you, but the goals are often the same:

- Identify what was involved in the project that made it unique.
- Identify any factors that worked particularly well. This could be the client, your style of communication, a new kind of documentation—anything that contributed to the project's success.
- Identify any factors that made the project harder than it needed to be. I tend to spend the most time on this. When I reflect on a project, I want to know what I can improve on, what skills I need to improve, and so on.
- Document the things that will be particularly useful for later projects. This may be code, or it may be a way of dealing with clients; whatever it is, make sure you have it set aside somewhere where you can find it again.

The key to doing a successful retrospective is to find a process that works for you. Sometimes long-form prose works, such as a blog entry or journaling. Sometimes, if I'm stuck, I'll use a mind map to get all my thoughts onto the page before I commit anything to prose. (For more on mind maps, check out Chapter 3.)

Including Clients in the Retrospective

The choice of whether to include clients in your post-project reflections is up to you. Asking clients for feedback, especially if the project didn't go as well as you had hoped, can be hard. Nobody likes to hear they were harsher than they needed to be in a particular conversation, or that their design solutions weren't especially good.

Regardless of whether you allow clients to take part in the retrospective process, getting feedback from them is an essential part of the growth process, and it can also provide useful information for future projects. Designer Todd Nienkerk of Four Kitchens says, "We frame the conversation by saying that we won't take anything personally and by leading off with some thoughtful self-criticism to get the conversation started. As you say, it can sting, but it's important to learn what needs attention and growth."

There are several ways to include client feedback in your post-project reflection. The easiest way is through simple surveys; whether you do them through an online service such as Survey Monkey or through a simple thank-you note with a questionnaire, asking the right questions can result in some very valuable feedback. While surveys can be valuable, I often find that a simple conversation, over the phone or over coffee, works best. First, the client will be more likely to actually give you feedback (often a challenge with other means of communication); second, it gives you a valuable chance to deepen your relationship with the client and to find out if there are additional projects in the pipeline for which you can create a pitch.

Documenting What You Learned

An important benefit of the project retrospective is being able to document what you've learned. This could be a new way of collaborating with clients, a new productivity tool, or a new module you can't wait to share your glee about. How you set up this documentation is, again, up to you, but the best documentation has the following qualities:

- It's searchable (so that you can find notes when you need them).
- It's shareable (so that when you're chatting with another Drupal buddy who's dealing with a problem you've had before, you can send him or her a link to it).
- It has the option of being private. Let's face it: if a project really sucked, the last thing you want to do is blog about it publicly. But there's knowledge to be gained from it regardless, and you want to be able to document what you've learned so that you can remember it next time.

Every team has their own way of collecting documentation. Some will make their own wikis in Drupal, or use OpenAtrium,[2] a Drupal-based project intranet created by Washington, DC-based Drupal shop Development Seed. Others will collect documentation in a personal blog, built in Drupal or WordPress.

Evernote[3] is a free cross-platform application that allows you to easily collect, tag, and share notes via email and it syncs your notes over the Internet without forcing you to be online in order to create or edit your notes. You can also organize your content into distinct notebooks (see Figure 22-1), which is incredibly useful when you want to separate, for example, theming notes from modules you want to check out. And it's available for iPad, iPhone, and Android, so collecting notes is super-easy if you don't always have your computer on you.

Code snippets are also handy to collect. You can also save these in Evernote, publish them as blog posts, or, if you're using Coda,[4] my favorite site editor for Mac, save snippets directly in the program's Clips library (see Figure 22-2) and double-click on them to add them to your file as you're coding. This is especially useful for common Drupal theme hooks, or for commonly used CSS, JavaScript, or HTML snippets.

2. *http://openatrium.com*

3. *http://evernote.com*

4. *http://panic.com/coda*

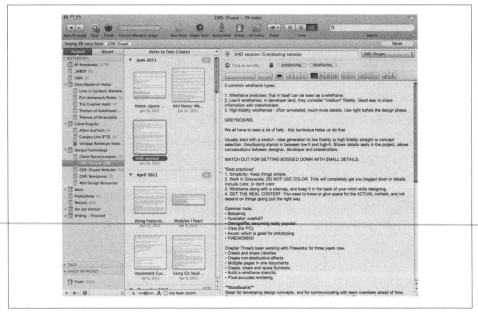

Figure 22-1. Evernote lets you collect and organize notes in topic-specific notebooks. I keep my Drupal notes in two notebooks: one for more general Drupal knowledge, and another for specific modules.

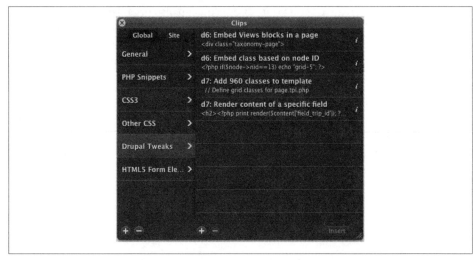

Figure 22-2. Coda's Clips library allows you to save and organize code snippets that you can easily add to your site's theme files. This is extremely useful once you start learning how to mess with theme hooks and .tpl files.

Documenting for the Community

Dries Buytaert, creator of Drupal, has been quoted many times as saying that the Drupal community needs designers. But what the community also needs is more people to help document Drupal modules, best practices, and other things that can help Drupal newbies not cry their way through their first several Drupal projects. While many development teams have made a habit of blogging their Drupal knowledge, too many contributed modules on Drupal.org (*http://drupal.org*) have woefully inadequate documentation, which makes it harder for folks new to Drupal who aren't hardcore programmers to access the brilliance of these modules. If, at the end of a project, you find yourself with knowledge of a particular module that isn't being shared, consider contributing documentation on Drupal.org (*http://drupal.org*), or on your own blog. The community will love you for it.

PART VII

Sample Documents

Project Brief

This brief borrows heavily from Happy Cog's project planner (*http://www.happycog.com/*), with a bent towards both branding and Drupal projects. I made this available as a download from the zen kitchen's website; clients would download it in Word, fill it out and send it back to us before we got back to them with a proposal. This can be very handy for getting a head start on the discovery process.

Hey There! It's Nice to Meet You.

This handy worksheet is designed to help us get a feel for your organization's background, goals, and design needs, and to help make sure that everyone is on the same page so that we can create the most accurate proposal possible for your project. The information in this document is also an important part of the zen kitchen's proven design process—your answers here serve an important role in clarifying direction, messaging and audience up front. This makes it easier for us to produce award-winning strategic design for our clients.

When you're finished, save the document as *{organization name}*_planner.doc (replacing *{organization name}* with the name of your particular organization), and email the document to *email@site.com*. Please allow up to 1 week for a response. In a hurry? Just let us know and we'll let you know if we can help you sooner.

While this project planner includes information that will help us for identity, print and web projects, it also includes some information that is specific to certain types of projects. Feel free to leave out any information that doesn't apply to your project; however, the background information, look and feel, and other supporting information is something that we need for all types of projects.

Who are you?

Your name:
First and last name.

Your title:
Answer here.

Organization name:
Answer here.

Where is your office located? *(not necessarily where your organization is, where you are):*
Answer here.

Email address and URL *(if you have one):*
Enter email address here.

Enter URL here.

Business phone including area and/or country code:
Phone number here.

So, how did you hear about us?
Answer here.

Responding to inquiries generally takes up to a week. If you need us to move more quickly than that, please indicate below:
[ ] I'm in a rush and I need a Proposal/Statement of Work from you as soon as possible

About your project

Tell us about your project. What components will be involved? *Check (√) all that apply.*

[ ] Logo/Identity Design
[ ] Business cards, stationery, etc.
[ ] Brochure, postcards, sales or tradeshow materials
[ ] Design for events
[ ] Annual or Corporate Citizenship/Responsibility/Sustainability Report
[ ] Website Design
[ ] Email marketing
[ ] Print advertising

Have you ever worked with a designer or design firm before? What was that experience like? What type of project? What worked? What didn't?
Answer here.

Background

Tell us in a few words about your organization. What do you produce? Why does your customer need it?
Answer here.

How many people does your organization employ? Who besides you (if applicable) will be decision-makers on this project?
Answer here.

Goals and Objectives

What is your organization looking to achieve with strategic design? *(i.e., increased visibility? More sales? Build customer loyalty? General image upgrade? Other?) Please be specific and try to stick with one major goal with 1–2 secondary goals.*
Answer here.

How will you define success for this project?
Answer here.

Target Audience

List some key facts about your intended market or user. Include both demographic data *(age, income, education, etc.)* ***and psychographics*** *(What magazines do they read? What websites do they visit frequently? What are their values and attitudes?).*
Answer here.

Does your target audience already know about your product or service? If so, how do they feel about it? How would you like to change that perception *(if at all)?*
Answer here.

What motivates them to use your product or service?
Answer here.

For websites: Whom do you consider the primary and secondary users of your site? What are they there for? What information do you want to give them?
Answer here.

Competition

Whom do you consider your peers and competitors? How do they present themselves? *Give us their URLs if you have them.*
Answer here.

What are the key benefits/advantages to going with you instead of your competitors?
Answer here.

How about your competitors? Do consumers perceive any advantages to going with them? (It's okay to be honest here. Part of good design is knowing what your competitors do well so we can differentiate from them.)
Answer here.

Brand Attributes

Describe briefly, in as few words as possible, the type of feelings that you want to evoke in the audience with your brand and/or web presence, and the brand attributes that you want to convey. *(Example feelings may include: warmth, reassurance, excitement, empowerment. Example brand attributes: honesty, integrity, trustworthiness.)*
Answer here.

Using adjectives and short phrases, tell us about the look and feel you're going for. *(Examples: edgy, modern, clean, organic, traditional, classic, user-friendly. Try to avoid terms like "web 2.0" and "cutting edge.")*
Answer here.

In terms of look and feel, are there any sites or design projects you've seen that you feel convey the type of image you're going for? *Share a few of them and tell us why they appeal to you.*
Answer here.

Functionality and Technical Requirements

For all projects

Are there any current brand standards that we should be aware of adhering to: fonts, colors, etc.? If not, would you like to talk about having us develop them for you?
Answer here.

How much of the copy do you have completed for this project?
[ ] All of it
[ ] Some of it
[ ] We'd like to hire you to create it

For print projects

How will you be handling distribution of design? *(Are brochures mailed or handed out? Will ads run on a specific schedule?)*
Answer here.

Do you have a printer currently, or do you want us to handle it for you? (Note: design estimates do not include printing costs, which will be handled separately by the client. Also, as a sustainable design firm, the zen kitchen promotes and works exclusively with companies that utilize sustainably minded printing methods.)
Answer here.

For web projects

Is your current site powered by a content management system (CMS) or publishing platform? How are updates generally handled?
Answer here.

If "yes," which platform are you using?
Answer here.

What do you like/dislike about it?
Answer here.

Does your site plan involve support for community features, social media, RSS feeds, profiles, commenting, blogs, forums, sharing, user generated content, etc? Give us a brief rundown of what you'd like to see.
Answer here.

Does your plan include hosting video, audio, or other media-intensive components? This could involve podcasting, photo sharing, etc.
Answer here.

Does your plan include selling products, event management, or other features that would require a user to give you money through the site?
Answer here.

About how many pages do you estimate your site will have? What might the top-level navigation look like (main sections, secondary sections, etc.)?
Answer here.

Would you prefer to do this project in a single pass or split it up into phases (each requiring its own budget)?
Answer here.

If splitting up into phases, please tell us the general breakdown of each phase that you have in mind.
Answer here.

Anything else we should know?
Answer here.

To deliver the best experience to the most users and to build pages that will last, we use modern standards-based methods. As a result, our sites may not look exactly the same in an old, noncompliant browser like Internet Explorer 6 as they do in newer browsers like Firefox, Safari, and Internet Explorer 7 and 8. Designing your site to work in older, noncompliant browsers will add significant development time and cost to the project budget, and some modern technologies that aren't supported by the browser may have to be removed from the project scope.

[ ] My site has to look and work exactly the same way in older as it does in newer browsers.

[ ] I understand that the site may not look as good or work as well in outdated browsers.

Time and Money

If you're working within a time frame, or have been given a mandatory launch date, list it here. If the project will launch in phases, list proposed milestones and dates.
Answer here.

Please tell us your budget for this project. (Note: sharing a realistic assessment of what you have to spend on this effort will help us scope our engagement appropriately. While disclosing your budget might not be something you typically do, sharing this information with us now will greatly reduce the likelihood of both sides spending significant time and resources "shooting in the dark.")
Answer here.

Thanks Again!

We very much appreciate you taking the time to fill out our project planner. We realize it's a lot to ask up front, but it's a huge help when it comes time to put together numbers that accurately reflect the work involved in your unique project.

When you're finished, save the document as *{organization name}*_planner.doc (replacing *{organization name}* with the name of your particular organization), and email the document to *email@site.com*. Please allow up to 1 week for a response. In a hurry? Just let us know and we'll let you know if we can help you sooner.

THIS INFORMATION IS USED TO DEVELOP AND IMPLEMENT PROCEDURES IN CREATING THE PROJECT REQUESTED. BY SIGNING THIS AGREEMENT, YOU AGREE ALL INFORMATION SUBMITTED IS CORRECT.

Name (print)
Approval Signature
Date
Designer Approval

Work Agreement (with Professional Relationship Clause)

NOTE: The terms of this standard Work Agreement were crafted by Jessica Manganello, founding attorney at New Leaf Legal (*http://newleaflegal.com*). They're available for you to adapt under the Creative Commons license; however, if you need a great legal team to help you work out your own contract terms, I highly suggest giving the team at New Leaf a call sometime.

Work Agreement

Description	Amount
Brand and Messaging Strategy, including:	*$XXX*
One half-day kickoff meeting to brainstorm audience profiles, needs and perceptions, key messages, and platforms	
Brand immersion and research	
Compilation of research findings and recommendations into a comprehensive findings analysis and preliminary messaging report	
Refinement of findings and positioning into comprehensive brand position and key messaging report	
Project Management and client communication (including up to 2 follow-up meetings)	
Design of Drupal website, including:	*$XXX*
Wireframes, user flows, and site maps to flesh out user experience priorities	
Creation of site look and feel, including 3 rounds of revisions and 1 complete change of direction (if needed)	
Project Management and client communication	
Configuration of Drupal website, including:	*$XXX*
Installation and configuration of Drupal CMS	
Establishment of user roles and permissions, including content editors and administrators	

Description	Amount
Project Management and client communication	
Theming of Drupal website, including:	*$XXX*
Application of site look and feel across all site page templates	
Creation of up to 5 unique page templates	
Estimate Total	*$XXXXX*

Terms and Conditions

This work agreement is based on the specifications listed in the above Project Scope. If, upon receipt of all materials to be supplied by client, the project is determined to differ significantly from the original specifications, the client will be notified promptly and an updated estimate will be produced. This estimate does not include expenses and reimbursements aside from those listed in the Estimated Costs and Project Scope. If such expenses arise, the client will be informed prior to expenditures made and a separate invoice will be submitted for reimbursement.

Payment Notes

Payment will be made in 5 installments monthly starting upon project sign-off. The first installment of *$XXXX* is due before project starts; 4 installments of *$XXXX* each will be due on the fifth of each month starting one month after project kickoff.

All estimates are valid for 30 days from the date of estimate.

A finance charge of 5% per month will be applied to overdue balances. A charge of $25 per item will be charged for checks returned by the bank.

Professional Relationship

In order to provide a rewarding working experience for both Client and Designer, Designer seeks to maintain a professional relationship with the Client. Designer and Client agree to:

- Promptly meet deadlines for producing material, payments, and/or work product and communicate clearly if those deadlines cannot be met with alternative timelines for delivery.
- Promptly review and reply to communications from parties involved in this project.

Deliverables Timeframe

- Milestones and dates/times will be determined in initial project meeting once contract is approved and deposit is received. Once project starts, a detailed action plan will be submitted to client and we will establish deadlines for delivery on content one piece at a time.

- Failure of client to provide the required materials within the established deadlines will result in a delay of all deliverable deadlines. This delay will be equal to the number of days late the materials were received by the Designer, unless otherwise specified in writing, via email, by Designer.

Additional Terms

Rejection/Cancellation of Project

The client shall not unreasonably withhold acceptance of, or payment for, the project. If, prior to completion of the project, the client observes any nonconformance with the design plan, the Designer must be promptly notified, allowing for necessary corrections. Cancellation or Rejection by Client must be made upon 10 days written notice to Designer. Rejection of the completed project or cancellation during its execution will result in forfeiture of the deposit and billing for all additional labor or expenses incurred prior to the date of cancellation, at the standard rate of $*XXX* per hour.

All elements created by the Designer for the project must then be returned to the Designer within 30 days of cancellation. All materials supplied by the Client will be returned in their original condition within 30 days of cancellation. Any usage by the Client of design elements created by the Designer after cancellation of the project will result in appropriate legal action. Client shall bear all costs, expenses, and reasonable attorney's fees in any action brought to recover payment, enforce the terms and/or protect Designer's Intellectual Property under this contract.

Designer reserves the right to cancel this contract at any time upon 10 days written notice for any reason, including but not limited to: Client's failure to provide materials or payment within 30 days of the agreed upon deadlines or failure of Client to comply with the terms of this agreement including the terms of the Professional Relationship clause. Upon Designer's cancellation of the contract, Designer will return all unused funds and deposits to the Client and return all materials to the Client within 30 days of cancellation.

Modifications

Modification of the Agreement must be written, except that the invoice may include, and the Client shall pay, any fees or expenses that were orally authorized by the Client in order to progress promptly with the work. Oral agreements and other communications will be confirmed in writing, including electronically, and thereby incorporated into this agreement.

Ownership of Artwork

The Designer retains ownership of all original artwork, whether preliminary or final. No use of same shall be made, nor any ideas obtained therefrom used, except upon compensation to be determined by the Designer. The Client shall return such artwork within 30 days of use. In the case of logo work, the Client shall retain ownership of artwork once the invoice has been paid in full and can use said logo in all of their materials, including materials created by other designers. Said artwork, however, may not be modified for any use without the express consent of the Designer.

The Designer retains the right to use the completed project and any preliminary designs for the purpose of design competitions, future publications on design, educational purposes, and marketing materials. Where applicable the Client will be given any necessary credit for usage of the project elements.

Reproduction of Work

The Client assumes full reproduction rights upon payment for completed project. The work may be reproduced as is by the Client at any given time. Any revisions to the work prior to reproduction must be negotiated between the Designer and the Client.

Author's Alterations (AA's)

AA's represent work performed in addition to the original concept and specifications. Such work includes, but is not limited to: inclusion of material in project in addition to material originally discussed; additional design concepts or revisions of project beyond the number allotted in the Project Scope section of this contract; significant color/paper/quantity changes beyond what was originally discussed.

Such additional work shall be charged at a rate of $*XXX* per hour plus any additional expenses incurred by the extra work (including rush shipping and/or printing charges), and will be supported with documentation upon request.

No additional payment shall be made for minor changes required to conform to the original assignment description as noted in the creative brief, including spelling and grammatical errors.

The terms of this paragraph do not apply to the agreed upon alterations, modifications, or edits listed in the Deliverables Timeframe.

The Designer shall not be held responsible for delays in production caused by Author's Alterations.

Proofs

Proofs will be sent to Client via emailed PDF unless otherwise noted in the Project Scope section of this contract. Client will be responsible for carefully reviewing said proofs and offering feedback in a timely and constructive manner. Delays in receipt of appropriate feedback by Client will result in delay of project deliverables. A reasonable variation in color between color proofs and the completed job shall constitute acceptable delivery. The Designer cannot be held responsible for errors under any or all of the following conditions: if the Client has failed to return proofs with indication of changes; if the Client has failed to approve proofs in writing via email or signed Approval Form; if the Client has instructed the Designer to proceed without submission of proofs.

Completion/Delivery of Project

The estimated completion date of the project is to be determined. Any shipping or insurance costs will be assumed by the Client. Any alteration or deviation from the above specifications involving extra costs will be executed only upon approval with the Client. Any delay in the completion of the project due to failure of client to meet the deadlines set forth in this contract for receipt of materials to begin work on the project, proof revisions/approvals, etc., will delay the completion/delivery date. The Client will allow a reasonable time for printing and shipping of final project (generally 2–3 weeks). The Client will be responsible for any "rush charges" assessed by the printer and/or shipping company due to failure of client to meet the deadlines set forth in this contract for receipt of materials, proof revisions/approvals, etc.

In addition, unusual transportation delays, unforeseen illness, or external forces beyond the control of the Designer, shall entitle the Designer to extend the completion/delivery date, upon notifying the Client, by the time equivalent to the period of such delay.

Releases

The Client shall indemnify the Designer against all claims and expenses, including reasonable attorney's fees, due to uses of design or artwork, for which no release was requested in writing or for uses that exceed authority granted by a release. The Client further indemnifies the Designer against any liability, claims, or rights of any third party arising out of this contract, including reasonable attorney's fees and expenses. Client is liable for any costs, including attorney's fees, incurred by Designer in enforcing this agreement and any of its terms.

Any revisions to the work prior to reproduction must be negotiated between the Designer and the Client.

Limitation of Liability

The Client agrees that it shall not hold the Designer or his/her agents or employees liable for any incidental or consequential damages that may arise from the Designer's failure to perform any aspect of the Project in a timely manner, regardless of whether such failure was caused by intentional or negligent acts or omissions of the Designer or a third party.

Warranty of Originality

The Designer warrants and represents that, to the best of his/her knowledge, the work assigned hereunder is original and has not been previously published; that consent to use has been obtained on an unlimited basis; the undersigned from third parties is original or, if previously published, that consent to use has been obtained on an unlimited basis; that the Designer has full authority to make this agreement; and that the work prepared by the Designer does not contain any scandalous, libelous, or unlawful matter.

This warranty does not extend to any uses that the Client or others may make of the Designer's product that may infringe on the rights of others. Client expressly agrees that it will hold the Designer harmless for all liability caused by the Client's use of the Designer's product to the extent that such use may infringe on the rights of others.

Project Proposal

NOTE: The format of this proposal was inspired by Chicago design firm Rogue Element, whose founder Alison Manley is a colleague and friend. It's been adapted several times to fit individual project plans, but the basic format is the same.

Project Proposal

to: Client Name
Client Address
Client Phone Number
for: Project Name
1.0 Project Background & Objectives
2.0 Statement of Work
3.0 Development Process
4.0 Budget Estimate
5.0 Background & Capabilities
6.0 Terms and Conditions

Section 1.0: Project Background and Objectives

The Consulting Firm is the next evolution of a former partnership as a solo endeavor. In this evolution, The Consulting Firm's founder is getting back to what she does well—providing education, consulting, and guidance to technology companies in staying compliant with evolving environmental policy. For this, she needs:

- A comprehensive brand platform and core messaging strategy that will guide the brand's communication efforts;

- A social media and blogging strategy that will position the Founder more effectively as a thought leader in the field of environmental compliance for technology, without taking up her entire schedule;

- A website and identity that will help facilitate the Founder's thought leadership efforts, and lead her audience to the brand.

Objective 1: Build upon the history of the Founder's experience with her prior firms to effectively position The Consulting Firm as a leader in environmental compliance information and consulting for technology products.

Effective positioning requires a deep understanding of both your brand's target prospects, and an understanding of the landscape that the prospect is dealing with. We will work with the Founder to get a clear picture of the competitive landscape, and establish the right positioning for the brand.

Objective 2: Create a blogging and social media engagement strategy that allows the Founder to more firmly establish thought leadership in the field.

We will work with the Founder to create a content strategy that will allow her to showcase her considerable knowledge in this space, without "giving the cow away" for free. We'll also work with her to set up strategies and tools to manage her online presence without requiring a full-time investment.

Objective 3: Create a website that will serve as a marketing vehicle for The Consulting Firm, and integrate the Founder's content leadership efforts.

Using the flexibility of the Drupal content management system, we will create a dynamic website that will allow the Founder to keep content fresh and updated as the business evolves.

Section 2.0: Statement of Work

Brand Messaging and Positioning Strategy

- All deliverables as outlined in the Project Development Process (section 3.0);
- Up to 12 hours of collaboration via Skype and in-person meetings to clarify and confirm goals, messaging, and brand direction;
- Research and development of brand platform (proposed positioning statement, audience, and competitive analysis), and core messaging, using the process outlined in the Project Development Process.

Blogging, Social Media, and Content Strategy

- All deliverables as outlined in the Project Development Process (section 3.0);
- Up to 12 hours of collaboration via Skype and in-person meetings to clarify and confirm goals, messaging, and direction;
- Research and development of social media strategy (blog platform, areas of focus, content guidelines);
- Assistance with setting up profiles and third-party integrations.

Logo and Website Development

- Setup and delivery of logo, brand guidelines, and Drupal website.

Client Responsibilities

To move the project forward efficiently, you will be expected to provide the following:

- Timely delivery of focused feedback, content, and edits according to the production schedule;
- Access to preliminary research and competitor materials;
- Participation in face-to-face meetings at key milestones during the project, including the project kickoff meeting and brainstorming sessions.

Section 3.0: Development Process

At the zen kitchen, we believe that the best design results from active and open collaboration between creatives and clients. Our proven, research-driven process helps us consistently create effective, award-winning design that works hard for your business.

Phase I: Strategy, Goal-Setting, Requirements and Research

All of our projects begin by working with you to drill down to the core of your messaging, audience, and goals. During this first phase, we will refine our understanding of your business, your target audience, and the competition. It is also our objective to clearly identify the project's goals, and define what success will look like. Finally, we will further define the functional, technical, and informational requirements for your project, which will enable us to design the right solution for your needs before getting into the actual web development. The deliverables for this stage will include:

- A finalized design brief describing our understanding of the project's goals, functional requirements, and audience;
- A detailed schedule to guide the process, provided through our project management system.

Phase II: Creative Exploration and Design Development

Through creative thinking, collaborative discourse, and a healthy dose of intuition, we develop ideas to visually express your core message. Every choice, from layout and color to type size and style, is made with your communication goals in mind. The best ideas are further refined into initial concepts, which we will present to you. From there, we discuss and refine to turn these concepts into comprehensive design directions. The deliverables for this stage will include:

- Three to four strategic design concepts for evaluation;
- Refinement of your chosen design direction.

Phase III: Implementation and Testing

Once the design direction is approved, it's time to implement. At this phase we push pixels, lay out pages, configure, code, and collaborate to make sure that each element we produce aligns with your communication goals. During this phase, we also work with you to create and/or gather needed text and images, and incorporate them into the production flow.

We proof and refine the design, test, debug, proof again, and prepare for final production or launch. For all of our websites, we perform cross-browser checking on IE7 (and above), Firefox for PC and Mac, and Safari to ensure that the design works perfectly cross-browser. We work closely with all vendors—print, web, or otherwise—to ensure that your finished product meets our (and your) standards of excellence.

The deliverables for this stage will include:

- Production management and delivery of the finished project;
- Documentation and training as needed for brand guidelines, updating web content, etc.

Phase VI: Measure and Refine

Our work isn't done after the project delivers. We want to know how it's working. We work with you to gather feedback and evaluate not only how the process went, but also what the response has been from the target audiences. At this point, we'll also work together to identify areas of the project that can be refined for future iterations, and develop a plan for the next phase of production.

Section 4.0: Budget Estimate

The following is a proposed budget based on the scope of the project as outlined in this proposal. All fees are our best estimates based on our conversations about the project, and may change as the project moves forward.

The zen kitchen will regularly provide detailed invoices and status updates about project budget, milestones, etc. via our project management system.

Description of Work	Estimated Fees
Brand and Messaging Strategy, including:	$XXX
One half-day kickoff meeting to brainstorm audience profiles, needs and perceptions, key messages, and platforms	
Brand immersion and research	
Compilation of research findings and recommendations into a comprehensive findings analysis and preliminary messaging report	
Refinement of findings and positioning into comprehensive brand position and key messaging report	
Project Management and client communication (including up to 2 follow-up meetings)	
Design of Drupal website, including:	$XXX
Wireframes, user flows, and site maps to flesh out user experience priorities	
Creation of site look and feel, including 3 rounds of revisions and 1 complete change of direction (if needed)	
Project Management and client communication	
Configuration of Drupal website, including:	$XXX
Installation and configuration of Drupal CMS	
Establishment of user roles and permissions, including content editors and administrators	
Project Management and client communication	
Theming of Drupal website, including:	$XXX
Application of site look and feel across all site page templates	
Creation of up to 5 unique page templates, e.g., custom homepage templates or interior section templates	
Estimate Total: $XXXXX	

Section 5.0: The Zen Kitchen Background and Capabilities

Section 5.1: Who Is the Zen Kitchen?

The zen kitchen combines creative problem-solving with solid business sense and a passion for sustainability, to create beautiful, elegant, and powerful marketing communications for our clients. The zen kitchen is a small strategic design studio with big project experience that combines a passion for sustainable design and a holistic approach to creativity with clients who make a difference. We work with you closely to uncover the truth behind your unique story and communicate it clearly, elegantly, and effectively to the people you need to hear it.

Section 5.2: What Can the Zen Kitchen Do for You?

The zen kitchen has strong experience in creative project management and maintains a strong, nimble network of writers, photographers, programmers, illustrators, printers, and fabricators to help you scale up to any size project without the costly overhead of larger agencies. From concept to execution, we can give you everything you need—and nothing you don't. Our capabilities include:

- Identity and brand standards systems design;
- Website design, including WordPress and Drupal development;
- Print collateral design including: annual reports, restaurant menus, brochures, corporate communications, sustainability reports, and capital campaigns;
- Packaging design for food and personal care;
- Environmental graphics and display design.

Section 5.3: Why Choose the Zen Kitchen?

We like to think our approach to marketing and design is simple: just ask questions. But beyond that, we think it's important to ask the right questions, and listen carefully for the answers. Anyone can figure out who your target audience is. Figuring out what's relevant to them, and shaping your messaging to fit that relevance without coming across as inauthentic or cheesy—or worse, being accused of greenwashing? That's what we do best. When you work with the zen kitchen, you get:

Intuitive chefs who help you make the most of what you've got. An intuitive chef never obsesses over a recipe. She knows the ingredients so well she can taste the combinations in her mouth, creating something spectacular with whatever's on hand. We do that for your brand. First, we help you understand what your audience really wants, and then we use fonts, logos, colors, and content to create an experience that matches what you give your customers.

Friendly straight-shooters who get things done—and done right. It's impossible for us to settle for anything less than delightful. And we won't let our clients settle, either. Hidden beneath this friendly, approachable exterior is a relentless commitment to your customers. Yes, we're pushy. But don't worry—we know you'll thank us later.

Section 6.0: Terms and Conditions

This work agreement is based on the specifications listed in the above Project Scope. If, upon receipt of all materials to be supplied by client, the project is determined to differ significantly from the original specifications, the client will be notified promptly and an updated estimate will be produced. This estimate does not include expenses and reimbursements aside from those listed in the Estimated Costs and Project Scope.

If such expenses arise, the client will be informed prior to expenditures made and a separate invoice will be submitted for reimbursement.

Payment Notes

Payment will be made in 5 installments monthly starting upon project sign-off. The first installment of $*XXXX* is due before project starts; 4 installments of $*XXXX* each will be due on the fifth of each month starting one month after project kickoff.

All estimates are valid for 30 days from the date of estimate.

Payment Notes

A finance charge of 5% per month will be applied to overdue balances. A charge of $25 per item will be charged for checks returned by the bank.

Professional Relationship

In order to provide a rewarding working experience for both Client and Designer, Designer seeks to maintain a professional relationship with the Client. Designer and Client agree to:

- Promptly meet deadlines for producing material, payments, and/or work product and communicate clearly if those deadlines cannot be met with alternative timelines for delivery.
- Promptly review and reply to communications from parties involved in this project.

Deliverables Timeframe

- Milestones and dates/times will be determined in initial project meeting once contract is approved and deposit is received. Once project starts, a detailed action plan will be submitted to client and we will establish deadlines for delivery on content one piece at a time.
- Failure of client to provide the required materials within the established deadlines will result in a delay of all deliverable deadlines. This delay will be equal to the number of days late the materials were received by the Designer, unless otherwise specified in writing, via email, by Designer.

Additional Terms

Rejection/cancellation of project

The client shall not unreasonably withhold acceptance of, or payment for, the project. If, prior to completion of the project, the client observes any nonconformance with the design plan, the Designer must be promptly notified, allowing for necessary corrections. Cancellation or Rejection by Client must be made upon 10 days written notice to Designer. Rejection of the completed project or cancellation during its execution will result in forfeiture of the deposit and billing for all additional labor or expenses incurred prior to the date of cancellation, at the standard rate of $*XXX* per hour.

All elements created by the Designer for the project must then be returned to the Designer within 30 days of cancellation. All materials supplied by the Client will be returned in their original condition within 30 days of cancellation. Any usage by the Client of design elements created by the Designer after cancellation of the project will result in appropriate legal action. Client shall bear all costs, expenses, and reasonable attorney's fees in any action brought to recover payment, enforce the terms and/or protect Designer's Intellectual Property under this contract.

Designer reserves the right to cancel this contract at any time upon 10 days written notice for any reason, including but not limited to: Client's failure to provide materials or payment within 30 days of the agreed upon deadlines or failure of Client to comply with the terms of this agreement including the terms of the Professional Relationship clause. Upon Designer's cancellation of the contract, Designer will return all unused funds and deposits to the Client and return all materials to the Client within 30 days of cancellation.

Modifications

Modification of the Agreement must be written, except that the invoice may include, and the Client shall pay, any fees or expenses that were orally authorized by the Client in order to progress promptly with the work. Oral agreements and other communications will be confirmed in writing, including electronically, and thereby incorporated into this agreement.

Ownership of artwork

The Designer retains ownership of all original artwork, whether preliminary or final. No use of same shall be made, nor any ideas obtained therefrom used, except upon compensation to be determined by the Designer. The client shall return such artwork within 30 days of use. In the case of logo work, the client shall retain ownership of artwork once the invoice has been paid in full and can use said logo in all of their materials, including materials created by other designers. Said artwork, however, may not be modified for any use without the express consent of the Designer.

The Designer retains the right to use the completed project and any preliminary designs for the purpose of design competitions, future publications on design, educational purposes, and marketing materials. Where applicable, the client will be given any necessary credit for usage of the project elements.

Reproduction of work

The client assumes full reproduction rights upon payment for completed project. The work may be reproduced as is by the client at any given time. Any revisions to the work prior to reproduction must be negotiated between the Designer and the client.

Author's alterations (AA's)

AA's represent work performed in addition to the original concept and specifications. Such work includes, but is not limited to: inclusion of material in project in addition to material originally discussed; additional design concepts or revisions of project beyond the number allotted in the Project Scope section of this contract; significant color/paper/quantity changes beyond what was originally discussed.

Such additional work shall be charged at a rate of $*XXX* per hour plus any additional expenses incurred by the extra work (including rush shipping and/or printing charges), and will be supported with documentation upon request.

No additional payment shall be made for minor changes required to conform to the original assignment description as noted in the creative brief, including spelling and grammatical errors.

The terms of this paragraph do not apply to the agreed upon alterations, modifications, or edits listed in the Deliverables Timeframe.

The Designer shall not be held responsible for delays in production caused by Author's Alterations.

Proofs

Proofs will be sent to Client via emailed PDF unless otherwise noted in the Project Scope section of this contract. Client will be responsible for carefully reviewing said proofs and offering feedback in a timely and constructive manner. Delays in receipt of appropriate feedback by Client will result in delay of project deliverables. A reasonable variation in color between color proofs and the completed job shall constitute acceptable delivery. The Designer cannot be held responsible for errors under any or all of the following conditions: if the Client has failed to return proofs with indication of changes; if the Client has failed to approve proofs in writing via email or signed Approval Form; if the Client has instructed the Designer to proceed without submission of proofs.

Completion/delivery of project

The estimated completion date of the project is to be determined. Any shipping or insurance costs will be assumed by the client. Any alteration or deviation from the above specifications involving extra costs will be executed only upon approval with the client. Any delay in the completion of the project due to failure of client to meet the deadlines set forth in this contract for receipt of materials to begin work on the project, proof revisions/approvals, etc., will delay the completion/delivery date. The Client will allow a reasonable time for printing and shipping of final project (generally 2–3 weeks). The Client will be responsible for any "rush charges" assessed by the printer and/or shipping company due to failure of client to meet the deadlines set forth in this contract for receipt of materials, proof revisions/approvals, etc.

In addition, unusual transportation delays, unforeseen illness, or external forces beyond the control of the Designer, shall entitle the Designer to extend the completion/delivery date, upon notifying the client, by the time equivalent to the period of such delay.

Releases

The Client shall indemnify the Designer against all claims and expenses, including reasonable attorney's fees, due to uses of design or artwork, for which no release was requested in writing or for uses that exceed authority granted by a release. The Client further indemnifies the Designer against any liability, claims, or rights of any third party arising out of this contract, including reasonable attorney's fees and expenses. Client is liable for any costs, including attorney's fees, incurred by Designer in enforcing this agreement and any of its terms.

Any revisions to the work prior to reproduction must be negotiated between the Designer and the client.

Limitation of liability

The Client agrees that it shall not hold the Designer or his/her agents or employees liable for any incidental or consequential damages that may arise from the Designer's failure to perform any aspect of the Project in a timely manner, regardless of whether such failure was caused by intentional or negligent acts or omissions of the Designer or a third party.

Warranty of originality

The Designer warrants and represents that, to the best of his/her knowledge, the work assigned hereunder is original and has not been previously published; that consent to use has been obtained on an unlimited basis; the undersigned from third parties is original or, if previously published, that consent to use has been obtained on an unlimited basis; that the Designer has full authority to make this agreement; and that the work prepared by the Designer does not contain any scandalous, libelous, or unlawful matter.

This warranty does not extend to any uses that the Client or others may make of the Designer's product that may infringe on the rights of others. Client expressly agrees that it will hold the Designer harmless for all liability caused by the Client's use of the Designer's product to the extent that such use may infringe on the rights of others.

Index

We'd like to hear your suggestions for improving our indexes. Send email to *index@oreilly.com*.

About the Author

Dani Nordin is the founder of the zen kitchen, an independent user experience design and research practice focused on helping forward-thinking organizations and development shops create great things in Drupal. Her background runs the gamut from print design and branding to layout, site planning, and user experience for the web. She has been an active member of Boston's Drupal community since 2008.

Colophon

The animal on the cover of *Drupal for Designers* is a butterfly blenny (*blennius ocellaris*). It is a small fish, only growing to approximately 8 inches in length. The butterfly blenny is characterized by a long, comb-shaped dorsal fin and tentacles around its nasal area.

The *Blenniidae* family is quite numerous and recognized by a long, tapering body and dorsal fin. However, blennies vary widely in appearance, behavior, and eating habits.

Butterfly blennies are nocturnal fish. They inhabit shallow water from Morocco to the English Channel, feeding on small invertebrates and mollusks. Blennies make their homes among seaweed and large rocks, often using castoff shells as homes and as places to keep their eggs safe. Sometimes, they have even been known to inhabit old cans. Blennies are protective of their eggs: the male watches over them constantly and refuses to leave them until they hatch.

The cover image is an original engraving, loose plate. The cover font is Adobe ITC Garamond. The text font is Linotype Birka; the heading font is Adobe Myriad Condensed; and the code font is LucasFont's TheSansMonoCondensed.

Get even more for your money.

Join the O'Reilly Community, and register the O'Reilly books you own. It's free, and you'll get:

- $4.99 ebook upgrade offer
- 40% upgrade offer on O'Reilly print books
- Membership discounts on books and events
- Free lifetime updates to ebooks and videos
- Multiple ebook formats, DRM FREE
- Participation in the O'Reilly community
- Newsletters
- Account management
- 100% Satisfaction Guarantee

Signing up is easy:

1. **Go to: oreilly.com/go/register**
2. **Create an O'Reilly login.**
3. **Provide your address.**
4. **Register your books.**

Note: English-language books only

To order books online:
oreilly.com/store

For questions about products or an order:
orders@oreilly.com

To sign up to get topic-specific email announcements and/or news about upcoming books, conferences, special offers, and new technologies:
elists@oreilly.com

For technical questions about book content:
booktech@oreilly.com

To submit new book proposals to our editors:
proposals@oreilly.com

O'Reilly books are available in multiple DRM-free ebook formats. For more information:
oreilly.com/ebooks

Spreading the knowledge of innovators   oreilly.com

Have it your way.